THE AGE OF MAGNIFICENCE

THE AGE OF MAGNIFICENCE

The Memoirs of the Duc de Saint-Simon

Selected, Edited and Translated by

TED MORGAN

PARAGON HOUSE
NEW YORK

First Paperback edition, 1990

Published in the United States by

Paragon House
90 Fifth Avenue
New York, NY 10011

Copyright © 1963 by G.P. Putnam's Sons

Reprinted by arrangement with G.P. Putnam's Sons

10 9 8 7 6 5 4 3 2 1

Library of Congress Cataloging-in-Publication Data

Saint-Simon, Louis de Rouvroy, duc de, 1675–1755.
[Memoirs, English. Selections]
The age of magnificence : the memoirs of the court of
Louix XIV / by the Duc de Saint-Simon ; selected, edited,
and translated by Ted Morgan. — 1st pbk. ed.
Reprint. Originally published: New York : Putnam, 1963.
Includes bibliographical references.
ISBN 1-55778-327-6 : $12.95
1. Saint-Simon, Louis de Rouvroy, duc de, 1675–1755.
2. France—Court and courtiers—History—17th century.
3. Louis XIV, King of France, 1638–1715.
I. Morgan, Ted, 1932– . II. Title.
DC130.S2A35213 1990
944'.033'092—dc20
[B]   89-72186
CIP

This book is printed on acid-free paper.
Manufactured in the United States of America

For Nancy, My Unofficial Co-anthologist.

CONTENTS

PART ONE

SCENES AND GLANCES

PART TWO

PORTRAITS

PART THREE

THE KING

PART FOUR

SAINT-SIMON: HIS LIFE AND CAREER AT COURT

PART FIVE

SAINT-SIMON AND RELIGION

PART SIX

SAINT-SIMON AS A WRITER

EDITOR'S NOTE

In culling from the 9,857 pages of the Pléiade seven-volume edition of the *Memoirs* the excerpts that make up the present volume, it has often been necessary for conciseness and coherence to cut from one passage to the other and even from one sentence to another. These cuts are indicated by an ellipsis. In a few instances, different passages in the *Memoirs* dealing with the same topic (Saint-Simon's friendship with the Regent and several of the portraits are examples) have been combined under a single heading. The entry titles are mine and the dates following them are the year of the *Memoirs* under which the entry appeared, ranging from 1691 to 1723. The entries have been grouped by subject in six chapters and thus do not appear in chronological order.

The guiding principle in the translation has been that anything other than punctuation which would cause the reader to pause should send the translator back to his workbench. This readability rule leads to occasional changes in the sentence structure of the memoirs. Saint-Simon's sentences flow freely and with many meanderings, sometimes rushing with a torrential absence of syntax, sometimes broken by clumps of semicolons. While not adhering with blind obedience to the text, I have made efforts to keep to the original rhythm of the sentences whenever possible, even leaving intact certain repetitions, improprieties, and awkwardnesses of style, in the belief that the translator's job is not to currycomb the original, but to convey flavor as well as meaning.

Saint-Simon's frequent use of idiomatic expressions, some of his own coinage, may often be matched in English. "The scales fell from his eyes" is the identical counterpart of the French. Other expressions, such as *rôtir le balai* (literally "roasting the broom," to describe a loose woman), needs a paraphrase that may be less vivid. Words whose meaning has changed over the centuries have been restored their original coloring thanks in part to the Royal French-English dictionary, published by Mr. A. Boyer of London in 1751. Affectionate gratitude is expressed to Madame la comtesse Gabriel de Lastours for sharing her vast fund of knowledge on Saint-Simon and the court of Louis XIV.

Principal Personages at the Court of Louis XIV

Louis XIV: Born in 1638, ruled France for seventy-two of his seventy-seven years. Married Marie-Thérèse of Austria, who died in 1683 after bearing him six children, five of whom died in infancy; the sixth was the Grand Dauphin. The King recognized eleven illegitimate children, five by the duchesse de la Vallière, and six by the marquise de Montespan. The eight who survived infancy were legitimized and given titles. The daughters were married off to peers with an assist from the King. In later life, the King married Madame de Maintenon secretly, but they had no children.

Monseigneur: Louis, the Grand Dauphin, eldest son of the King, who had the following three sons:

Louis, duc de Bourgogne: Eldest grandson of Louis XIV, and Dauphin from 1711, when Monseigneur died, until his own death a year later. His wife, the duchesse de Bourgogne, was a favorite of the King.

Philippe, duc d'Anjou: Grandson of Louis XIV who became Philip V of Spain in 1700.

Charles, duc de Berry: Grandson of Louis XIV who married the daughter of Philippe II d'Orléans.

Louis, duc d'Anjou: Great-grandson of Louis XIV, who became Louis XV in 1715.

Monsieur: The King's brother, in this case (after 1660) Philippe, duc d'Orléans. His wife (first Henrietta of England, then Charlotte Elizabeth of Bavaria) was called MADAME.

MADEMOISELLE: The eldest granddaughter of a king of France. Anne-Marie-Louise d'Orléans, duchesse de Montpensier and the granddaughter of Louis XIII, was LA GRANDE MADEMOISELLE.

THE REGENT: Philippe II d'Orléans, son of MONSIEUR, and nephew of Louis XIV, who became Regent at the death of the King in 1715.

MONSIEUR LE PRINCE: Henri-Jules de Bourbon, prince de Condé, prince of the blood and member of a collateral branch of the Bourbons. His wife, Anne of Bavaria, was MADAME LA PRINCESSE.

MONSIEUR LE DUC: Louis III de Bourbon-Condé, eldest son of MONSIEUR LE PRINCE. His wife, Mlle. de Nantes, a bastard daughter of Louis XIV, was MADAME LA DUCHESSE.

DUC DU MAINE AND COMTE DE TOULOUSE: Legitimized bastards of Louis XIV by the marquise de Montespan.

FIRST MADEMOISELLE DE BLOIS: Legitimized bastard daughter of Louis XIV by the duchesse de la Vallière, who married a prince de Conti.

SECOND MADEMOISELLE DE BLOIS: Legitimized bastard daughter of Louis XIV by the marquise de Montespan, who married Philippe II d'Orléans.

GRAND PRIEUR: Honorary appointment granted by the order of Malta to supervise the priories and monasteries of France. It was given under Louis XIV to the chevalier de Vendôme, illegitimate great-grandson of Henri IV.

DUC DE VENDÔME: General of the armies and illegitimate great-grandson of Henri IV.

MONSIEUR LE GRAND: The King's Master of the Horse (or Grand Equerry), Louis de Lorraine, comte d'Armagnac.

Important Dates in the Memoirs
of the Duc de Saint-Simon

1675. Birth of Louis de Rouvroy, second duc de Saint-Simon.

1685. Morganatic marriage of Louis XIV and his longtime mistress, Madame de Maintenon. Revocation by Louis XIV of the Edict of Nantes which had granted Protestants religious freedom.

1691. The young Saint-Simon studies philosophy and the arts of war at an academy for the nobility. On October 28 he is presented to the King, who gives him a commission in the Gray Musketeers although finding him on the frail side.

1692. Saint-Simon is at war when he learns of the death of his father, who had risen to the peerage after starting as an equerry for Louis XIII.

1694. Saint-Simon writes his first notes for eventual memoirs, regretting that he has no training as a historian.

1695. Saint-Simon marries Mlle. de Lorge, daughter of a marshal of France.

1700. The duc d'Anjou, grandson of Louis XIV, becomes King of Spain as Philip V and the first French Bourbon to sit on the Spanish throne.

1702. Saint-Simon quits the army and incurs the King's displeasure for the first time.

1711. Death of the eldest son of Louis XIV, Monseigneur, the Grand Dauphin, at the age of fifty. A papal bull denounces the heresy of Jansenism which is spreading in France.

1712. Death of Louis, Dauphin and duc de Bourgogne, son of the late Grand Dauphin, and of his wife, the duchesse de Bourgogne. The court suspects they were poisoned by the duc d'Orléans. His son, the duc d'Anjou, will become the next king, Louis XV.

1714. It becomes known that the will of Louis XIV makes special provisions for his two bastard sons by the marquise de Montespan—the duc du Maine and the comte de Toulouse. They will be made princes of the blood in line for succession to the throne.

1715. The King is dead. Long live the King. Since Louis XV is only five, the duc d'Orléans is appointed Regent. Saint-Simon is named to the Council of Regency.

1718. The triumph of Saint-Simon over the royal bastards elevated to princely rank comes in a special session of Parlement called by the Regent. The bastards are stripped of their rank and deprived of the right of succession. Voltaire's play *Oedipus* is shown for the first time and causes scandal with the line: "Tremble, unfortunate kings, for your reign is past."

1721. Saint-Simon is sent as extraordinary ambassador to Spain to ask the Infanta's hand for Louis XV.

1723. Death of the Regent. Saint-Simon leaves court and begins writing his memoirs.

1743. Death of the duchesse de Saint-Simon.

1746. Death of the duc de Ruffec, Saint-Simon's eldest son, born in 1698.

1754. Death of Saint-Simon's second son, the marquis de Ruffec, born in 1699.

1755. Death of Saint-Simon on March 2.

NOTE ON THE GENEALOGICAL TABLES

THE key marriages of the era in the opinion of Saint-Simon were those of the duc d'Orléans (nephew of Louis XIV and later Regent), and the duc de Berry (grandson of Louis XIV). Louis XIV arranged the marriage between Orléans and one of his bastard daughters, the second Mlle. de Blois, uniting royal and bastard blood. The Regent and his bride were first cousins, since their respective fathers were the King's brother and the King.

Having taken in bastard blood, the Orléans branch returned it in the next generation with the marriage of the Regent's daughter to a grandson of Louis XIV, the duc de Berry. The match served to reunite the royal and the Orléans branch, but the crisscrossing of royal and bastard blood and the two branches led to curious relationships. As one example, the duc de Berry's mother-in-law was also his aunt.

HENRI IV AND LOUIS XIV—LEGITIMATE DESCENDANTS (Abbreviated table)

HENRI IV (1533-1610)

(1) Marguerite de Valois (1552-1615)

(2) Marie de Medicis (1574-1642)

LOUIS XIII (1601-1643)
= Anne of Austria (1601-1666)

LOUIS XIV (1638-1715)
= Marie-Thérèse of Austria (1638-1683)

Louis le Grand (*Monseigneur*) (1661-1711)
= Marie-Anne-Christine of Bavaria (1660-1690)

Louis, duc de Bourgogne (Dauphin) (1682-1712)
= Marie-Adélaïde de Savoie (1685-1712)

Louis, duc d'Anjou (Louis XV, 1710-1774)

Philippe d'Anjou (Philippe V d'Espagne, 1683-1745)

(1) Marie-Louise de Savoie (1688-1714)

(2) Elizabeth Farnese (1692-1766)

Charles, duc de Berry (1686-1714)
= Marie-Louise d'Orléans (1695-1719)

Philippe d'Orléans (*Monsieur*, 1640-1701)

(1) Henrietta of England (1644-1670)

(2) Charlotte Elizabeth of Bavaria (1652-1722)

Philippe, duc de Chartres, d'Orléans, and Regent (1674-1723)

Second Mlle. de Blois (1677-1749)

Marie-Louise d'Orléans (1695-1719)
= Duc de Berry

LOUIS XIV—ILLEGITIMATE

Duchesse de la Vallière
(1644-1710)

Marquise de Montespan
(1641-1707)

Charles de Lincour,
Philippe Dersy, and
Louis de Bourbon, all
of whom died in infancy

Louis, comte de Vermandois,
legitimized (1667-1683)

Marie-Anne de Bourbon,
legitimized as the first
Mlle. de Blois (1666-1739)

Louis-Armand, prince de
Conti (1661-1685)

[all six legitimized]

Louis-Auguste,
duc du Maine
(1670-1736)

Louis-César
(1672-1683)

Louise-Françoise, Mlle.
de Nantes (1673-1743)

Louis III de Condé
(M. le Duc) (1668-1710)

Louise-Marie,
Mlle. de Tours
(1676-1681)

Françoise-Marie,
second Mlle. de
Blois (1677-1749)

Philippe d'Orleans,
the Regent

Louis-Alexandre,
comte de Toulouse
(1678-1737)

HENRI IV—ILLEGITIMATE (Abbreviated)

Gabrielle d'Estrées	Henriette d'Entraigues, marquise de Verneuil	Comtesse de Morel	Charlotte des Essarts
César, duc de Vendôme (1594-1665)	Henri, duc de Verneuil, cardinal of Metz (1601-1682)	Antoine, comte de Morel	Joan, a nun — Mary, a nun

[legitimized second house of Vendôme]

Catherine-Henriette

Alexandre, chevalier de Vendôme, Grand Prieur de France (1589-1629)

César, duc de Vendôme (1594-1665) ⚌ Françoise de Lorraine, daughter of the duc de Mercoeur

Elizabeth

François, duc de Beaufort (1616-1669)

Louis, cardinal de Vendôme, duc de Mercoeur (1612-1669) ⚌ Laure Mancini (1636-1657)

Philippe, chevalier de Vendôme, Grand Prieur de France (1655-1727)

Louis-Joseph, duc de Vendôme, general of the armies (1654-1712)

I

SCENES AND GLANCES

Introduction

*T*HE court of Louis XIV was an elaborate playpen with a closely regulated system of rewards and punishments. Like children, the courtiers were concerned mainly with their own amusement and the approval of their elders. They showed the child's pitiless cruelty toward the vulnerable, the child's irresponsibility, the child's capacity for boredom. They were practical jokers, which is the most childish form of humor; and they were tattletales and show-offs, the most childish of faults.

The King devised for his titled wards a life of games and other inoffensive pleasure. These were transported to the level of state functions by virtue of royal participation. Gambling was encouraged and interrupted only for the brief mourning of princes. The harder the times and the emptier the state's coffers, the more magnificent the balls, and elderly men couranted to exhaustion to prove they were devoted subjects. Trips from Versailles to the King's other residences in nearby Marly and Fontainebleau were more than trips—they were royal displacements, and an invitation was not a request but a royal summons.

The King's genius for authority gave the round of trivialities compelling importance, and for those who sensed the hollowness of court life there was no alternative. Versailles was the arbiter of taste, the seat of the government, the envy of Europe. An Italian visitor to the court wrote home that one "might be ashamed to be part of this but would have been even more ashamed not to be part of it."

The King dispensed generous quantities of fool's gold to loyal courtiers. Hereditary duchesses were allowed to sit on uncomfortable wooden stools in his presence while other women stood. What more unmistakable sign of prestige than the relief of a ducal

*derrière? Important persons invited for a weekend found their
name inscribed in chalk on the doors of the rooms they had been
assigned, preceded by the word* POUR. *Others had only their
names on the door, and not getting the "pour" was a terrible
social defeat. Marshals of France were addressed as "dear cousin"
by the King in his correspondence. The diligent and highly born
courtier had the right to hold the King's candle as the monarch
was getting into bed. He could leave his hat on in the King's
presence in the gardens of Marly. He noted that the King inclined
his own hat in greeting at a more pronounced angle than for his
neighbor. If he was exceptionally fortunate, he might have both
panels of a door opened for him in Versailles.*

*The humiliations of court life were equally calibrated. A fall
from the King's favor was as irredeemable and tragic as the fall
of Lucifer. The courtier was no longer given the candle to hold,
or invited to Marly, although his wife might be. He was not asked
to hold the King's napkin at communion. The decisive sign of
banishment would come when the wretch, returning to his apartment at Versailles, found someone else occupying it, and stumbled
out to what Saint-Simon considered a horrible fate, "a life of
obscurity."*

*The King's genius lay in convincing the court that outside its
own narrow confines, there was nothing worthwhile. He created
an honors system with as much real value as the paper stars studi-
ous children are given to paste in their exercise books, and just as
highly sought and appreciated.*

*The court of Versailles, however, is not as hopelessly archaic
as it may seem by twentieth-century standards. The careful nur-
turing of artificial status is part of the fabric of our own society.
In certain large corporations, a repairman is called an engineer.
It may make him feel better, but it does not necessarily lead to
promotion. In other firms, office boys have beautifully embossed
name cards on their desks, which may give them the illusion of
identifying with their betters but does not fatten their pay check.
And the tacit or overt rules affecting the dress, private lives, and
social behavior of executives in some corporations seem to have
been passed on from despot to despot since Louis XIV and
adapted to the times.*

The King's encouragement of vices to keep his courtiers occu-

pied is another lesson instinctively understood by every age. Recently in New York, a matron was arrested for holding marijuana parties for teen-agers; she wanted to keep them off the streets, she explained. Once we have stripped the courtiers of their seventeenth-century costumes, once we have forgotten the blue boys, the silver flower pots, the formal gardens, the Hall of Mirrors and the Petit Trianon, once we have abstracted the behavior from the scenery, we find a mixture of malice, viciousness, futility, and ignorance that is the legacy of every society.

A BAD DANCER (1692)

I cannot leave unmentioned a very ridiculous adventure that happened to the same man on two occasions. He was Montbron's son, who was no more made to dance at Versailles than his father was intended to be Knight of the Order,[1] although the father became one in 1688, and was governor of Cambray, lieutenant general, the only lieutenant general in Flanders, and bore a name which he could never prove was his. This young man, who up to then had attended court little or not at all, was leading Mlle. de Moreuil. He had been asked if he danced well and had replied with a smugness that made everyone eager to find fault. They were satisfied. He lost his countenance at the first bow: He was out of step from the start. He tried to hide his mistake by drooping to one side and waving his arms: This proved even more ridiculous and prompted laughter which soon came in bursts and then turned to jeers despite the respect owed the presence of the King, who could hardly keep from laughing himself. The following day, instead of fleeing or keeping silent, he claimed that the presence of the King had upset him, and promised to outdo himself at the ball to follow. He was a friend of mine, and his behavior made me suffer. I would have warned him but I feared he would not receive my advice gracefully. As soon as he began to dance at the second ball, everyone stood up pushing to see, and the jeering grew so loud that it led to clapping. Everyone, even

[1] The Order of the Holy Ghost, one of Europe's highest honors.

the King, laughed heartily, and most of them explosively, in such a manner that I doubt whether anyone else ever suffered the like. After that, he disappeared, and did not show his face for a long time.

Two Surgeons (1692)

There were two house surgeons who became famous and rich: Bienaise, because of his aneurism or pricked artery operation, and Arnaud, with his operation for fallen organs. I cannot restrain myself from telling a tale about the latter. When he had become prominent in his profession, a very debauched young priest came to him in a condition that greatly interfered with his pleasure. Arnaud made him lie on a bed to examine him, and told him the operation was so urgent there was not a moment to lose and he should not even go home. The priest, who had not counted on anything so pressing, wanted to put it off; but Arnaud held fast and promised to be very careful. He had him seized by his assistants and along with the operation for fallen organs he performed another only too common in Italy with little boys who have beautiful voices. The priest was all screams, all fury, all threat. Arnaud told him with great calm that if he wanted to die without delay he had only to keep up his uproar; and that if he wanted to live and get well, he must calm down and regain his tranquillity. When he was well, he wanted to murder Arnaud, who kept out of his way; and that put an end to the poor priest's pleasure.

Funeral of the Grande Mademoiselle [1] (1693)

It was a state funeral, and her remains were watched over for several days by two ladies of quality and a princess or a duchess

[1] The Grande Mademoiselle (1627-1693), duchesse de Montpensier, was the daughter of Gaston d'Orléans, who was the brother of Louis XIII. She

who alternated every two hours; they wore mourning mantles and the King had them summoned by the master of ceremonies. . . . The comtesse de Soissons refused to go; the King was angry, threatened to banish her, and made her obey.

There occurred a very ridiculous mishap. In the middle of the day, and before the ladies present, the urn containing her entrails[2] shattered with a horrible sound and a sudden and intolerable smell on top of the sideboard where it had been placed. The ladies present were either swooning from fear or in flight. The heralds on duty and the friars reciting psalms joined the crowds and pushed their way outside. The confusion was extreme. Most of them reached the garden and the courts. The cause of the fracas was the fermentation of the entrails, which had been badly embalmed. All was perfumed and restored, and the commotion was made light of.

CENSORSHIP AT THE COURT THEATRE (1697)

The King abruptly banished the entire troupe of Italian players, and wanted no other. As long as they had kept the butt of their overflow of filth and profanity to their own kind, they were merely laughed at; but they decided to give a play called *The False Prude* where Mme. de Maintenon was easily recognized. Everyone rushed to see it; but after three or four consecutive performances had brought them a good profit, they were ordered to close the theatre and clear out of the kingdom within a month. There was quite a fuss, and although the players lost their establishment through boldness and folly, she who had them banished won nothing, because of the talk that surrounded such a ridiculous event.

was thus the first cousin of Louis XIV. She was granted the title "Grande Mademoiselle" to distinguish her from her great-niece, "Mademoiselle," the daughter of Philippe duc d'Orléans (Monsieur), the brother of Louis XIV.

[2] Entrails were removed from the body after embalming and placed in urns. With Very Important People the heart was cut out, preserved, and kept in a chapel.

GAMBLING AT COURT (1698)

In those days, the King gambled heavily, and *brelan*[1] was all the rage. One evening when the King was playing with Saissac, M. de Louvois came up and whispered in his ear. A moment later, the King gave his hand to M. de Lorge, told him to hold it and continue the game until he returned, and went into his cabinet with M. de Louvois. While the King was absent, Saissac bid against M. de Lorge, although it was against all the principles of the game, bet everything he had, and won against heavy odds. The stakes had been very high. That night, M. de Lorge felt bound to warn the King of what had taken place. The King had the card manufacturer and the blue boy[2] who had been holding the card basket discreetly arrested: It turned out that the cards were marked and, to obtain his pardon, the manufacturer admitted that he had been in league with Saissac to make them.

The next day, Saissac was ordered to give up his commissions and appointments and go home. After several years, he obtained permission to leave for England: There he gambled for several years and came out a heavy winner. He was allowed every freedom of movement upon his return except that of presenting himself to the King. He settled in Paris, where he held heavy gambling sessions at his home. . . . He was a very singular man, untroubled by contempt and affronts. One of his quirks was the refusal to wear mourning: He said it served no purpose and made him sad, and held to the principle all his life, even for his next of kin. They paid him back, for when he died, not one of his relatives went into mourning for him.

[1] *Brelan* was a game in which each of three players drew three cards and bet against the other players.
[2] Blue boys were young court valets named for the color of their costume.

GETTING RID OF A SQUATTER (1698)

Charnacé had a very long and perfectly beautiful road in front of his castle in Anjou; the road was obstructed by the house and small garden of a peasant who had been there before it was built and refused to sell to either Charnacé or his father in spite of all the advantages that were offered; many small landowners pride themselves on this kind of obstinacy in order to enrage as they please the people they depend upon and at whose convenience they must remain.

Charnacé had let it go a long time without mentioning it because he did not know what to do. Finally, weary of the cottage which marred the beauty of his road, he thought of a trick. The peasant who owned the cottage and lived there alone without wife or children was by profession a tailor, when he had occasion to practice. Charnacé sought him out and told him he had been summoned to the court for important duties and was in a hurry to get there, but that he needed a livery. They struck a bargain; but Charnacé stipulated that he wanted no delays and would pay extra if the tailor agreed to move in with him; he said he would lodge him, feed him, and pay him before sending him off. The tailor agreed and started working. While he was busy, Charnacé had the plan and dimensions of the house and garden taken with great precision, including the rooms, and the position of the furniture and utensils; he had the house taken apart and put back together four musket shots away from his road, with everything in it replaced in the same position, including furniture and utensils, and the garden replanted; at the same time he had the road leveled and cleaned so one could not tell the house had been there.

All this was done before the livery was ready, while, fearing exposure, Charnacé kept the tailor discreetly guarded. Finally, when both tasks were done, Charnacé entertained his man until the night was good and black, paid him, and sent him off content. The tailor started down the road: Soon, he found the way long;

he tried to find the trees and could not. He realized he had gone beyond the road and groped his way back, looking for the trees; he followed them, crossed over, but his house was not there. He could not understand what was happening. The whole night was spent in this exercise; the day came, with light enough to see, but he saw nothing; he rubbed his eyes, looking for other landmarks, trying to discover if his sight was at fault. Finally he thought the devil was after him and had carried off his house. After further wandering and searching, he noticed far from the road a house as similar to his own as one drop of water to another. He could not believe his eyes; but curiosity prodded him to the spot where the house stood and where he had never seen a house before. The closer he came to it, the better he recognized it as his own. His head was whirling; he tried the key: The door opened and he walked in to find everything as he had left it and in precisely the same place. He was nearly in a faint, and remained convinced it was sorcery. The day was not far along when he learned he was the joke of village and castle and discovered the truth behind the witchcraft, which made him furious: He wanted to sue and seek justice before the provincial overseer; but everyone laughed at him. The King heard the story, and also laughed, and Charnacé had a clear road.

Amusing Malice of the Duc de Lauzun (1698)

The comte de Tessé was the victim of an amusing adventure. He was colonel general of the dragoons. Two days before an inspection, M. de Lauzun asked him with that air of kindness, sweetness, and simplicity which he almost always assumed, whether as head of the dragoons he had decided what to wear to salute the King; they discussed his horse and his apparel, and after much praise Lauzun asked ingenuously: "But the hat; I have not heard you mention the hat." "No," replied the other, "I was planning to wear a cap." "A cap!" exclaimed Lauzun. "You're not serious? A cap! That is all right for the others; but for the colonel general to wear a cap! M. le comte, don't even think of it." "How so?"

asked Tessé. "What would be amiss?" Lauzun made him beg for an answer and gave the impression that he knew more than he would say. Finally, giving in to his entreaties, he said he would not allow him to commit such a grave error; and that since he had been the first holder of the commission he was in a position to know that one of its principal honors was to wear a gray hat when the King reviewed the dragoons. The astonished Tessé admitted his ignorance and poured out his thanks for such pertinent advice which had kept him from a terrible blunder; he hurried home and dispatched one of his servants to Paris for a gray hat. The duc de Lauzun had taken care to give Tessé the information in a cunning aside, so that no one else heard it; he was careful not to mention it and certain that Tessé would be too ashamed of his own ignorance to talk.

The morning of the review I attended the King's rising and saw M. de Lauzun remain there against his custom, for since he had full access,[1] he always left when the courtiers arrived. Tessé was also there, strutting and swaggering with a gray hat, a black plume, and a huge cockade. I was struck by his attitude and by the hat's color, to which the King had an aversion and which no one had worn for years, and I stared at him, for he stood almost directly across from me, while M. de Lauzun stood close behind him.

The King, after putting on his shoes and speaking to some of those present, finally noticed the hat. He was so surprised he asked Tessé where he had got it. The other, all self-congratulation, replied that it had come from Paris. "And what for?" asked the King. "Sire," replied the other, "because Your Majesty has honored us with his visit today." "Well!" replied the King, showing more and more surprise, "what has that to do with a gray hat?" "Sire," said Tessé, embarrassed by this reply, "the privilege of a colonel general is to wear a gray hat for the occasion." "A gray hat!" said the King. "Who the devil told you that?" "M. de Lauzun, Sire, for whom you created the commission." At that moment, the good duc burst out laughing and withdrew. "Lauzun has made a fool of you," answered the King somewhat sharply. "Take my advice and send that hat immediately to the superior

---

[1] Full access or grande entrée was a privilege granted a few courtiers to be at the King's side at all times from his rising to his bedtime.

of the Premonstratensians." [2] I never saw a man more abashed than Tessé. His eyes downcast, he looked at his hat with a sadness and shame that made the scene perfect. None of the spectators restrained their laughter, and the King's familiars had their say. Finally Tessé had enough sense to leave.

PROFOUND IGNORANCE OF BRETEUIL (1698)

Breteuil was a know-it-all, although he kept within the bounds of respect, and everyone took pleasure in tormenting him. One day at a dinner given by M. de Pontchartrain, who always entertained the cream of society, he began to lay down the law. Mme. de Pontchartrain spoke up, and finally told him that for all his knowledge she was sure he did not even know who had written the Our Father. Breteuil began to laugh and joke, but Mme. de Pontchartrain insisted, and continued to press him and bring him back to the point. He defended himself as well as he could until he was able to leave the table. Caumartin, who had noticed his embarrassment, followed him into the drawing room and kindly whispered: "Moses." Breteuil, who was a fathead, thought he had the upper hand and triumphantly brought the Our Father up again over coffee. This time Mme. de Pontchartrain did not have to prompt him. After rebuking her for pretending to doubt him and for the shame to which he had been subjected in so trivial a matter, he pronounced with great authority that no one could be ignorant of the fact that Moses had written the Our Father. The burst of laughter was general. Poor Breteuil was so mortified he could scarcely find the exit; everyone had something to say about his gullibility. He and Caumartin were on bad terms for a long time, and the Our Father remained a sore point.

His friend the Marquis de Gesvres, who sometimes vaunted his erudition and learned phrases by heart so that he could repeat them whenever the opportunity arose, was in the King's study one day chatting and admiring the excellent paintings with a critical eye; among others there were Crucifixions of Our Lord

[2] Members of the Premonstratensian Order wore gray.

by several great masters, but M. de Gesvres held that the same artist was responsible for many of the crucifixions, and indeed for all those that were there. Everyone made fun of him and gave him the names of the different painters, who could be recognized by their style. "Not at all," said the marquis, "the painter's name is INRI.[1] Don't you see his signature on all the paintings?" One can imagine what followed such dull-witted nonsense, and what became of such a perfect fool.

A CYNIC'S ANGER PURGED (1699)

Decent people at court mourned a cynic who had lived and died among them, and who saw only what he wanted to see: He was the chevalier de Coislin, brother of the duc and of the cardinal of the same name and, like them, half brother of the maréchale de Rochefort. He was a very decent man in all things, worthy and poor, although he was never in need thanks to his brother the cardinal. He was extremely crossgrained and disagreeable. He never left Versailles, although he made a great principle of never seeing the King, to the point that he was seen crossing the street when he found himself accidentally in the King's path. . . . He had his room and board at the cardinal's Versailles apartment. There were always many guests, and if there was one he did not like, he would have a tray brought to his room; if he was at the table and someone arrived who displeased him, he would throw down his napkin and go off to his room and sulk. One could never be safe from his outbursts, and his brother's hospitality was far more appreciated after his death, although most people had become accustomed to his behavior. . . .

One anecdote will serve to epitomize him. He had followed the King on a trip with his brothers and a fourth person whose name I forget. Although he never saw him, he always followed the King so he could be with his brothers and friends. The duc de

---

[1] Of course, the abbreviation INRI on crucifixes stands for *Iesus Nazarenus Rex Iudaeorum* (Jesus of Nazareth, King of the Jews).

Coislin was so extravagantly polite that it was sometimes embarrassing. During the trip, he heaped compliments on his hosts,
which made the chevalier de Coislin lose his patience. It happened
that they were staying with a gentlewoman of wit, bearing, and
good looks. That evening the duc outdid himself in attentions and
the next morning redoubled his compliments. M. d'Orléans (who
had not yet been made a cardinal) was impatient to leave; the
chevalier was raging, but the duc kept wagging his flattering
tongue. The chevalier, who knew how long his brother would
be at it, purged his anger with a solid vengeance. When they had
traveled three or four leagues, the chevalier brought up the handsome hostess and his brother's compliments; he started to laugh,
and said he had reason to believe that despite his endless flattery
his brother had not left a favorable impression. The duc was perplexed and said he could not imagine why. "Would you like to
know why?" the chevalier de Coislin said bluntly. "I was so exasperated by your flummery that I went into your bedroom and
dropped a huge turd smack in the middle of the floor; at this very
moment, our beautiful hostess is convinced that despite your exquisite manners the house gift was left by you." The other two
laughed heartily, but the duc de Coislin was so angry he wanted
to get a horse and ride back to expose the real villain and pour
out his shame and excuses. Though it was raining very hard, it
was all they could do to restrain him, and almost more than they
could do to reconcile the brothers.

The Holder of the Pen (1701)

Rose, another private secretary in the King's cabinet, who had
held the pen for more than fifty years, died at the age of eighty-
six or eighty-seven in perfect health of mind and body. He was
also president of the King's auditors; he was very rich and
miserly, and a man of great wit, with incomparable sallies and repartees; he was a man of letters, with a flawless and admirable
memory, and a complete grasp of court and business affairs; he
was gay, free, bold, often impudent, but knew how to keep his

place politely and respectfully with those who did not step on his toes, and he was very old-fashioned. . . . His duties had put him in close contact with the King, and he knew things of which the ministers were ignorant. To hold the pen is to be an official forger and to do out of duty what would cost the life of any other man. It consists in copying the King's handwriting so accurately that the real thing cannot be distinguished from the forgery, and in writing all the letters the King should or must write in his own hand, but does not trouble to. Many are sent to sovereigns and other high-ranking foreigners; or to subjects, such as army generals and other important persons singled out for secret business or as a mark of kindness or distinction. It is impossible to paraphrase a great King with more dignity, more pertinence toward each recipient and each matter, than in the letters composed by Rose and signed by the King in his own hand; his penmanship was so like the King's that one could not tell them apart. An infinity of important matters had passed through Rose's hands: He was extremely faithful and discreet, and the King trusted him completely. . . .

Rose had been the butt of M. de Duras' cruelty and bore him a grudge. It was during a court expedition. For some reason, Rose's carriage had broken down and, impatient with the delay, he continued on horseback. He was not an experienced horseman: The horse did not take to him, and threw him into a mud puddle. Pinned under the horse in the middle of the puddle, Rose cried for help. M. de Duras, whose carriage was slowly making its way through the mud, put his face to the window, and by way of encouragement, began to laugh and shout that it was a fortunate horse indeed that could roll around on a bed of ROSES; he went on his way and left him there.

The duc de Coislin was more charitable and picked Rose up. He was incoherent with anger. The worst was yet to come at the King's bedtime. M. de Duras, who feared no one and whose tongue was as wicked as Rose's, told the story to the King and all the court, and gave them a good laugh. Rose was so furious that from then on he avoided M. de Duras and whenever he tried to malign him before the King, the King would laugh and bring up the mud puddle.

BÉCHAMEIL'S VANITY (1703)

Béchameil was a good-looking man of prepossessing appearance who thought he looked like the duc de Gramont. The duc's nephew, the comte de Gramont, saw him while walking through the Tuileries and told his companions: "I'll bet that if I give Béchameil a kick in the rump he will thank me for it." No sooner said than done. The startled Béchameil turned around, and the comte de Gramont apologized for having mistaken him for his uncle the duc. Béchameil was delighted, as were Gramont's two companions.

THE DUKE OF ALBA'S VOW (1703)

Trouville found the Duke of Alba[1] lying on his right side between two untidy sheets; he had neither moved nor made his bed for several months. He claimed he was unable to move, and yet his health was good. The fact was that his mistress had grown tired of him and run away; he searched desperately for her throughout Spain, and had masses and other devotions said for her return. Such is the enlightenment of religion in the country of the Inquisition. Finally he vowed to stay in bed lying on his right side until she was found. At last, he admitted his folly to Trouville, but claimed it was a practical and effective way of getting back his mistress. He continued to receive the best people at court, and was prized for his conversation. But because of his vow, he did not attend the funeral of Charles II or the coronation of Philip V, and always gave excuses for not paying court to the latter; he kept up this extravagant behavior to his death, without

[1] Antoine-Martin of Toledo (1669-1711), was a descendant of the celebrated Duke of Alba who governed the Netherlands for Spain under Philip II in the sixteenth century.

having budged from his right side. His mania was so singular and yet so persistent that I think it should be noted, for otherwise he was a sober, sensible, and intelligent man.

A Singular Holdup (1703)

There was a good deal of thievery in those days: Fieubet and Courtin were waylaid and frisked, and as a result Fieubet was heavily out of pocket. When the thieves had gone, Fieubet damned his misfortune, but Courtin was pleased because he had been able to slip his watch and fifty pistoles[1] into his codpiece. At that instant, Fieubet jumped from the carriage and yelled so at the thieves that they came back to see what he wanted. "Sirs," he said, "you look like honest and needy men. It is not right that you should be the dupes of this gentleman, who did you out of fifty pistoles and his watch," and turning to Courtin, he said with a laugh: "Sir, you told me your hiding place; believe me, you had better give them up without a search." Courtin's stupor and indignation were such that he let his money and watch be taken without a word of protest; but no sooner had the thieves fled than he tried to strangle Fieubet, who was the stronger and laughed heartily. Fieubet told the tale to everyone at St. Germain, and their mutual friends had all the trouble in the world patching it up between them.

A Headdress Catches Fire (1703)

The marquise de Charlus, sister of Mézières and mother of the marquis de Levis who has since become a duke and peer, died old and rich. She was always dressed like an old ragpicker, which made her suffer many painful affronts from people who did not

[1] A pistole was worth ten pounds, and a pound was worth about one dollar in our currency.

know who she was. As a relief from serious affairs, I will recount another sort of adventure that happened to her. She was very miserly and loved to gamble. She would have spent the whole night gambling even if her house was on fire. In Paris, every evening, the daughter of M. le Prince, Mme. la princesse de Conti, held *lansquenet*[1] sessions at high stakes. One Friday evening, Mme. de Charlus was there with quite a crowd and was taking time out for supper. She was no better dressed than usual. In those days women wore a very high detachable headdress called a commode, which could be taken on or off like a man's wig or nightcap. Mme. de Charlus was sitting near the archbishop of Reims, Le Tellier. She opened a soft-boiled egg and leaned forward to take some salt, but a nearby candle set fire to her headdress without her realizing it. The archbishop, seeing her in flames, threw himself on the headdress and knocked it to the ground. Mme. de Charlus was so surprised and indignant that she threw her egg at the archbishop and splattered his face. He only laughed, as did everyone else at Mme. de Charlus' dirty, gray, and hoary head, and at the archbishop's omelet. Mme. de Charlus, furious at what she considered an insult and at having had her head peeled in public, would not listen to reason and heaped abuse on the archbishop. Her headdress was burned and Mme. la princesse de Conti gave her another; but before she had a chance to put it on her head everyone was able to admire its charms, while she kept grumbling furiously.

Two Curious Masks (1704)

Lieutenant General Bouligneux and Camp Marshal Wartigny, valorous and singular men, were that year killed at the battle of Verue. The previous winter, the court had derived great amusement from wax masks that represented different courtiers; they were worn under other masks so that when the first mask was removed it revealed the wax mask, which was mistaken for a face.

---

[1] *Lansquenet* was a card game imported from Germany and named after a Landsknecht (servant of the country, or German mercenary infantryman).

The game was taken up again the next winter and the surprise was great when the masks were found unchanged except for those of Bouligneux and Wartigny. Their masks had maintained their resemblance but had the pale and drawn look of death. They were worn at a ball and frightened everyone so that rouge was applied to their cheeks to freshen them up. But the rouge somehow vanished and the deathly pallor could not be repaired. The incident seems so extraordinary that I have felt it worth reporting. I would certainly not have mentioned it had not the whole court been a startled witness to this singular event. Finally the two masks were thrown away.

Luxury on the Battlefield (1707)

The luxury of court and town had spread to such a degree in the army that all sorts of previously unheard-of delicacies were brought to the bivouacs. It had become the custom to serve hot meals to the troops, even during short stopovers. The meals brought to the trenches during a siege were abundant and varied, and included ices, fruit, and a profusion of liquors, which gave a festive note. The expense ruined the officers, who outdid themselves rivaling for magnificence. The number of servants and horse-drawn crews was quadrupled to carry everything and it was a problem to feed them.

All those who undertook such ruinous expenses complained, without daring to reduce them. Finally, in the spring, the King limited the number of horses to forty for a lieutenant general, thirty for camp marshals, twenty-five for brigadier generals, and twenty for colonels. But this ruling went the way of so many others. No country in Europe has such fine laws and sensible statutes, and observes them so little: You cannot keep a single one, for they are usually broken and forgotten during the first year.

DEATH OF A DRUNKARD (1707)

About this time, Vaillac died. He was one of the King's good cavalry generals, and would have gone far as a lieutenant general had not wine, drunkenness, and unavoidable loss of reputation rendered his talents and services useless. He could hold his wine, and was the last in any gathering to pass out. Some rascals once got him married to a trollop when he was too dead drunk to know what he was doing, without the benefit of promises, banns, or a marriage license. When he had slept it off and woke up, imagine his surprise to find this creature in his bed. He asked her with astonishment how she had got there and what she was doing. The trollop reacted with even more surprise and said indignantly that she was his wife. Our friend was so bewildered he thought he was going mad, could not understand what he was being told, and began to call for help. But the prank had been well prepared and all he saw swore up and down that they had been witnesses at his wedding the previous night; he insisted they were liars, that he could not remember a single thing, and that he would never have thought to bring the dishonor of such a marriage upon himself. There was such a row it nearly came to blows, so the adventure ended there and was never mentioned again. It is claimed as authentic that having been well wined and dined by the magistrates of Basel thanks to his fame as a drinker, he proposed a parting toast on horseback; they brought him bottles and a glass: He said this was no way to drink wine and, throwing off one of his boots, he had it filled and then drained it. But this sounds like a tall tale, and was embroidered to the point that it was said the magistrates had the scene painted in their city hall.

Madness of La Chastre (1709)

La Chastre was the brother of the maréchale d'Humières. He was a gentleman of quality and cut a good figure, which made him stand out; he was a very worthy, worldly, and brave man, extremely vain, and had been an ardent lady's man all his life. His nickname was *The Handsome Shepherd*, and he was often the butt of ridicule. He was a lieutenant general, but lacked intelligence, and had no talent for war or anything else. His natural impetuousness gradually increased and led to unfortunate outbursts. One evening, in the middle of a play at the Versailles theatre, he thought he saw the enemy: He shouted orders, drew his sword, and brandished it at the players and the audience. La Vallière, who was close by, grabbed him around the waist and convinced him that he was ill and needed help to get away. This ruse got La Chastre out of the theatre, but he still wanted to rush his enemies. The incident, which took place in front of Monseigneur and the whole court, created quite a commotion. But there were many more to come. He had one of his first seizures while visiting M. le prince de Conti in Paris. The prince was sitting in a lounge chair by the fire, though quite far from the fireplace, and was forced to keep his feet up because of the gout. As luck would have it, M. le prince de Conti was left alone with La Chastre. A fit seized him, and as usual he saw the enemy and wanted to charge: He yelled, drew his sword, and attacked the chairs and the screen. M. le prince de Conti, who expected nothing of the sort, was extremely startled and tried to speak to him; but he continued to yell: "Have at them! Rally round! Over here!" and that sort of thing, and kept thrusting and slashing about. M. le prince de Conti, who was too far from the fireplace to ring or to arm himself with the fire tongs or the coal scoop, was frightened to death, and expected to be taken for an enemy and attacked at any moment: He said that he had never spent such a bad moment. Finally someone came in, saw La Chastre, and calmed him down: He sheathed his sword and left. M. le prince de Conti faithfully kept the matter secret; but he ordered the servant who had come upon them never again to leave him alone with La Chastre.

MELTING THE SILVER (1709)

The duchesse de Gramont told her husband to offer his silver table service to the King in the hope that his example would be followed; she hoped to be given credit for the idea and rewarded for having thought of such a prompt, sound, and considerable means of assistance. Unfortunately for her, the duc de Gramont first mentioned her suggestion to his son-in-law, the maréchal de Boufflers: The maréchal was enthusiastic and thought it an admirable idea; he lost no time in offering his own abundant and admirable silver and beat the drum so loud for everyone to do the same that it appeared to be his idea. The old Gramont woman and the duc de Gramont were never even mentioned and were furious at having been overlooked. Boufflers had asked his old billiards companion Chamillart to bring the matter up before the King. Chamillart took to the idea and convinced the King it was a good one, and Boufflers went straight to the King, who thanked him and his father-in-law. . . .

This rattle of silver caused a great hurly-burly at court: No one dared hold out, but everyone regretted giving in. Some had been keeping their silver as a nest egg, and were grieved to lose it; others feared the uncleanliness of pewter and earthenware; those addicted to silver were forced to use a revolting imitation which only benefited its inventor. The following day, the King told the financial council that he was very much in favor of receiving everyone's silver. This expedient had already been studied and rejected by Pontchartrain when he was controller general, and he was no more in favor of it now that he was chancellor. The argument for donations was that now the King's finances were in far worse shape and there were less means of replenishing them. This speciousness did not sway Pontchartrain: He argued that the profit would be small compared with each individual's loss; that once the silver had been collected, it would fail to provide substantial relief; that each individual would be embarrassed and grieved, and even those who gave with good will would regret it; that the thing was shameful in itself; that confusion would arise because courtiers and other donors would be using earthenware, while people in Paris and the provinces would either keep using their silver or despair and resort to hiding it if they were forbidden to; that the state's finances, after exhausting this apparently extreme and final expedient, would fall into disrepute since there would seem to be no further solutions; and finally that the news would spread abroad and excite the enemy's audacity, contempt, and hopes, perhaps reviving the jeers of the war of 1688 when so many valuable pieces of massive silver furniture that decorated the gallery and the large and small apartments at Versailles were sent to the Mint, even the silver throne that always dazzled visitors. The admirable workmanship was even more of a loss than the silver and would be again in the present case, for many of the silver place settings were luxuriously designed. Desmaretz strongly agreed with these views, even though he bore the burden of the country's finances, which the project would have lightened by several million francs. Despite these excellent and obvious reasons, the King persisted in wanting to accept the silver of those who would offer it freely; it was decided by voice vote that any good citizen could give his silver either to Launay, the King's goldsmith, or to the Mint. Those who wanted to make an outright gift sent it to Launay, who put down their names and the number of marks[1] in a ledger. The King looked over this list, at least at the beginning, and promised the donors he would give them back the same weight when his affairs permitted it, which none of them believed or expected. He also promised to make them exempt from the recently passed hallmark tax for any new silver they would have made. Those who wanted to be paid for their silver sent it to the Mint. The names, dates, and marks were noted, and each was paid according to weight. Some were pleased to be able to sell their silver without disgrace, and made a handsome profit because silver was extremely scarce; but the loss of admirably rich mouldings and embossed and raised designs with which wealthy and fashionable people decorated their silver was irredeemable. When all the

[1] A mark is eight ounces.

accounts were in, there were less than a hundred names on Launay's list, and all the silver donated and sold brought in less than three million francs.

The court and the Paris bigwigs did not dare excuse themselves, and there were a few others who went along to make themselves noticed; but there were no others from Paris, and few from the provinces. Most of those who stopped using their silver put it away with the prospect of selling it according to their needs or bringing it out when times were better. I admit I was in the rear guard, so mightily tired of taxes I was not about to submit to a voluntary one. But when I saw I was practically the only one of my kind still eating off silver plates, I locked up the finest of it and sent the Mint a thousand pistoles' worth that my father had left me. As it was old and rather plain, I regretted the silver less than the inconvenience and uncleanliness. Even an accomplished courtier like M. de Lauzun could not mask his deep resentment, for he had a great deal of admirable silver. I was with him, the duc de la Rocheguyon, and others when the duc de Villeroy asked him whether he had contributed. "Not yet," he replied almost in a whisper. "I don't know who to ask the favor of taking it, and after all, how can I be sure it is not meant to go under the duchesse de Gramont's petticoats?" We thought we would die laughing, and he left us on a pirouette. Within eight days everyone distinguished and worth knowing was eating off china, and there was a run on it that emptied the shops, whereas all the second-raters continued using their silver. The King urged the use of china; he sent his gold table service to the Mint, and M. le duc d'Orléans also sent the little he had. The King and the royal family switched to silver and gold-plated silver; the princes and princesses of the blood used china. The King learned soon after that many had made fraudulent claims, and he reacted with unusual bitterness, which changed nothing. He would have done better to chastise the duc de Gramont and his nasty wife, who were the despicable causes of his shameful and useless outburst. They were not the dupes of their proposal: They stored their beautiful and magnificent silver, and the woman took her old silver to the Mint herself, and got a pretty price for it. . . . Those who had given their silver were not long in favor: After three months, the King realized the shame and feebleness of this fine expedient, and admitted he was sorry he had ever agreed to it. Such was then the march of events, for the court and for the State.

How Wars Were Started (1709)

The war of 1688 had a strange cause. The story, as authentic as it is curious, is so characteristic of the King and his minister Louvois[1] that it must find its place here. At the death of Colbert, Louvois became superintendent of construction. The porcelain-faced small Trianon, which had been built for Mme. de Montespan, bored the King, who wanted palaces everywhere. One of his major interests was construction. He had an unfailing eye for accuracy, proportion, and symmetry, but, as we shall see, his eye was not matched by his taste. The new Trianon had scarcely begun to rise when the King noticed a defect in a ground-floor casement window. Louvois, who had a violent nature and was too spoiled to tolerate his master's reprimands, argued loud and long that the window was flawless. The King turned his back and went to inspect other parts of the building. The next day he saw that fine architect Le Nostre, who has become famous because of the gardens he introduced in France and brought to the highest level of perfection. The King asked him whether he had been to Trianon, and he said he had not. The King explained what had shocked him, and asked Le Nostre to go see for himself; the next day, same question, same answer, and the day after that. The King realized Le Nostre did not dare put himself in a position where he would have to take sides. He grew angry, said he would be at Trianon with Louvois the next day, and ordered Le Nostre to be there too. There was no holding back. The following day, the King brought up the matter of the window. Louvois argued, and Le Nostre held his tongue. The King commanded him to measure the window. Louvois was furious at this inspection, grumbled aloud, and insisted bitterly that the window was like all the others. The King waited without

[1] The marquis de Louvois (1641-1691) was secretary of state for war and superintendent of construction, arts, and manufactures.

showing how pained he was by Louvois' attitude. Finally, he asked Le Nostre the result of his inspection, and Le Nostre began to mumble. The King was furious, and ordered him to speak up. Le Nostre admitted that the King was right and that the window was crooked.

He had no sooner finished than the King turned to Louvois and told him he could no longer stand his stubbornness. He said that if he had not noticed the window, the Trianon would have gone up crooked and everything would have had to be torn down as soon as it was finished; in other words, he really gave Louvois a tongue-lashing. Louvois was infuriated by the scolding, which had been overheard by courtiers, workmen, and valets. Saint-Pouenge, Villacerf, the chevalier de Nogent, the two Tilladets, and other of his trusty friends were alarmed to see him in such a state. "It's all over with the King, the way he just treated me," he said. "I am lost because of a window. My only way out is to start a war that will make him forget his buildings and make me indispensable. By God, he shall have it!" He kept his word; the war began several months later, and spread despite the efforts of the King and the other great powers. For all her military strength, the war ruined France internally, added no further conquests, and was the cause of many shameful events.

A TERRIBLE WINTER (1709)

The winter had been so terrible, as I have already said, that no one could remember any that came close to it. A two-month freezing spell had in its first days frozen the rivers solid up to their mouths and the seaside to the point where you could ride over it with heavily laden carts. A premature thaw melted the snow which had covered the ground all winter, but it was followed by another freezing spell as violent as the one three weeks before. The cold was so fierce that it broke bottles of Queen-of-Hungary water[1] as well as the strongest elixirs and spirits. I saw

[1] The eighteenth century equivalent of eau de Cologne.

this happen in heated rooms surrounded by chimney flues in several Versailles apartments. And dining with the duc de Villeroy in his small bedroom, icicles fell into our glasses from bottles on the mantelpiece although they had been brought from a small kitchen near his room where a great fire roared. His son lives today in this same apartment. The second frost ravaged the countryside. The fruit trees perished. There remained not a single walnut, olive, apple, or grape, or so few they are not worth mentioning. A great many other trees died, and the gardens perished, as well as all the grain that had been sown. It is impossible to imagine the desolation of this general ruin. Everyone hoarded his old grain; the price of bread went up as hopes for the harvest fell. The most farsighted sowed barley on land where there had been wheat, and most of the others imitated them. These were the most fortunate, and it was to prove their salvation. The police decided to prohibit this practice, and was to change its mind too late. Various edicts concerning wheat were issued, police searched for secret granaries and inspectors were not sent through the provinces until three months after their arrival had been announced. These methods made poverty and the cost of living reach new heights, although it could be easily reckoned that there was enough wheat in France to feed the whole country, even if there was no harvest. There were many who believed that the gentlemen who direct the country's finances had taken advantage of the situation to appropriate wheat in every market of the kingdom and later sell it at good profit to the King and to themselves.

This belief was strengthened by an accident that could not be concealed: A considerable number of shiploads of wheat which the King had bought spoiled in the Loire, and the wheat had to be thrown overboard. What is certain is that the price of wheat was the same in marketplaces throughout the kingdom, but that in Paris commissioners raised the price and often made the merchants raise it against their will. When the people demanded how long the high prices would last, this all too transparent reply escaped from commissioners in a market near Saint-Germain-des-Prés, two steps away from my home: "As long as you please." By this they were implying, out of indignation and compassion, as long as the people would tolerate that wheat could only enter Paris with d'Argenson's[2] agreement; and no other way was found to bring it in. D'Argenson, who was to be Lord Privy Seal under the Regency, was then police commissioner, and was at the same time made Councillor of State without giving up his police post. Rigorous coercion was practiced on all the bakers, and what I am saying was true all over France. What d'Argenson did in Paris, the provincial administrators did in their jurisdictions. In every marketplace, the wheat that was not sold at a fixed price before the market's closing was requisitioned. Those who sold it at a lower price out of pity were cruelly punished.

Boufflers Calms Two Riots (1709)

The high price of everything, especially bread, was responsible for riots all over the kingdom. Paris experienced many, although the regiments that guard the marketplaces and other danger points had been reinforced by fifty percent, and d'Argenson risked his life on several occasions. Monseigneur had been attacked several times on his way to or from the Opéra by the populace and crowds of women crying for bread; although well guarded, he had quite a fright, for his guards had not dared disperse the mob for fear of arousing it further. He got out of it by throwing money to the crowd and making promises he could not keep, so that he did not dare go back to Paris. The people of Versailles yelled in the streets and the King himself heard strong words under his windows. The numerous speeches and complaints against the government and even against the King's person were brazen and immoderate; people met in streets and public squares and told each other they should not endure such suffering, since nothing could be worse than starvation. To appease the populace, the poor and the idlers were signed on to level a big mound on the boulevard between the gates of Saint-Denis and Saint-Martin, and the only salary they received was a little stale bread. It happened that on Tuesday morning, August 20, there was a shortage

[2] The marquis d'Argenson was Paris chief of police. He became Lord Privy Seal in 1718 and minister of state in 1720.

of bread. A woman began to scream at the top of her voice, which excited the others. The soldiers distributing the bread threatened her, which made her scream all the louder, so they grabbed her and imprudently had her put in irons. All the other workers rushed to her assistance, freed her from the irons, and ran through the streets, looting bakeries and cake shops: The shops closed one after the other as the mob increased and went from street to street clamoring for bread and taking it where they could find it, but without molesting anyone. The maréchal de Boufflers had anything but this on his mind when he went to see his notaire that morning in the same neighborhood.

Startled by the riot and learning its cause, he wanted to go and calm the mob; the duc de Gramont, who was also at the notaire's, could not dissuade him, so decided to join him. A hundred paces from the notaire's cabinet they saw the carriage of the maréchal d'Huxelles coming from the direction of the riot, and stopped him for news. He told them it was all over and, after trying to keep them from going on, he drove away in the manner of someone who wanted no part of noise and disorder. But the maréchal and his father-in-law plunged ahead, and found increasing turbulence, with people shouting at them from windows to turn back lest they be roughed up. When they reached the head of Saint-Denis Street, the tumult and the shouting made the maréchal de Boufflers decide to continue on foot. He and the duc de Gramont mingled with the vast and furious mob, and he addressed it with firm and quiet eloquence, asking the reason for the commotion, promising that there would be bread, and explaining that this was not the way to ask for it. His words carried, and as he continued to make his way through the crowd there were cries of *Long live M. le Maréchal de Boufflers!* He saved the day. Had it not been for him blood would have been spilled and things would have gotten out of hand, for d'Argenson was about to march on the crowd with detachments of mounted French and Swiss guards and musketeers. No sooner was the maréchal back at his home on the Place Royale with his father-in-law than he was told the sedition was even greater at the Faubourg Saint-Antoine: He hurried there with the duc de Gramont and calmed that crowd as he had the other. Then he went home for a bite to eat before going to Versailles.

THE USHER'S MISTAKE (1711)

One morning while Mme. la duchesse de Berry was dressing, the new usher from the King's chambers announced Mme. la duchesse d'Orléans, who had come to borrow some article of clothing. The scatterbrained and inexperienced usher opened both sections of the double door.[1] Mme. la duchesse de Berry's face grew crimson and she trembled with rage; she was very short with her mother. Once alone, she called Mme. de Saint-Simon and asked her if she had noticed the usher's impertinence, and said she wanted him removed forthwith. Mme. de Saint-Simon agreed the usher was at fault and promised to instruct him on the proper opening of doors so there could be no further mistakes; that is, both sides only for the sons and daughters of France, an honor to which none other should or would pretend. But she added that it would be enough to reprimand the usher instead of having him removed, for he had been loaned by the King, and his first mistake after all had been only to grant her mother too great an honor. Mme. la duchesse de Berry insisted, wept, and threw a tantrum; Mme. de Saint-Simon let her go on, softly scolded the usher, and gave him a lesson in etiquette.

AN APRIL FOOL'S JOKE (1711)

The Elector of Cologne liked to take part in every kind of ceremony. He even liked to preach, and one can imagine what kind of preacher he was. He decided, on the first day of April, to take to the pulpit; he had invited everyone in Valenciennes, and the church was full. The Elector made his appearance, looked over the entire attendance, and suddenly began to scream: "April

[1] It was a major breach in court etiquette to open both sides of a door except for the King and princes of the blood.

fool! April fool!" while his musicians chimed in with trumpets and kettledrums. He had had his fun, and vanished. It was a typical German prince's joke, and those who witnessed it were more surprised than amused.

Two Trivial but Amusing Adventures (1713)

Sometimes the most serious and melancholy matters are peppered with droll incidents, and the contrast could make an undertaker laugh. I cannot resist reporting two such incidents that I witnessed during a parliamentary session, one of which caused me a good deal of concern. Because of my rank, I was seated on the lower benches between the duc de Richelieu and the duc de La Force. They had been there quite a while, waiting for the duc de Berry, who was not long in arriving. Soon after, I noticed old Richelieu fidgeting, and he asked me whether it would be a long session. I said I thought so as there was to be a procession of speakers addressing the King. He did not take it well, and began to grumble. He could not sit still, and kept fidgeting and grumbling, and finally said he had to get out because he was dying to go to the toilet. I pointed out to him the impropriety of a departure which required his crossing the empty floor where all present would surely see him. But that did not satisfy him, and he started up again. I knew my man from experience; he was such a rare bird that I have mentioned him elsewhere. I knew he took senna[1] almost every morning, and that he often took an enema, which he would carry around three or four hours before releasing it wherever he happened to be. I was alarmed for his breeches, and consequently for my nose. I tried to devise a way to rid myself of such a dangerous neighbor, but saw to my horror that the crowd was too thick to get through. To make a long story short, his whines and threats continued during the entire session, increasing so toward the end that more than once I thought I was lost. . . .

The other amusing incident was not so menacing. Monsieur

[1] A laxative obtained from the bark of Cassia, a cinnamon-like tree.

de Metz had his back to my knees . . . and soon after the start of the session he grew impatient. He complained about the use-lessness of the speeches, he wanted to know whether the speakers were determined to have us spend the night there, and he finally said he was dying to take a piss. He was amusing, and had a natural sense of the comic that went to the heart of the most serious matters.

I suggested that he piss on the ears of the counselors below him on the lower benches. He shook his head, spoke out loud, challenged the attorney general between his teeth, and fidgeted so that the duc de Tresmes and the duc de Charost, on either side of him, kept telling him to behave himself. We almost died laughing. He wanted to get out but saw that it was impossible; he swore he would never be caught again at such a gathering; several times he threatened to relieve himself in his breeches; he entertained us during the whole session and I never saw a man so relieved as when it was over.

Punishment of an Inattentive Courtier (1715)

We had been given lodgings at Versailles on the ground floor of the first pavilion, near the chapel. One day as we were sitting down to lunch we were surprised to see Blouin,[1] followed by several wardrobe attendants. He said the King had requested that I yield my apartment to the Prince de Cellamare and move to lodgings across from and above the chapel. He did not explain how these lodgings happened to be vacant. He assured me I would like the new apartment and that the King wanted me to be comfortable. He added that the King was so eager to have me move right away he had ordered his own wardrobe attendants to help mine with the moving. We lunched, Mme. de Saint-Simon went out, and I attended to the moving. My servants told me quite a few wardrobe attendants were on hand, that Blouin had looked in again, and that everything had been done in the wink of an eye. I could not imagine the reason for such haste, but

[1] Louis Blouin, superintendent of Versailles and Marly.

upon retiring I discovered it. My servants told me I had been moved to the apartment of Courtenvaux, who since he was captain of the Swiss guards, had permanent lodgings along with the other chief attendants of the King's chambers, wardrobe and chapel. At ten o'clock, a chaise post arrived: It was Courtenvaux, who was surprised to see light coming through the windows of his room and sent someone to find out why. His footman went up, was very surprised to find my servants already settled, and came to tell his master. He sent word it was his apartment and that he intended to spend the night in it. My servants told his footman why I had moved, said they would not budge, and suggested that Courtenvaux see Blouin and find out what was going on. There was nothing else for Courtenvaux to do. Blouin, speaking for the King, told him he had been absent from court without leave for eighteen days and that it was not the first time. He said the King had had enough of his absences, had purposely given his apartment to someone else to teach him a lesson, and that he would henceforth be banned from Marly. Such is the pettiness above which the Crown cannot rise.

A State Visit [1] (1717)

The Czar was admired for his great curiosity in matters of government, trade, education, and police. His curiosity touched on everything, disdained nothing, and always had a wise, closely reasoned, and definite purpose. He only considered what was most worthwhile, and displayed a sound and brilliant intelligence as well as great powers of understanding. Everything he did brought out the vast scope of his knowledge and his powers of reasoning. It was astonishing to see how he blended a majesty at once lofty, proud, delicate, sustained, and natural, with a monarch's courtesy, which everyone felt in varying degrees depending on their rank. He had a kind of familiarity which stemmed from an independent spirit; but he had not shaken off the strong imprint of his country's ancient barbarism, which made him im-

---

[1] Visit of Czar Peter the Great to France.

patient, abrupt, and incapable of tolerating contradiction, although his opinions wavered; he set a rather coarse table, and the coarseness increased after the meal was over, for he displayed the brazenness of a king who felt himself everywhere at home; he wanted to do and see everything in his own way, and everyone had to bend to his wishes and demands. His supremely independent spirit often made him prefer rented carriages, even hackney coaches, or a carriage belonging to courtiers he scarcely knew who were paying him a visit; he wanted to see things at his own leisure and not be made a spectacle of. He would jump into a carriage and have himself driven around or outside town. One of his victims was Mme. de Matignon, who had come to gape at him. He drove off in her carriage to Boulogne and other country spots and she was mightily surprised to find herself on foot. Whenever the Czar escaped, it was up to the maréchal de Tessé and his suite to chase after him, but sometimes they could not find him.

He was a very tall man, extremely well built, on the thin side, with a rather round face, a high forehead, and fine eyebrows; his nose was short without being too short, and had a wide tip; he had rather thick lips and his complexion was reddish-brown; he had beautiful black eyes, large, alert, piercing, and well set. When he wanted it to be, his expression was majestic and gracious, otherwise it was stern and fierce, with a recurring tic that twisted his whole face and frightened people. He would take on a wild and terrible look, but it only lasted a moment, and his face would go back to normal. Everything in his manner showed intelligence, thoughtfulness, and grandeur, and did not lack a certain grace. He wore only a cloth collar, a round, brown wig with hardly any powder, which did not reach his shoulders, a brown jerkin with gold buttons, a jacket, breeches, stockings, and neither gloves nor cuffs; he wore the star of his order over his coat and the cordon under it,[2] and his coat was often completely unbuttoned; he left his hat on the table, and never put it on his head, even when going outdoors. For all his simplicity, even if one saw him unaccompanied in a shabby carriage, his air of natural majesty was unmistakable. It was inconceivable how much he ate and drank at meals, without mentioning the amount of beer, lemon-

[2] The Order of Saint Andrew.

ade, and other beverages he and his suite put away between meals. The Czar's average for a meal was a bottle or two of beer, as much or more wine, followed by liqueur wines, with half a quart and sometimes a quart of spirits after the meal. His suite was even more voracious when it was at table at eleven in the morning and eight in the evening. No matter how much was brought, they always cleared the table. The Czar enjoyed and was much amused by a chaplain who ate at his table and whose appetite was half again as keen as any other. Prince Kuriakin[3] went to the Hôtel de Lesdiguières every day but slept at the Embassy. The Czar had a good understanding of French and could have spoken it if he wished; but for prestige, he always had an interpreter. He spoke Latin and many other tongues very well. He had been given a company of King's guards, but rarely allowed them to escort him. He would not leave the Hôtel de Lesdiguières for any reason, or give any sign of life, until he had received the King's visit.

Saturday morning, the day after his arrival, the Czar received the Regent's visit. The monarch emerged from his study, advanced to meet him, kissed him with an air of great superiority, showed him the door of his study, and turned and entered without further ceremony. The Regent followed with Prince Kuriakin to serve as interpreter. The Czar and the Regent sat in two facing armchairs and, although they did not talk business, the conversation lasted close to an hour. The Czar came out of the study followed by the Regent, who gave him a deep bow which was indifferently returned, and left him at the same spot where he had found him.

The King [Louis XV] went to see the Czar the following Monday, May 10. The Czar was at the door to greet him, watched him get out of his carriage, and led him to his room, where there were two identical armchairs. The King sat on the right, the Czar on the left, and Prince Kuriakin served as interpreter. The astonishment was general when the Czar grabbed the King under both arms, lifted him in the air, and kissed him. Despite his age,[4] the King displayed no fear at this unexpected greeting. For the King's benefit, the Czar strikingly displayed graciousness, tenderness, and a natural courtesy which also brought out his grandeur, his equality of rank, and the slight

[3] Boris Kuriakin was then Russian Ambassador to Paris.
[4] He was then seven years old.

superiority due to his age. He praised the King highly and convinced everyone he had been charmed by him. He kissed him several times. The King very prettily paid his brief compliment, and conversation was provided by M. du Maine, the maréchal de Villeroy, and other distinguished persons present. The meeting lasted about a quarter of an hour. The Czar saw the King out as he had seen him in, and watched him get into his carriage. . . .

After lunch, the Czar went to the Palais Royal to see Madame, who had sent her first gentleman usher to pay him her compliments. She had received him as she would have the King, except for the armchair. M. le duc d'Orléans came to take him to the Opéra, where they were alone on the front bench of his box, which was decorated with a tapestry. Soon after they had arrived, the Czar asked whether beer would be served. A big goblet full was immediately brought on a saucer. The Regent rose to take it and presented it to the Czar, who accepted it with a smile and a polite nod, drained it, and put it back on the saucer, which the Regent still held. The Regent then offered the Czar a napkin on a plate, which he took without rising as he had the beer, to everyone's surprise. During the fourth act, he left to have supper, but would not allow the Regent to escort him. The next day, Saturday, he hopped into a rented carriage and went to visit workmen, where he saw all sorts of curious things.

May 16 was Pentecost, and he went to the Invalides, where he wanted to see and examine everything. At the soldiers' mess, he tasted their soup and wine, drank to their health, smacked them on the shoulder and called them comrades. He much admired the church, the infirmary, and the pharmacy, and seemed charmed by the order of the establishment.

On Friday June 11, he went from Versailles to Saint-Cyr, where he visited everything, including the young ladies in their classrooms. He was received as the King would have been. He also wanted to see Mme. de Maintenon, who tried to escape his curiosity by taking to her bed and drawing all her curtains but one, which was only half closed. The Czar came into her room, opened all the window curtains, and then all the bed curtains. He looked at Mme. de Maintenon long and hard, but they did not exchange a single word. Then he left without making the slightest bow. I learned that she had been most surprised and mortified; but there was no recourse to a King who was no longer alive.[5]

Tuesday June 15 he went to Paris early to visit d'Antin. I was working with M. le duc d'Orléans that day and he was surprised to see me getting up to leave after half an hour had gone by, and tried to hold me back. I told him I would always have the honor of seeing him, but not the Czar, who was leaving and whom I had never seen, and that I was therefore going to d'Antin's to gape at leisure. No one was allowed in except the guests and a few ladies who were with Madame la Duchesse and her daughters the princesses who had also come to gape. I went into the garden, where the Czar was strolling. The maréchal de Tessé, seeing me from afar, came up to present me to the Czar. I begged him not to, and asked him not to tell the Czar I was there. I wanted to watch him freely and lie in wait for him as often as I wished so as to observe him unnoticed, which would have been impossible had I been identified.

I asked him to warn d'Antin and, after taking this precaution, I was able to satisfy my curiosity to my heart's content. I found the Czar open in conversation, although he always remained the master. D'Antin led him into a study and showed him various papers and oddities, and he asked several questions. It was there I saw the tic I have mentioned. I asked Tessé if he had it often; he said several times a day, and more when he did not take care to control himself. Going back into the garden, d'Antin tried to spirit him past the lower apartment, warning him that Madame la Duchesse and her party were there and were dying to see him. He did not reply and let himself be led. He slowed down and turned his head toward the apartment, where they were all standing up like sentries on the lookout. After taking a good look at them, he gave a slight nod, without having fully faced them, and passed by proudly. From the manner in which he had received other ladies of the court, I believe he would have displayed

[5] After the death of Louis XIV, Madame de Maintenon went to finish her days at Saint-Cyr, the school for young ladies she had founded. Harold Nicolson writes in *The Age of Reason* that the meeting between the Czar and Madame de Maintenon was "a strange picture assuredly of the old woman flat in her little convent bed and the giant Peter staring at her silently, holding apart the curtains with his vast moujik hands. The picture of a fading past, confronted with a colossal symbol of the future."

greater courtesy had Madame la Duchesse not shown such eagerness to gape. He purposely failed to inquire who she and all the
other ladies were. I was there for nearly an hour and did not take
my eyes off him. Toward the end, he seemed to notice it, which
made me even more circumspect for fear he would ask who I
was. As he was going in I quickly took my place in the banquet
hall, where the table had been set. D'Antin was up to his old tricks
and had unearthed a portrait of the Czarina, a very good likeness,
which he had hung over the fireplace, along with a poem in her
praise. The Czar was surprised and very pleased, and he and his
suite agreed that it was a good likeness.

The Czar left on Sunday, June 20. He refused an escort, even
when leaving Paris. He slept at Livry and went straight to Spa,
where the Czarina was waiting for him. The luxury he saw had
greatly impressed him; he said it pained him to realize that such
luxury would eventually doom France, and he spoke with sym-
pathy of France and the King. He was charmed by the style of
his welcome, everything he had seen, and the freedom of movement he had been given.

One could go on forever about a czar so particularly and so
truly great. The singularity and rare variety of so many great
talents will make him remembered to all succeeding generations
as a monarch worthy of the highest admiration, despite the great
defects of the barbarism of his origin, his country, and his education.

The Regent Buys an Extraordinary Diamond (1717)

In a most unusual feat, an employee of the Great Mogul's diamond
mines found a way to hide a diamond of prodigious size up his
ass. What is even more wonderful is that he was able to reach
the coast and find passage on a ship without being subjected to
the usual controls for suspect passengers, such as purges and
enemas to make them give up what they might have swallowed
or concealed. He was clever enough to convince everyone that
he had never been near the mines or had anything to do with

precious stones. His good fortune was such that he was able to reach Europe with the gem. He showed it to several princes, who could not afford it, and finally took it to England, where the King could not decide whether to buy it. He had a crystal copy made in England, and took the copy and the diamond to France. He showed them to Law,[1] who proposed the gem to the Regent for the King [Louis XV]. The price frightened the Regent, and he refused to buy it. Law, who had many grandiose schemes, came to see me in great distress, and showed me the copy. I agreed with him that it did not suit the greatness of the King of France to balk at the price of a unique and priceless gem and that the greater the number of potentates who had refused it the more reason not to let it out of our hands. Law was delighted with this opinion and begged me to speak to M. le duc d'Orléans. The Regent insisted that the main obstacle was the state of the country's finances. He was afraid he would be blamed for such a considerable expenditure at a time when he had trouble meeting the most pressing demands and when so many people were suffering. I praised his motives and agreed that it would be reprehensible to throw away a hundred thousand francs to adorn oneself with a pretty diamond while he had obligations he could not meet; but I added that what was true for a simple individual did not hold for the greatest king in Europe; that for the honor of the Crown, the unique opportunity to buy the most priceless diamond in Europe should not be missed; that it would be a glory for which the Regency would always be remembered; and that whatever state the finances were in, the saving would not relieve them much, while the expense would hardly be noticed.

I would not leave M. le duc d'Orléans' side until he agreed to buy the diamond. Meanwhile Law convinced the seller that he would never find a buyer for his diamond at so high a price and that he would suffer an even greater loss by having it cut. He knocked down the price to two million francs, with the seller keeping the chips when the stone was cut. The man was paid interest on the two million until the capital could be raised, with two millions' worth of precious stones as security. M. le duc

[1] The Scotsman John Law (1671-1729), head of the royal bank, founder of the company of the Indies, controller general of finances in 1720, bankrupt in 1721.

d'Orléans was pleasantly surprised by public approval for such a beautiful and unique acquisition. The diamond was called *The Regent*. It was as big as a greengage plum, almost round, with a thickness proportionate to its size, perfectly white, free of any spot, cloud, or flaw, of the first water, and weighed more than 125 carats. I congratulated myself on having persuaded the Regent to make such an illustrious purchase.

ARRANGEMENT OF A ROYAL WEDDING [1] (1721)

"There, there, master," Fréjus was saying, "you must agree to it with good grace." Fréjus was whispering urgently to the King, and I could only half hear what he was saying. The others stood in mournful silence, and those of us who had just come in were very surprised by the sight; since I knew what was at stake I was especially surprised. Finally I realized they were trying to make the King announce his marriage plans to the Regency Council; I did not dare try to learn how it was going by signaling to M. le duc d'Orléans or the cardinal Dubois. All these stratagems lasted nearly a quarter hour. After a final whisper, M. de Fréjus told M. le duc d'Orléans that the King would attend the Council but needed a little time to get hold of himself. This news brought the color back to their faces. M. le duc d'Orléans said there was no rush and that everything must be done in its own time; drawing close to the King, he spoke to him softly, then said out loud: "The King will come; I believe we would do well now to leave him alone." We all left except M. le Duc, the maréchal de Villeroy, and the bishop of Fréjus. On the way to the council chamber,

[1] The marriage between eleven-year-old Louis XV and the three-year-old Infanta of Spain was arranged in 1721 to cement crumbling relations between the two Bourbon houses. The king of Spain, Philip V, was the grandson of Louis XIV, who had him put on the throne. Since Louis XV was the great-grandson of Louis XIV, the Infanta was his first cousin. The marriage never took place. After the death of the Regent in 1723, M. le Duc (the duc de Bourbon) became prime minister and opposed the match. The Infanta was in France for the marriage, but he had her sent back to Spain, thereby putting an end to cordial relations between the two countries. He pushed Louis XV into marriage with the Polish princess Maria Leczinska.

I approached M. le duc d'Orléans, who put his arm under mine and pulled me into a narrow passageway for a confidential chat. He said that at the mention of marriage the King had begun to cry and they had all the trouble in the world getting him to agree; they found him equally reluctant to announce it before the Regency Council, which is where we had come in. He had no opportunity to tell me more, and we entered the council chamber together. The King's wedding was such a personal matter that it could not be arranged without him, and it was essential that he either announce it himself or be present when it was announced. The other members of the Council, surprised by such a long and unusual conference in the King's chambers, approached us out of curiosity but did not dare question us; they all seemed preoccupied. M. le duc d'Orléans bantered with them as best he could and said the King would not be long. The three maréchaux and I, who had come in with M. le duc d'Orléans, separated but did not mingle with the others. We did not wait long. The King came in with Monsieur le Duc and the maréchal de Villeroy, and everyone took his seat. Cardinal Dubois, who no longer attended the Regency Council since he had been given the *zucchetto* [cardinal's cap], had left after the conference in the King's cabinet.

As we sat there, all eyes were on the King, whose own eyes were wide and red, and who appeared very solemn. There were a few moments of silence, during which M. le duc d'Orléans looked everyone over; they all seemed full of great expectations. Then, asking them to notice that the King had arrived, he asked the King if he was ready to tell the Council about his marriage. The King's answer was *yes*, uttered in a dry and rather low voice, which was heard by the four or five closest to him on either side. M. le duc d'Orléans then announced the marriage and the forthcoming arrival of the Infanta, adding that the match was a suitable and important one, and would strengthen the necessary union of two related royal branches, which had fallen out due to unfortunate circumstances. He was brief but vigorous, for he spoke marvelously, and then asked for opinions. One can well imagine what opinions were given. Only the maréchaux de Bezons, d'Huxelles, and d'Estrées, and the bishop of Troyes spoke at some length. The maréchal de Villeroy approved in a few

words, adding sadly that it was too bad the Infanta was so young.
I spoke at greater length than anyone, but with gravity. The
comte de Toulouse and M. le Duc approved gracefully, with few
words. M. le duc d'Orléans took a few more words to say that
he had expected nothing less than a unanimous vote for such a
suitable marriage. Turning toward the King, he bowed and
smiled as though inviting the King to smile as well, and told him:
"There then, Sire, your marriage has been approved and voted,
and a great and happy affair is done."

Advice to a Young King (1721)

Every year on the feast of Saint-Louis there was an evening concert in the garden. The maréchal de Villeroy[1] turned the concert
into a festive occasion and added fireworks. That was more than
enough to attract the crowds, which were so dense there was not
enough room to drop a pin. The windows of the Tuileries, the
roofs of the Carrousel, and the square were full of people. The
maréchal de Villeroy was delighted by the crowds, although they
annoyed the King, who hid in corners at every opportunity; the
maréchal would pull him by the arm, and lead him first to the
windows giving on the crowded courtyard, the Place du Carrousel, and the roofs strewn with onlookers, then to the windows
overlooking the gardens and the numberless throngs waiting for
the festivities. Whenever they saw him, the crowds shouted
Vive le Roi! and the maréchal held the King in front of the
windows despite his attempts to hide: "Look here, my master,"
he said, "at this crowd and all these people; it is all yours; it all
belongs to you; you are its master. Have a look at them then to
make them happy; for they are all yours; you are the master of
all that." A fine lesson for a governor to inculcate! He repeated
it every time he led the King to the windows, for fear it might
be forgotten. And it was true that the king remembered it well.
I wonder how many other lessons of this sort he learned from

[1] The duc and maréchal de Villeroy (1644-1730) was tutor (or governor)
of Louis XV from 1717 to 1722.

those responsible for his education. Finally the maréchal led him to the canopied terrace where he heard the end of the concert and watched the fireworks. The lesson so frequently and publicly repeated by the maréchal de Villeroy brought him great notoriety but little honor.

PALL-MALL [1] AT THE COURT OF SPAIN (1722) [2]

From the Atoche[3] the King usually went to Retiro Park with those who had accompanied him to mass. They stopped at the pall-mall court, which was beautiful, wide, and extremely long. The King always played three full games with his equerries and the marquis de Santa-Cruz or some other lord. His partner was always the Queen, who changed sides when she had to so as to be always on his left. The pall-mall court was extremely agreeable and charming. Only lords and the Queen's lady in waiting were allowed there; everyone else had to stand outside. One followed the royal couple and the Queen made conversation with pleasant familiarity, amusing the King with her sallies. Valouse[4] made them even more amusing by displaying his embarrassment. The Queen also directed her wit at the duc del Arco, and took pleasure in provoking arguments between him and Santa-Cruz, which resulted in diverting exchanges. The grand equerry sometimes took the liberty of giving the Queen as good as he got. If one of the players made a pirouette or some other error of play, everyone laughed and teased him, so that the time spent at the pall-mall always seemed too short. The King was usually solemn but sometimes smiled; sometimes he would say a word or two. He was a good player and a good sport, and the Queen admired him greatly. When the game was over the carriages came to the end of the court to pick up the players.

[1] A precursor of croquet, in which a wooden ball was driven with a long-handled mallet.

[2] In 1722, Saint-Simon was named special ambassador to Spain to ask for the Infanta's hand for Louis XV. It was his first and last diplomatic mission.

[3] The Atoche was a Dominican convent outside Madrid with a renowned chapel.

[4] The marquis de Valouse was head of the King's personal staff.

An Audience at the Court of Spain (1722)

The audience soon turned on general matters. I had the honor of hearing from the King and Queen about Cardinal Borgia, who had arrived from Rome several days before, and about his description of Italy. In the course of this conversation, the King began to laugh, glanced at the Queen, and said the cardinal had told them the funniest story in the world. I smiled, in the manner of someone who would like to know but does not dare ask. He again looked at the Queen and said: "It might not be right to tell," then: "Should we tell him?" "Why not?" replied the Queen. "All right," said the King, "but on condition you repeat it to no one, without exception." I promised and I kept my word: I am mentioning it here for the first time, after the death of the king of Spain and all those concerned, for the readers of these memoirs, if they ever see the light of day after I am gone; at that time no one will be annoyed by the disclosure. The King granted me the honor of telling me that the cardinal de Borgia had told him that the cardinal de Rohan was little esteemed and had a poor reputation in Rome, despite all his magnificence and the charm of his flattering manners. Despite his age, conceit and self-admiration had led him to take frequent milk baths to make his skin softer and more beautiful; he had tried to keep it a secret but had been found out, to the indignation of the pious and the contempt and raillery of others; with that, the King, the Queen, and I began to laugh with all our hearts; for the King had told the story in the most amusing way, and had commented on it equally well.

A Hunt at the Court of Spain (1722)

Hunting was the King's everyday pleasure and the Queen was forced to make it hers; it never varied. Once, their Catholic

Majesties granted me the singular honor of an invitation, and I took my own carriage. I was able to see the hunt well, and who has seen one has seen them all. As the red and black deer cannot be found in the plains, they must be sought in the mountains. This country is too harsh for riding the stag, wild boar, and other animals that are hunted in France and elsewhere. The plains are so dry, so hard, so full of unexpected crevasses, that the best hounds would soon be worse off than the hares, with their feet scraped and perhaps badly injured. At any rate, the country is so full of strong-smelling grass that the dogs would not find their noses of much use. The King had long since given up riding, so that the hunt was limited to battues.

One of the duc del Arco's duties as grand equerry was to manage the hunts, and choose the spot where the King and Queen should go. Two great blinds of foliage were built back to back, closed except for large openings at the right height for firing. The King, the Queen, the captain of the guards on duty, the grand equerry, and four men to load the guns were alone in the first blind with about twenty guns and ammunition. In the other blind there were the prince of Asturias who had come in his own carriage with the duc de Popoli and the marquis del Surco, the marquis de Santa-Cruz, the duc de Giovenazzo, who was major-domo and grand equerry to the Queen, Valouse, two or three guards officers, myself, a great many guns, and several men to load them. A single lady of the palace on duty for the day trailed the Queen in another carriage which she never left, with a book and some sewing for consolation. No one in the suite ever went near her. Their Majesties and the suite traveled at full speed with carriage relays to reach the blinds, for there were at least three or four leagues to cover, and it was at least twice as far as from Paris to Versailles. One alighted as soon as the blinds were reached, and all the carriages, horses, and the poor lady of the palace were taken far out of sight so they could not frighten the animals.

Two, three, even four hundred peasants had been recruited and had built enclosures during the night; at dawn they started their hallooing from far off to frighten the animals, make them rise and assemble, and prodded them gently toward the blinds. In the blinds, no one was allowed to move or talk the least bit, or wear

any gaudy clothes; everyone stood in silence. The waiting lasted
a good hour and a half, and did not appear very diverting to me.
Finally we heard great halloos from afar, and soon after we saw
herds of animals passing repeatedly within gun range, and immediately the King and Queen began to fire at will. This sort of
butchery, or if you will, this pleasure, lasted more than half an
hour: Numberless stags, does, roe deer, wild boar, hares, wolves,
badgers, foxes, and weasels passed before us and were killed or
wounded. You had to let the King and Queen fire first, and since
they often permitted the grand equerry and the captain of the
guards to fire, you could not really tell who was firing, and you
had to wait until the King's blind had completely stopped firing;
then you had to let the prince fire, who had very little left to
fire at, while the rest of us had still less. I did manage, however,
to kill a fox, although I must admit I fired a bit earlier than I
should have. I was somewhat ashamed and apologized to the
prince of Asturias, who started to laugh, and the others with him,
so that I followed their example. It was all done with great tact.
The hunt nears its end when the peasants close in on the blinds,
and it ends when they reach them, still hallooing, for there is
nothing more behind them. Then the carriages return; the two
teams of hunters meet outside the blinds; the dead animals are
brought before the King and loaded behind the carriages. During
this time conversation turns on the hunt. That day we took away
a dozen or more animals, not including several hares, foxes, and
weasels. The recruited peasants were paid; the King usually gives
them a little extra as he is getting into his carriage. Night fell
soon after we had left the blinds. Such is the pleasure of their
Catholic Majesties every working day.

INCONCEIVABLE BOLDNESS OF THE DUC DE LAUZUN
(1723)

The duc de Lauzun[1] was a small flaxen-haired man, well-made,
haughty, imposing and full of wit, but with an unattractive face,

[1] Antoine, duc de Lauzun (1632-1723), was at various times a general and
commander of the King's household, but he was disgraced twice, in 1665
and 1671.

from what his contemporaries have told me. He was ambitious, impulsive, harebrained, jealous of everything, extravagant, restless, melancholy, solitary, savage, crass, and did not have an agreeable or elegant turn of mind; his manner was noble, but he was mean and malicious by nature, even more from jealousy and ambition, although he was a good family man and a loyal friend, which is rare; he was quick to make enemies, even among those he scarcely knew, and quick to find fault and make people look ridiculous; he was extremely brave and dangerously bold; as a courtier, he was insolent, mocking, capable of the most obsequious servility, full of ideas, industry, intrigue and baseness to attain his ends, full of cruel and salty sallies that spared no one, and consequently feared by everyone at court, including ministers. . . .

The duc Mazarin, who had retired from court in 1669, wanted to get rid of his commission as grand master of artillery; Lauzun was among the first to learn this and asked the King for the commission; he was promised it on the condition that he keep it a secret several days. . . . The day it was to be announced no announcement came and the surprised Lauzun went to speak to the King at his bedtime. The King told him it was too soon, and that he would see; Lauzun was alarmed by the King's equivocation and curtness. He was a favorite with the ladies, well versed in the jargon of seduction; he poured out his anxiety to Mme. de Montespan and asked her to relieve it. She promised miracles but kept him dangling several days.

Weary of waiting and unable to guess the source of his trouble, he made a resolution that would seem incredible if it did not bear witness to what the court was like in those days. He was sleeping with Mme. de Montespan's favorite maid, for nothing was too low that could inform or protect him; thanks to her he conceived the most hazardous boldness that was ever imagined. The King, for all his mistresses, always shared the Queen's bed, although he often reached it very late; after lunch, to be more comfortable, he would often slip into a mistress's bed.

Lauzun had the maid hide him under the bed into which the King was about to get with Mme. de Montespan. From their conversation he learned that Louvois had opposed his appointment and the King would not give him the artillery out of spite and anger that the secret had been broken and to put a stop to the quarrels he always had to arbitrate between Lauzun and Louvois. He heard everything the King and his mistress said; after having promised Lauzun her good offices, she did everything she could to damage his cause. The rash Lauzun could have been undone by a cough, the slightest motion, or the merest accident. The thought of it is enough to make one choke with fright.

He was more fortunate than wise, and was not found out. Finally the King and his mistress got out of bed. The King dressed and went off to his apartments; Mme. de Montespan went to her dressing table to prepare for a ballet rehearsal that the King, Queen, and court were attending. The maid pulled Lauzun out from under the bed, and he apparently felt not the slightest need to freshen up in his own apartment. He went directly to Mme. de Montespan's apartment and waited outside her door.

When she left for the rehearsal, he offered his arm and asked with a soft and respectful voice if he could flatter himself that she had remembered him to the King. She assured him she had not forgotten, and proceeded to describe everything she had told the King in his favor. From time to time he interrupted with incredulous questions to trap her all the more; finally, leaning close to her ear, he told her she was a liar, a hussy, a drab, a whore for dogs, and repeated her whole conversation with the King word for word. Mme. de Montespan was so upset she was too weak to reply and it was all she could do to reach her destination and overcome the trembling in her legs and body. When she arrived at the rehearsal she fainted. All the court was there. The anxious King ran up to her; it was not easy to revive her. That evening she told the King what had happened and said she was sure the devil had given Lauzun an exact report on their conversation. The King was extremely annoyed at the way Mme. de Montespan had been insulted and extremely perplexed at the way Lauzun had so quickly learned the substance of their conversation.

Meanwhile, Lauzun was furious at having lost the artillery commission, so that he and the King were openly at odds for a few days. Lauzun, who had full access, sought and obtained an audience with the King. He mentioned the artillery and boldly accused him of going back on his word. The King replied that he was no longer bound to his promise since he had made it secretly and Lauzun had given away the secret. With that, Lauzun turned his back on the King, stalked off, drew his sword, broke the blade with his foot, and shouted in fury that he would never again serve a prince who had broken his word so contemptibly. The King, who could hardly contain his anger, accomplished in that moment what was probably the noblest act of his life: He turned to the window, opened it, and threw his cane out, saying that he would regret having to strike a gentleman of quality. Then he left the room. . . .

Lauzun was in love with Mme. de Monaco. . . . He was very jealous and she had displeased him. One summer afternoon at Saint-Cloud, he found Madame and her court sitting on the floor to cool off, and Mme. de Monaco was there half reclining, with one of her hands palm up on the floor. Lauzun began to gossip with the ladies and turned in such a way that he was able to grind his heel into Mme. de Monaco's palm; then he turned on his toes and left. Mme. de Monaco had the courage not to cry out.

Soon after he did much worse. He found out that the King was sleeping with her, and that Bontemps, at a certain time of day, brought her wrapped in a cloak by way of a concealed stairway to a back door of the King's rooms; across from this back door there was a privy. Lauzun arrived there ahead of time and locked himself in the privy. Through its keyhole, he saw the King open his door and put the key on the outside. Lauzun waited a moment, then locked the door and took the key back into the privy with him. Soon after, Bontemps and the lady arrived, and were most surprised not to find the key in the door. Bontemps knocked softly several times, then loud enough for the King to hear. He told the King the lady had arrived, and asked him to open, for the key was not there. The King replied that he had put the key in the lock; Bontemps began looking for it on the ground while the King tried the door. All three were mightily surprised and puzzled; through the door, they discussed how such a mishap could have occurred; the King wore himself out pushing at the door and trying to force the lock. Finally, they had to say good night through the door. Lauzun, who did not miss a word and could see them through the keyhole of the privy, where he was snugly locked in, laughed softly with all his heart and delighted in mocking them. . . .

His natural melancholy and the time he had spent in prison had made him a solitary dreamer, so that even when the most distinguished guests were present, he left them with Mme. de Lauzun and disappeared for the entire afternoon. He never bothered with books, for he was not much of a reader except for a few works of fantasy. He only knew what he had seen. To the end, he was interested in court gossip. I have regretted a thousand times his fundamental incapacity to write what he had seen and done. It would have been a treasury of curious anecdotes, but he was capable of neither method nor application. I often tried to worm a few scraps out of him. Another aggravation was that he would begin to tell a story, reach the name of someone concerned, and go off on a tangent about that person, and then another person, and then a third, until finally he was telling a dozen stories at once, as in a novel. The way he went from one to the other without ever finishing was enough to make you swoon, and it was impossible to learn anything from him, or retain anything. In any case, his conversation was always influenced by politics or by his mood and was only agreeable because of his occasional sallies and malicious witticisms. Several months before his last illness, when he was more than ninety years old, he was still breaking in horses. One day in the Bois de Boulogne he was riding a colt that he had just broken in. The King was on his way to La Muette and he rode past him many times. Onlookers were astonished by his skill, steadiness, and grace. One could go on about him endlessly.

II

PORTRAITS

Introduction

*T*HE *portraits are drawn up like balance sheets for human
lives. Saint-Simon begins with a list of qualities, in which wit
and worldliness are the customary reward for assiduous court
attendance. Wit, seen as a combination of courtier's talents and
enlightened self-interest, escaped a very few—one of the notable
exceptions is the King, whose mind is described as third-rate—
but then, of everyone at court, he had the least need for wit. After
listing virtues that saints might envy, Saint-Simon just as scru-
pulously begins to recite a litany of malevolence. We find that
outward appearance disguised a monster, and that vice, not virtue,
is its own reward. The portrait gallery sometimes becomes a freak
gallery.*

*Historical fairness must not be expected in these character
sketches of the court's principals. Saint-Simon's vindictiveness
and pet hatreds lurk at every corner. Because de Mesmes, First
President of Parlement, had his chair seat stuffed in his declining
years, Saint-Simon brands him a "Nero" trying to usurp a
privilege. Men were "monsters of perversion" because they disagreed with him. Finally, it is not accuracy but the quality of
his virulence we admire most in the portraits—they flow like a
river of vinegar, astringent, pungent, and sour.*

*The court was marked by inbreeding and infirmity, congenital
and acquired. Wigs, high heels, powders, perfumes, lace and
brocade were artificial remedies for nature's neglect that could not
hide the pervasive physical debility. The men often died young,
their insides rotting from syphilis and overeating. Louis XIV
measured only five feet four (as we know from the size of his
armor), and towered over Saint-Simon. By modern standards,
Monsieur le Duc and Monsieur le Prince were dwarfs. The maré-*

chal de Luxembourg had humps in back and in front. The duc de Bourgogne had a spine shaped like a pretzel. The duc du Maine had a clubfoot. The duc de Vendôme submitted to the mercury cure for syphilis, and returned to court without his nose, as a result. The prince de Vaudémont's bones were decalcifying so fast he had trouble walking.

The women were no better off, but Saint-Simon was kinder to them. To be beautiful, it was enough not to be misshapen. His efforts to salvage a redeeming feature in his female portraits are heroic. He will say "her teeth were rotting, but it did not prevent her from being beautiful," or "the upper part of her face was beautiful, but her nose was crooked and she had a goiter."

Morally, the court was as fetid as the swamp Versailles had been built upon. Beneath the surface glitter of court ritual, a grotesque submarine world polluted the waters. It was like a painting with the top half by Boucher and the bottom half by Bosch, like the incident where the duchesse de Bourgogne in a magnificent evening gown is chatting brightly with the King and Madame de Maintenon while behind her a maid is administering an enema. It was a world where doctors bled their enemies to death, poison was as common as snuff, a valet became a viscount because he supplied the King with aphrodisiacs, the King's homosexual brother recruited lovers among the marshals of France, the King's nephew deflowered his own daughter when she was fourteen, and cardinals were praised for their virtue because they were discreet about their vices. At Versailles, corruption was in the public domain. Backstairs maids knew more than ministers of state, and the King received his information from both sources. Scandal was so commonplace it ceased to be scandalous, and reputations followed courtiers to the grave. Someone scrawled on the tombstone of the duc. d'Orléans' mother: His Jacet Otium—"Here lies Indolence" (mother of vice). Few of Saint-Simon's characters rise above the mire. Among the most attractive is the child-bride of the duc de Bourgogne, whom we see peeping over the King's shoulder as he reads reports from his ambassadors, going through his desk drawers, and exercising her prerogatives as favorite granddaughter-in-law. She was playful, but not very selective in her choice of games. After she had been at court two years, she drove one of her lovers to suicide, having by that time reached

*the age of fourteen. Good literature, we know, does not come
from good intentions, and Saint-Simon's most virtuous subjects are
also his dullest. The integrity of the duc de Beauvillier, the courage
of the maréchal de Boufflers, are far less compelling than the
coarseness of the duc de Vendôme and the tantrums of the
duchesse de Berry.*

MONSIEUR (1701)

*"Monsieur" was the distinctive appellation of the King's brother,
first gentleman of the kingdom after the King. Philippe, duc
d'Orléans (1640-1701), was the second son of Louis XIII and
Anne of Austria. He was the court homosexual, and took pleasure
in providing a flaccid reflection of his brother. Encouraged in
his perversion by ministers bent on keeping him away from
public affairs, he began as a youth to dress in female costume and
cover his pudgy fingers with rings. His first marriage to the
languorous Henrietta of England was a source of constant humiliation, for "Madame" soon became more interested in her royal
brother-in-law than in her husband. After her death, he married
the bovine Princess Elizabeth Charlotte of Bavaria. He was continuously exploited by his lovers, notably the chevalier de
Lorraine. When Lorraine was banished from court, Saint-Simon
writes that Monsieur "fainted, then burst into tears and threw
himself at the King's feet." Despite his effeminate airs, Monsieur
had great physical courage and was a gifted general. It was said
that at the battle of Cassel in 1677 "he fought like a grenadier."
It was his last battle, for Louis XIV was piqued by his success
and forbade him to risk his life again.*

Monsieur was short and potbellied, and wore such high heels
he looked as though he was on stilts. He was forever dressing up
like a woman, with rings, bracelets, and gems everywhere, a long,
black, powdered wig frilled in the front, ribbons wherever he
could put them, and all kinds of perfumes. He was always

meticulously clean. It was said that he wore rouge, but imperceptibly. He had a very long nose, a fine mouth and eyes, and a full but very long face. All his portraits are a good likeness. . . .

Although he was very courageous, had won the battle of Cassel and shown valor at every siege in which he took part, he had all the bad qualities of women. He had more poise than wit, no learning except in genealogy, and was perfectly incompetent. No one was flabbier in mind and body, weaker, more timid, more easily gulled and dominated, and more despised and badly treated by his favorites . . .

The court lost a great deal when it lost Monsieur. He was the soul of its amusement and pleasure, and without him it seemed lifeless and dull. Aside from his stubbornness concerning foreign princes, he liked the order of rank, privileges, and distinctions. He watched over their enforcement, and gave the good example. He loved society, and attracted it with his amiability, courtesy, and the way he gave to each according to his rank. He showed a flattering awareness of birth and dignity, age and merit, and social condition by varying the degree of his courtesy and attentiveness; and he kept a natural dignity and poise. . . .

On Wednesday, June 8, Monsieur went to Marly to lunch with the King, and entered his study as usual when he saw the Council of State leaving it. He found the King upset because M. de Chartres was making his daughter unhappy.[1]

At that time, M. de Chartres was in the middle of a violent love affair with Mlle. de Séry, one of Madame's ladies in waiting. Referring to this, the King dryly reproached Monsieur for his son's behavior. Monsieur, who was already in a bad mood, and needed only this to lose his temper, replied bitterly that some fathers had little authority to criticize their children after the lives they had led. The King, shaken by the retort, fell back on his daughter's patience, and said her husband's mistresses should at least be kept out of her sight. But Monsieur, who was beyond restraint, reminded the King with irony of how he had treated the Queen, allowing his mistresses to ride with her in the same carriage. The King, outraged, went even further, and they began to yell at each

[1] M. de Chartres, son of Monsieur, future duc d'Orléans, and Regent under Louis XV, had married a bastard daughter of Louis XIV, the second Mlle. de Blois (who was therefore his first cousin and whose mother was the marquise de Montespan). He was flagrantly unfaithful.

other. . . . Finally, beside himself, Monsieur told the King that his son had been promised miracles when he married and had not even obtained a governorship; that he had sought some occupation for his son to keep his mind off passing fancies, and that the young man had even gone to the King with requests, as the King well knew; since there had been no result, he did not see why he should prevent his son from consoling himself with amusements. He added that now he saw how true the prediction was that he would reap no profit from this marriage, but only shame and dishonor. The King, growing angrier and angrier, retorted that the field of battle would soon make him cut down on his amusements, and that since he was unwilling to bend to the royal will, he would cut off his pension.

Upon that, the King was notified that the meat was ready, and they went to eat. Monsieur's face was a fiery red, and his eyes snapped with anger. His face was so congested that several ladies at the table and several courtiers standing to the rear who wanted to be noticed said that he seemed to need a good bleeding. The same thing had been said recently at Saint-Cloud and he admitted himself that he was bursting to be bled. Despite their quarrels, the King had urged him several times to have it done. But he did not want to be bled by his surgeon Tancrède, who was old, bled badly, and often missed the vein; and out of kindness to Tancrède, he refused to be bled by anyone else. It killed him. At this talk of bleeding, the King said he would take him in his room after lunch to have him bled. The meal passed uneventfully, and Monsieur ate as much as he did at every meal, to say nothing of the large amounts of hot chocolate he drank in the morning, and all the fruit, pastries, jams, and candies of all kinds which he munched all day long, and with which he filled his pockets and the drawers of his desks.

That evening after supper, while the King was still in his study with Monseigneur and the princesses, Saint-Pierre arrived from Saint-Cloud with a message from M. le duc de Chartres. He came into the study and told the King that Monsieur had felt very bad during supper, had been bled and given an emetic, and was now feeling better. The fact was that Monsieur had supped as usual with the ladies at Saint-Cloud. Toward the sweet, as he was pouring a glass of wine for Mme. de Bouillon, he began to mumble and point at something. As he sometimes enjoyed speaking in Spanish, several ladies asked what he was saying, but others cried out—it only took an instant—and he fell in a fit of apoplexy on M. le duc de Chartres, who held him up. He was carried into his apartment, bled, and given large quantities of emetic. But he gave almost no sign of life despite efforts to revive him. . . .

The King reached Saint-Cloud a little before three in the morning. Monsieur had not had a moment of consciousness since his stroke. He had one last glimmer the next morning, when Father du Trévou, his confessor, arrived to say mass. The most horrible spectacles often offer ridiculous contrasts. When Father du Trévou returned, he cried: "Monsieur, don't you recognize your own confessor? Don't you recognize good little Father du Trévou speaking to you?" Those least affected had the indecency to laugh.

The King seemed very afflicted. Easily moved to tears, he wept openly. He had always loved Monsieur tenderly, despite their recent quarrels, which made his affection more moving. Perhaps he was blaming himself for having precipitated his death with that morning's scene. Finally, Monsieur was only two years younger than the King, and had always been in as good or better health. The King heard mass at Saint-Cloud, and at eight in the morning, since there was no hope left for Monsieur, Mme. de Maintenon and Mme. la duchesse de Bourgogne urged him to leave, and left with him in his carriage. As he was leaving, he said a few words of kindness to M. de Chartres. They were both sobbing, and the young prince took advantage of the moment and cried, throwing his arms about the King's legs: "Sire, what will become of me? I am losing Monsieur, and I know you do not love me." The King, surprised and touched, kissed him and spoke to him with great tenderness.

Arriving at Marly, the King stayed with Mme. la duchesse de Bourgogne in Mme. de Maintenon's apartments. Three hours later, the King saw M. Fagon, whom he had ordered not to leave Monsieur's side unless he died or miraculously recovered, and asked him: "Well, Monsieur Fagon, is my brother dead?" "Yes, Sire," he replied, "no remedy would act." The King wept abundantly. He was pressed to have a bite in Mme. de Maintenon's apartments, but wanted to lunch with the ladies as usual, and during the brief meal his tears flowed often. After that, he shut himself up with Mme. de Maintenon until seven o'clock, when he went for a stroll in the gardens. . . .

Madame was in her dressing room. Although she had never had much affection or esteem for Monsieur, she felt his loss and her own downfall, and cried out in her grief: "There will be no convent! I won't hear of it! I will not go to any convent!" The good princess had not lost her shrewdness. She knew the stipulation in her marriage contract that once widowed, she would have to choose between a convent and a life of seclusion in the castle of Montargis. . . .

Everyone thought that after such a terrible spectacle, with so many tears spilled and so much tenderness displayed, the last three days of the Marly trip would be most mournful. But on the day after Monsieur's death, when the ladies of the palace went in to see Mme. de Maintenon, they heard the King, who was there with Mme. la duchesse de Bourgogne, singing opera overtures in the next room. A little later, the King saw Mme. la duchesse de Bourgogne sitting sadly in a corner of the room, and asked Mme. de Maintenon with surprise what was making her so melancholy. He joked with her and sought to amuse her, and summoned several ladies of the palace to amuse them both. That was not all. After lunch, that is to say a little after two o'clock, and only twenty-six hours after the death of Monsieur, Msgr. le duc de Bourgogne asked the duc de Montfort if he wanted to play Three-of-a-kind. "Three-of-a-kind!" cried out Montfort in extreme astonishment. "How can you think of such a thing when Monsieur's body is still warm!" "Forgive me," replied the prince, "I realize that, but the King does not want anyone to be bored at Marly and has ordered me to make everyone play. Fearing that no one would dare start things off, he asked me to give the good example." They began to play, and soon the drawing room was filled with gaming tables.

Monseigneur (1711)

Louis le Grand, the Dauphin (1661-1711), was the only legitimate son of Louis XIV who survived childhood. He was terrorized by his father, and played a minor role at court. Those who asked him to intercede for them with the King were told with self-deprecation that it was "the best way to spoil everything." He married Marie-Anne-Christine of Bavaria, who died in 1690, and was thereafter under the influence of Mlle. de Choin, a coarse but devoted woman who lived in Paris and came for brief stays to Meudon, where Monseigneur held his own unpretentious court, in the shadow of Versailles.

Monseigneur was on the tall side, and very fat without being lumpy. His manner was noble and distinguished, without coarseness, and his face would have been pleasant if M. le prince de Conti had not accidentally broken his nose when they were children. He was a fine-looking blond, with a full, red, weatherbeaten, and placid face, the handsomest legs in the world, and singularly slender and tiny feet. When he walked, he felt his way, groping with his toes, for he was afraid of falling. He would ask for help when the path was not perfectly straight and smooth. He was a good rider and looked well on a horse, but he was not hardy. Casaus[1] always led the way at hunts, and if Monseigneur lost sight of him he thought he was lost. He never went above a canter, and he would often wait for the hunt under a tree, try halfheartedly to rejoin it, and failing, return. He had been fond of good food, but within the limits of propriety. Since his digestion had failed him (doctors thought it was apoplexy) he held himself to one meal a day, although his appetite was as good as the rest of the royal family's. Almost all his portraits are a good likeness. He had common sense, but no character or intelligence of any sort, which became clear in the affair of the king of Spain's will. His dignity was in part natural, in part bearing, and in part

---

[1] Henri de Casaus, Monseigneur's equerry.

imitation of the King. His stubbornness knew no bounds, and his life was a tissue of organized pettinesses. Laziness and a kind of stupidity made him seem gentle, but he had a hard core. His apparent kindness applied only to trivial matters with his valets and subordinates. He was prodigiously familiar with them, but otherwise insensitive to misery and pain, more from carelessness and habit than an evil nature. He was incredibly taciturn and secretive, and it was believed that he never discussed affairs of state with the Choin woman (probably because neither of them was interested).

Dullness of mind and fear made this prince more reserved than most; at the same time, he seemed excessively conceited (which is not easy for a Dauphin), hungry for respect, and sensitive and attentive to almost nothing but the respect he was due. He once told Mme. Choin, when she asked why he was so silent, that since the words of men like himself carry great weight and require great apologies when they are not measured, he usually preferred to hold his tongue. It was also convenient for his laziness and complete apathy, and this excellent but annoying maxim was apparently the lesson received from the King or the duc de Montausier[2] which made the deepest impression on him. He was extremely careful about his personal expenses and wrote down every one. He knew what the least important items cost, although he spent an inordinate amount on construction, furniture, jewels of all sort, trips to Meudon, and wolf hunts, which he had convinced himself he enjoyed. He had always gambled for high stakes, but since growing interested in construction, he only played for farthings. He was shockingly avaricious, except on rare occasions, when he gave a pension to a valet or some other servant, or alms to his parish priest or the Capuchin friars of Meudon. It is inconceivable how little he gave his beloved Choin: not more than four hundred louis[3] per quarter, always in gold despite the rate of exchange, which made sixteen hundred louis a year. He handed them to her himself, without ever miscounting by a single pistole, and that was all she got, except for a jewel

---

[2] The duc de Montausier (1610-1690) had been Monseigneur's tutor.

[3] A louis was worth 24 pounds (livres), and a pound was worth about one dollar in our currency.

or two a year. To do her justice, it must be agreed that no one was more disinterested, either because she knew that with Monseigneur she had to be, or because of her character, as the rest of her life seems to show. It would have been different if they had married, but their intimates swore they never had. She was fat and swarthy, with a pushed-in nose, and looked like a servant, although she had an intelligent expression. Long before the events I am recounting, she had become fat, old and stinking. . . .

Monseigneur's meager intelligence, if he ever had any at all, was stifled by the severity of a hard and austere education. It increased his natural shyness and his complete aversion for mental gymnastics, even more than for work and study. He admitted that since being freed of his masters, the only thing he read were the articles in the *Gazette de France* on deaths and marriages.

Everything about him, his natural shyness, severe education, and complete lack of intelligence, contributed to make him tremble before the King, who did everything he could to maintain and prolong a climate of terror as long as Monseigneur was alive. Louis XIV was always the King, almost never the father. If a small measure of fatherliness slipped out in their most intimate moments, it was never pure, but always mixed with royalty. They were seldom alone, so that these moments usually came in the presence of the bastards or members of the King's household. Instead of being relaxed and at ease, Monseigneur was constrained and respectful, and did not dare say anything out of place, although he could see the duc du Maine doing it every day successfully, and knew that Mme. la duchesse de Bourgogne was allowed the most familiar banter and took the most surprising liberties. He felt a secret jealousy, but it did not make him more outgoing. Intelligence did not provide him with weapons to match the duc du Maine, who was the son of the man and not of the King, so that royalty did not intrude on affection. And he was not in the same age group as Mme. la duchesse de Bourgogne, whose playfulness was forgiven because she was a child and charmed the King. There remained for him only his rank of son and successor, which was precisely what made the King reserved and placed him under the yoke. He did not have the least influence on the King. If he favored someone, that person would soon feel an unpleasant rebound. The King was so bent on showing how powerless Monseigneur was that he ignored his friends and even his favorites. They were chosen and named by the King himself, and he would have been the first put out if they had not shown Monseigneur great assiduousness. . . .

Instead of mistresses, which the King frowned on, he had brief and obscure encounters. Du Mont and Francine, who long managed the Opéra, furnished him young women, although he was almost incapable of making love. While we are on the subject, I cannot keep myself from giving an example of his prudishness. He desired one of the lovely young creatures of the Opéra. On the appointed day, she was brought to a cabinet in Versailles, accompanied by an ugly friend. Monseigneur, warned that they had arrived, opened the door, grabbed the nearest one, and pulled her to him. She fought him off, for she was the ugly one, and realized he had made a mistake. He thought she was being coy, pushed her into his room, and locked the door. Meanwhile, the other one was laughing, imagining that her friend would be sent back and she would be called.

A moment later, du Mont came in, was surprised to see her there alone, and asked her what she was doing and what had happened to her friend. She told him the story, and du Mont began to knock at the door, crying: "You've got the wrong one." No reply. Du Mont redoubled his efforts, but in vain. Finally, Monseigneur opened the door and pushed the creature out. Du Mont presented him with the other one, and said: "Here she is." But Monseigneur said: "I'm done. It will have to be for another time," and closed his door. . . .

From this long and curious description, we can see that Monseigneur was lacking in both virtue and vice, had no intelligence or learning and was fundamentally incapable of acquiring any. He was lazy, unimaginative, incompetent, undiscerning, born for boredom (which he communicated to others), a rolling stone moved by the impulsions of others, excessively stubborn and petty in everything, cautious and gullible at the same time, absorbed in his fat and obscurity, but devoid of malice. He had insidious friends and never realized it. He would have made a pernicious king.

THE DUC DE BOURGOGNE (1710)

Louis de France (1682-1712), duc de Bourgogne, grandson of Louis XIV and eldest son of Monseigneur, became Dauphin when his father died in 1711, only to die himself a year later (it was rumored that he had been poisoned by the duc d'Orléans, his first cousin). The duc de Bourgogne married Marie-Adélaide of Savoy when she was twelve years old, and she became the darling of the court. Their son, the duc d'Anjou, was the future Louis XV. The duc de Bourgogne's death was keenly felt by Saint-Simon. He saw in this sober, devout prince a proper heir to the throne, and, moreover, was in his good graces through his friendship with the duc de Beauvillier, who had been the duc de Bourgogne's governor and tutor.

The duc de Bourgogne was on the short side, with a long dark face, the top half of which was perfect, the most beautiful eyes in the world, and an expression that was lively, touching, striking, admirable, usually gentle, and always piercing. His general manner was pleasant, dignified, and refined, with enough intelligence for two. The lower half of his face was pointed and unseemly, with a long, turned-up, ugly nose. His chestnut hair was so curly and ample that it billowed excessively. His lips and mouth were pleasant when he kept them closed. But, although his teeth were not ugly, his upper jaw was so prominent that it covered the lower one, which was unfortunate when he spoke or laughed. He had the most beautiful legs and feet I ever saw, after the King, but they were too long for the rest of his body, as were his thighs. When he outgrew the care of women it was noticed that his spine was twisted. Everything was done to straighten it out, including the use of an iron collar and cross, which he wore indoors, even in public. But nature was the stronger, and he became a hunchback, particularly in one shoulder. This made him lame, not because he had one leg shorter than the other, but because there was no longer the same distance from his hips to his feet, and instead of standing straight, he listed. Nonetheless, he could walk just as easily, just as far, just as quickly, and just as willingly, and it did not spoil his enthusiasm for riding, although he rode very badly. It is surprising that although he had eyes to see with, a lofty intelligence, extraordinary virtue and eminent piety, the prince never saw (or never wanted to see) himself as crippled. It was a weakness that made everyone careful about loose talk and indiscretions, and that grieved the servants who had to dress him and fix his hair, for they did their best to conceal his flaws and never show that they noticed what was all too visible. . . .

It must be explained that the duc de Bourgogne was born with a nature that made everyone tremble. He was so fiery that he wanted to break the clocks when they rang the hour for unpleasant occupations, and lost his temper at the rain when it spoiled his plans. In his early years, I was often a witness to this rage at the slightest frustration. His passionate nature made him lean toward everything forbidden. His raillery was all the more cruel for its wit and saltiness, and he had a gift for repartee. All this was sharpened by a vivacity that bordered on impetuousness. In his early years, he could not learn anything unless he was doing two things at the same time. He loved pleasure with a violent passion, and devoted himself to it with inexpressible pride and haughtiness. He was feared for his discernment, as he could see the flaw in an argument and reason more closely and profoundly than his masters. When his anger abated, his reason took command; he realized his faults and admitted them, sometimes with a scorn that approached his anger. His intelligence was transcendent in all things, quick, active, penetrating and persistent. It was miraculous that in a short time, devotion and grace made another man of him, and changed these fearful faults into their opposite virtues. . . .

This violence in condemning his faults, this desire for perfection, this ignorance and fear that always accompanies new-found faith, made him go too far in the other direction, and inspired an austerity that annoyed everyone. Without realizing it, he adopted a constrained, criticizing manner, which increasingly alienated Monseigneur, and vexed even the King. I will give one example among thousands, which starting from an unimpeachable principle, made the King lose his temper and repelled the entire court. We were at Marly, and a ball had been announced for Twelfth Night. Msgr. le duc de Bourgogne did not want to attend, and gave enough warning so that the King, who was displeased, had a chance to ask him about it, at first jokingly, and then more and more bitterly, vexed at being criticized by his grandson. Mme. la duchesse de Bourgogne, her ladies in waiting and M. de Beauvillier tried in vain to change his mind. He said the King was the master, and it was not up to him to criticize anything he did. But, he added, the Epiphany was a triple holiday, meant particularly for Christians because of the vocation of the Gentiles and the baptism of Jesus Christ, and he did not intend to profane his devotion on this holy day by attending a spectacle which was barely tolerable on an ordinary one.

THE DUCHESSE DE BOURGOGNE (1710)

Marie-Adélaide of Savoy, the duchesse de Bourgogne (1685-1714), married the king's grandson when she was twelve. A year later, she had lovers, for she despised her hunchback husband. One of them, Andrault de Maulévrier, went mad because he lost her favor, and committed suicide by throwing himself out of a window. She could do no wrong, because she diverted the King.

Never had a princess arriving so young at a foreign court been better instructed or profited better from her instruction. Her shrewd father, who knew the court well, had described it to her, and taught her the only way to be happy in it. She was seconded by a facile and natural wit and many amiable qualities. Her position with her husband, the King, and Mme. de Maintenon attracted the compliments of the ambitious. She worked hard at adapting herself as soon as she arrived. This useful work continued ceaselessly, and she knew how to profit by it. She was sweet and shy, but clever; so kind that she was always afraid of hurting someone; and although she was frivolous and lively, she was capable of weighty and well-argued opinions. She felt the constraint of court life, but it did not seem to bother her, for she was naturally accommodating. She had regular but plain features: jowls, a prominent brow, an undistinguished nose, thick and avid lips, a good crop of chestnut hair and eyebrows, the most beautiful and eloquent eyes in the world, few teeth and all of them rotten (which she was the first to laugh at), a fine skin and complexion, a small but well-shaped bust, a long neck with a hint of goiter which rather suited her, a noble, gracious, and majestic bearing and expression, a lively smile, a perfectly shaped and graceful waist, long and rounded but narrow, and a walk like a goddess on clouds. She was extremely pleasing; the three Graces were reborn with her every step, gesture and word. Her manner was always simple and natural, often naïve, but seasoned with wit. She had charm and poise which she communicated to all those who approached her, and a natural desire to please even the most useless and petty persons. She gave the impression of devoting herself completely to whoever was with her. . . .

She approached the King and Mme. de Maintenon with a familiarity which none of his children, not even the bastards, ever dared match. In public, she was serious, measured, and respectful with the King, and showed a sense of reserved propriety toward Mme. de Maintenon, whom she called "Auntie," a pretty way of showing both respect and affection. In private, she talked, she jumped, she flitted about them, perched on the arms of their chairs, bounced on their knees, threw herself at their necks, kissed them, embraced them, caressed them, rumpled them, pulled at their chins, tormented them, went through their desk drawers and their papers, sometimes opening their mail when she saw they were in a good mood and discussing the contents with them. She was privy to everything, and was even present when couriers brought the most important news; she came to see the King at all hours, even when the Council was in progress; she could be an asset or a liability to ministers, although her natural bent was to oblige, help, make amends and do what she could for them, unless she was really set against someone, as she was against Pontchartrain, whom she described to the King as "that horrible man with the glass eye,"[1] or unless she was involved in a major

---

[1] Jérome Phelypeaux, comte de Pontchartrain, son of one of Saint-Simon's best friends, but himself one of his bitterest enemies, had lost an eye to smallpox. "It wept continuously and gave him a frightening aspect," Saint-Simon wrote.

cause, as she was against Chamillart. She spoke so freely that one evening, overhearing the King and Mme. de Maintenon affectionately discussing the court of England during the peaceful beginning of Queen Anne's reign, she said: "Auntie, you must admit that in England the queens govern better than the kings, and do you know why, Auntie?" And continuing her antics, she added: "Because under a king, women govern, and under a queen, men govern." The admirable thing is that both of them laughed in agreement.

I would not dare include the following anecdote in serious memoirs if it did not show the degree to which she was able to say and do what she pleased. I have already described with what familiarity the King and Mme. de Maintenon would come to visit her. They had come to chat with the princess one evening before attending a play at Versailles, when in came Nanon, a former chambermaid of Mme. de Maintenon's, whom I have already mentioned. The duchesse de Bourgogne, in evening dress and jewels, stood with her back to the hearth and leaned on a small folding screen. Nanon, keeping a hand under her apron, went behind her and kneeled down. Seeing them, the King asked what they were doing.

The princess laughed, and said she was only doing what the King did on theatre nights. The King insisted. "Do you really want to know?" she asked. "Since you haven't noticed, I am taking an enema." "What," cried the King, "do you mean you are taking an enema right there in front of us?" "That's right," she replied. "How do you do it?" the King wanted to know, and they began to laugh with all their hearts. The princess explained that Nanon brought the syringe all prepared under her aprons, lifted her skirts while she held herself as though she was warming her behind at the fire, and Nanon slipped in the nozzle. Then Nanon lowered her skirts and left with the syringe, so no one was the wiser; people usually thought Nanon was fixing the princess's dress. The King and Mme. de Maintenon were extremely surprised and thought it was most amusing. What is even more curious is that she kept the enema during the entire play. She was in no hurry to release it, and sometimes waited until after the King's supper. She said it refreshed her and kept the stuffiness of the theatre from giving her a headache. Being found out by the King did not make her give up the habit. One evening, while Msgr. le duc de Bourgogne was waiting for her in bed, she sat chatting on her *chaise percée* with Mmes. de Nogaret and du Châtelet (they told me about it the following day, and it was on her *chaise percée* that she spoke most openly), and discussed admiringly the good fortunes of Mme. de Maintenon and Mlle. Choin.[2] Then, she added: "I would like to die before Msgr. le duc de Bourgogne, and at the same time be a witness to what is sure to happen: He will marry a lay sister or one of those women at the turning-box for the Daughters of Saint Mary." She was as attentive to please Msgr. le duc de Bourgogne as the King, and took a lively interest in his glory and personal greatness. But she took too many risks, and took for granted his passion for her and the discretion of all those who approached him. . . .

One evening at Fontainebleau, she and the ladies in waiting of the princesses were in the same room as the King after supper. She had amused the King by jabbering in all sorts of languages and playing a hundred pranks, and noticed Mme. la Duchesse and Mme. la princesse de Conti looking at each other, using sign language and shrugging their shoulders with a contemptuous and disdainful air. After the King had left to feed his dogs in an anteroom and say good night to the princesses as usual she took Mme. de Saint-Simon by one hand and Mme. de Levis by the other, and said, pointing to Mme. la Duchesse and Mme. la princesse de Conti, who were only a few feet away: "Did you see that, did you see that? I know as well as they do that my behavior is silly and nonsensical; but it diverts him, he enjoys my romping." And then, leaning on their arms, she began to skip and sing: "I don't care! I snap my fingers at them! I will be their queen! I don't need them now or any other time! They will have to deal with me, for I will be their queen!" She jumped and threw herself about with joyous abandon. The ladies begged her to make less noise, for everyone could see her and the princesses could hear her; they even told her she was crazy, for they were very free with her. She jumped and sang all the more, crying: "I don't care about them, I don't need them, I will be their queen!" and only stopped when the King returned. . . .

[2] One had prospered as the King's mistress, the other as the mistress of the King's son, Monseigneur.

When she died, pleasure, joy, amusement, and all kinds of graces died. The surface of the court was covered with darkness, for she had given it animation, had filled, occupied, and penetrated it; the court survived, but it languished. Never was a princess so regretted and so worth regretting. The regret did not fade and a secret and unprompted bitterness lingered, along with a terrible and irremediable emptiness.

PHILIP V OF SPAIN (1700)

A grandson of Louis XIV, second son of Monseigneur, the duc d'Anjou (1683-1745) was only seventeen when Charles II of Spain designated him as successor to the Spanish throne and made him the first Bourbon to accede to it. Louis XIV, preoccupied above all with his own grandeur, could not resist placing a neighbor's crown on the head of his adolescent grandson. At the news, Monseigneur, son of Louis XIV and father of the duc d'Anjou, went around in a daze muttering to himself: "Son of a king, father of a king . . ." However, Louis XIV at the same time precipitated the War of the Spanish Succession, ending with the Treaty of Utrecht in 1714, which restored Spain's Dutch and Italian enclaves to the Austrian empire. Philip V ruled Spain for forty-five years, and died leaving it a second-rate power.

On Tuesday November 16, the King after having risen summoned the Spanish ambassador to his study, where M. le duc d'Anjou had already arrived by a back door. Pointing at him, the King told the ambassador he could salute his new king. The ambassador threw himself on his knees in the Spanish manner and delivered a rather long congratulation in his own tongue. The King said he would reply for his grandson, who did not as yet understand Spanish. Then the King, against his custom, had both sides of his study door flung open and ordered the crowd outside to enter. Passing a majestic eye over the well-filled room, he said, pointing to the duc d'Anjou: "Sirs, here is the king of Spain. He was beckoned to the crown by his birth and the late king's will. The whole nation wanted it and asked me for it. It was a command from Heaven, with which I was happy to comply." Turning to his grandson, he said: "Your first duty now is to be a good Spaniard. But remember that you were born French, and maintain the union between the two nations. In this way, you will make them happy and keep the peace in Europe." Then, addressing the ambassador and pointing at his grandson, he said: "If he follows my advice, you will soon be a great lord; and from now on, he could do no better than to follow yours . . ." [1]

On Saturday, December 4, the king of Spain spent a long time with the King before anyone else had seen him, and then went to see Monseigneur, with whom he stayed just as long. All three heard mass in the royal chapel, which was incredibly crowded with courtiers. After mass, they got into their carriage, with Mme. la duchesse de Bourgogne in back between the two kings, Monseigneur in front between Messeigneurs his two other sons [the duc de Berry and the duc d'Anjou], Monsieur at one door and Madame at another. The carriage was enveloped in the pomp of many more guards than usual, including gendarmes and light cavalry. The road all the way to Sceaux was strewn with carriages and people, and Sceaux itself, where they arrived shortly after noon, was crowded with courtiers and ladies, and guarded by three companies of musketeers. As soon as they had alighted, the King went into the farthest room on the ground floor with the king of Spain and had everyone else remain in the drawing room. Fifteen minutes later, he summoned Monseigneur, and soon after that the Spanish ambassador, who took leave of his master. A moment later he called in Monsieur le duc and Mme. la duchesse de Bourgogne, M. le duc de Berry, Monsieur and Madame, and after a brief interval, the royal princes and princesses. Both sides of the door were open, and one could see them all from the drawing room, weeping bitterly. The King told the king of Spain as he introduced the princes: "These princes are of my blood and of yours. Now our two nations must consider themselves one, with identical interests. Thus I hope that these

---

[1] According to Voltaire, Louis XIV at this point told the ambassador, Castel dos Rios: "The Pyrénées no longer exist." Saint-Simon missed a good quote.

princes will be as attached to you as they are to me; you could have no more faithful or more trustworthy friends." All this lasted a good hour and a half, but finally the time for parting came. The King led the king of Spain to the door, kissing him several times and holding him at length in his arms; Monseigneur did the same. The spectacle was extremely touching. . . .

Philip V was not gifted with superior powers of understanding or anything like what we call imagination. He was cold, close-mouthed, sober, afraid of the world and his own shadow, solitary and secretive, and insensitive to others. His only pleasure was the hunt and he made few other efforts to be worldly. Yet he had a measure of honest common sense and could be made to understand things. He could be inflexibly stubborn, but was nonetheless easy to influence and dominate. He loved war above everything. But as it did not matter to him whether or not he was in the field, he left everything to his generals.

He was extremely vainglorious, and could not bear resistance to his undertakings. I came to the conclusion that he loved adulation, for the Queen ceaselessly praised everything about him, and even asked me one day during a conversation at the end of an audience whether I had ever seen anyone more beautiful. His piousness was founded on custom, scruples, fears and petty observances. He knew nothing about religion, considered the Pope divine except when he was shocked by his behavior, and borrowed the easy shallowness of the Jesuits, whom he loved. Although his health was good, he constantly worried about it. A physician like Maître Coctier, whose fortune Louis XI made toward the end of his life, could have become rich and powerful with Philip V. Fortunately, his own physician was staunchly honest and honorable, and was succeeded by one who was under the Queen's thumb.

There was no physical flaw to prevent Philip V from being an agreeable speaker, but laziness and lack of self-confidence made him taciturn. He seldom joined in conversations, but left them to the Queen when they went to the Mall or to private audiences, or again to casual meetings. At the same time, no one was more aware of other people's failings and could describe them more amusingly. . . . I was finally able to win him over somewhat, so that my audiences always turned to conversation and several times I heard him speak and reason perfectly well. But if others were present, he refused to speak, and would say no more than a word or two, or ask a brief question.

The Duc de Berry (1715)

The youngest of three grandsons of Louis XIV (the other two were the duc de Bourgogne and Philip V, king of Spain), the duc de Berry (1680-1714) was remembered mainly for his stormy marriage with his second cousin, Marie-Elisabeth de Valois, daughter of the duc d'Orléans and granddaughter of the King's brother (Monsieur). The marriage was arranged by Saint-Simon, through his friendship with the duc d'Orléans. Saint-Simon had second thoughts about his matchmaking because of the duchesse de Berry's arrogant misconduct. She completely dominated her husband, who was so shy that when he was presented to Parle-ment, he lost his voice.

M. le duc de Berry was no taller than most men, tubby and blond, with a hearty and rather beautiful face that emanated glowing health. He was made for the court and its pleasures, and loved them all. He was the best of men, the kindest, the most compassionate and accessible, lacking in pride and vanity but not in dignity or in the awareness of his own rank. He was rather dull-witted and had no ideas or imagination. But his common sense was steadfast and he was capable of listening, understanding, and always making the right decision while discarding specious advice. He loved truth, justice, and reason. Although he was not noticeably pious, everything that attacked religion caused him great pain. He was not without firmness, and hated to be forced into anything. Such stubbornness was frightening in a third son of France, and it was impossible to make him understand that there was any difference between himself and his elder brothers. Their children's quarrels had been fearful. He was the most beau-tiful and friendly of the three brothers, and consequently the best loved and the most sought after and spoiled. When he was a child,

Madame and M. de La Rochefoucauld teased him daily, and his repartees were made much of because of his free and natural gaiety. He laughed at tutors, teachers, and scoldings, had not learned anything since being delivered from regular schooling, and could barely read and write. . . .

He feared the King to the point that he hardly dared approach him. If the King only looked at him or discussed topics other than hunting and gambling, he became confused, barely heard what was said, and was incapable of replying. One can judge that such fright did not foster close ties.

THE DUCHESSE DE BERRY (1715)

The tempestuous duchesse de Berry (1695-1719), daughter of Philippe d'Orléans and Mlle. de Blois, was a special thorn in Saint-Simon's side: first, because he had been the matchmaker between the Regent's daughter and the King's grandson, the duc de Berry, who soon regretted the marriage; second, because Mme. de Saint-Simon had against her better judgment and her husband's advice been pressured into serving as lady in waiting for the duchesse de Berry, and was an unwilling witness to her daily scandals; finally, because Saint-Simon's aim to give an unexpurgated view of life at court was thwarted by the duchesse de Berry. Even the exhaustive and unshockable memoirist balked at the incestuous relations between the duc d'Orléans and his daughter, which Saint-Simon hints at several times with unusual circumspection but never confirms.

The princess was tall and beautiful, with a good figure but little natural grace, and there was something in her eyes that made one fear what has since come to pass. She inherited her parents' eloquence, and could say whatever she wanted with clarity, precision, appropriateness, and a choice of terms and uniqueness of tone that never ceased to surprise. She was shy in small things and appallingly bold in others. Her arrogance bordered on folly, and she was capable of the lewdest indecencies. One can say that except for avarice, she was the incarnation of all the vices, and was all the more dangerous because of her matchless cunning and intelligence. I am not in the habit of inflating the descriptions I must present for the clear understanding of events, and it is easy to see how strictly reserved I am about ladies and amorous affairs not closely linked with important matters. In this case, I will be even more reserved, to keep my own self-respect as well as to respect the sex and dignity of the person discussed. . . .

She did all she could to make M. le duc de Berry, who was genuinely pious and completely honest, give up religion. She persecuted him for his diligent and self-sacrificing observance of lean and fast days. She mocked him so that sometimes he broke the fast, swayed by love and his good nature and embarrassed by her acid jests. Since she could not convince him without arguments that brought out how painfully scrupulous he was, she scoffed all the more and added to his grief.

His marriage with Mme. la duchesse de Berry began like that of most young newlyweds. His great love for her, plus his natural kindness and accommodation, did not take long in spoiling her completely. He realized it, but his love was stronger than himself. He had to deal with a proud, haughty, and pigheaded woman who despised him and let him know it, because she was much more intelligent than he and a perfectly determined and skillful deceiver besides. She made herself unbearable by bragging about her vices, mocking religion, and jeering at M. le duc de Berry because he was pious. . . . She lost no time in having affairs, which were conducted so indiscreetly that he found out about them. Her daily and interminable sessions with M. le duc d'Orléans, where it was clear that he was not wanted, put him in a rage. There were many stormy scenes between them. During the most recent one, which unfortunately took place at Rambouillet, Mme. la duchesse de Berry earned a kick in the backside for herself and the menace of being locked up in a convent the rest of her life. After he got sick, the duc de Berry would go begging to the King like a child, telling his troubles, and asking to be delivered of Mme. la duchesse de Berry. Enough said, for the details are horrid and wretched.

The angry and patently unjust demands she made on him in his own house pained his sense of fairness: If the house had been her own, he would not have objected. Other more serious matters pushed his patience to the brink of a terrible explosion. At each of the many informal meals she took, she became dead drunk, and threw up whatever she had eaten. On the rare occasions when she held her liquor, she was just as drunk. The presence of her husband, her parents, and ladies she scarcely knew did not restrain her. She even berated M. le duc de Berry for not keeping up with her. She often treated Monsieur her faher with an arrogance that had many frightening implications. Fear of the King kept her from dealing with Madame her mother in the same way. . . . She had frequent and open affairs, despite her high position.

The Duc d'Orléans (1715)

Philippe d'Orléans (1674-1723) was the reprobate nephew of Louis XIV. He was duc de Chartres until his father (Monsieur) died in 1701, when he took over the title of duc d'Orléans. When Louis XIV died in 1715, only a five-year-old great-grandson survived him. Philippe d'Orléans, as next of kin, was appointed regent for the young Louis XV. Although Orléans had done Louis XIV the favor of marrying one of his legitimized daughters by the marquise de Montespan (the second Mlle. de Blois), he was never in the King's favor, and his accession to the Regency was a genealogical irony.

The friendship between Orléans and Saint-Simon is one of the central relationships in the memoirs. Two more dissimilar men would be hard to find—the virtuous, pious, hard-working, and purposeful Saint-Simon was in continuous dismay at the antics of the debauched, profane, indolent and scatterbrained duc d'Orléans. Saint-Simon was a year older than Orléans, and the two had been brought up together, but in the memoirs he usually sounds like a patient father lecturing a wayward son. When Orléans was out of favor at court, Saint-Simon remained his only loyal friend. The unexpected turn of events that gave Orléans the power of the Regency could have brought Saint-Simon his share of bounty. For the first time, he had the opportunity to change what he had criticized, and mysteriously did not take it. Still, he played an important part in the Regency Council and directed the intricate political maneuvers that stripped the royal bastards of the power they had been willed by Louis XIV. There is more than a coincidence in the fact that Saint-Simon ended the Memoirs *the year of Orléans' death, 1723. The King's death had been an initial shock, for there was no one of his stature left to criticize. The death of Orléans was the end of personal interest in court life for Saint-Simon.*

M. le duc d'Orléans was of medium height at best, stout without being fat, with a noble and relaxed manner, a wide, pleasant and ruddy face, black hair, and a black wig. Although he would have been an ungainly dancer and would have done poorly at the academy,[1] there was infinite grace in his face, his gestures, and his manner. It was so natural that it adorned his most common and trivial acts. He had great poise when not under stress, and was kind, affable, open, and unceremoniously charming. The timbre of his voice was pleasant, and he had a particular and versatile gift for speaking with ease and clarity which nothing could disturb, and which disconcerted everyone. He exercised his natural eloquence in the most common and daily matters, but was equally at home with abstract sciences, which he could explain clearly, affairs of state, finance, justice, war, court, politics, ordinary conversation, and all sorts of arts and technical subjects. He could also discuss history and memoirs, and knew a great deal about noble houses. He could conjure up the lives of history's main figures, and was as familiar with the intrigues of former courts as with those of his own. To hear him, one would have thought he was vastly cultured, but nothing was farther from the truth. He skimmed over everything, but his memory was so singular that he forgot neither facts, names, nor dates, and he recalled everything with accuracy; his powers of assimilation were so great that he gave the impression of having deeply studied what he had touched but lightly. He excelled in vivacious and pointed impromptu remarks, such as retorts and witticisms. . . .

[1] The court academy where young noblemen were trained for life at Versailles.

Although he had no inclination for backbiting or malice, he could be dangerous in his judgment of others. He went out of his way not to judge, maintaining a modest discretion even on personal matters. He never talked about himself and when he discussed events in which he had taken part, he gave others their due. Yet he could not help deriding those he called "saints abroad and devils at home" and one could feel his natural contempt and revulsion for them. Another weakness was that he thought he resembled Henri IV in everything, even to his figure and the shape of his face. He tried to imitate his attitudes and spirit of repartee and nothing went straighter to his heart than flattery or praise along those lines. I was never able to make myself oblige him. I felt keenly that he sought resemblance to the great prince more in his vices than in his virtues, and that he admired the former as much as the latter.

Like Henry IV, he was naturally kind, humane, and compassionate. I have never known anyone more instinctively opposed to crime and the destruction of others, or more singularly incapable of harming anyone, than this man so cruelly accused of the blackest and most inhuman crime.[2] It can even be said that his kindness, humaneness, and tractability became defects, and I am not afraid to affirm that he turned the supreme virtue of forgiveness of enemies into a vice through his senseless, indiscriminate and irrational liberality, which was the source of so many drawbacks and unfortunate mishaps. . . .

I remember that about a year before the death of the King, I went to visit Mme. la duchesse d'Orléans at Marly early one afternoon, and found her in bed with a headache, with M. le duc d'Orléans sitting in an armchair at her side. I had no sooner sat down than Mme. la duchesse d'Orléans began to tell me what the prince and the cardinal de Rohan, who had arrived a few days before, were saying about M. le duc d'Orléans. She had evidence that they were discussing measures to be taken now and in the future against M. le duc d'Orléans, and were giving credit to the execrable imputations which the diligence of Mme. de Maintenon and the duc du Maine had spread. I was all the more shocked because for some reason, M. le duc d'Orléans had always sought

[2] It was rumored but never proved that M. le duc d'Orléans had poisoned the duc and duchesse de Bourgogne.

out the two brothers, shown them consideration, and believed he could count on them. "And what do you think of M. le duc d'Orléans," she added, "who although he knows the facts and can no longer doubt them, continues to treat the brothers as kindly as always?" At that I turned my gaze on M. le duc d'Orléans, who had said only a few words to confirm the story and who was negligently sprawled in his chair, and I told him heatedly: "As far as that goes, sir, the truth must be told: Not since Louis the Debonair[3] has there been anyone as debonair as yourself." At these words he sat up, his face crimson with anger except for the whites of his eyes, and mumbled resentfully that I had insulted him and that Mme. la duchesse d'Orléans (who was laughing) had given me the opportunity. "Take heart, sir," I added. "Placate your enemies and deride your friends. I am delighted to see you lose your temper, for it shows I put my finger on a sore spot. When one presses, the patient screams. I want to extract all the pus, to make you a new and more respected man." He grumbled some more and then calmed down. . . .

He loved liberty, as much for others as for himself. He praised England on this point, saying there were no exiles or sealed orders of arrest there, and the King could not keep anyone in prison and could prohibit only the entrance to his own palace. . . .

Debauchery and the boisterousness that went with it became a habit with him. He could not do without it, and thrived on noise, turbulence, and excesses. He threw himself into the weirdest and most scandalous debauchery as though he wanted to be unequaled as a rake. He spiced his orgies with blasphemous speeches and found a delicious refinement in holding them openly on the holiest days, such as Good Friday and similar days which he abused during the Regency. He admired those who were most expert, experienced and extravagant in their debauchery, and I saw him admire and then come to venerate the Grand Prieur because for the last forty years he had never gone to bed sober, publicly kept mistresses, and was continuously impious and blasphemous. It is not surprising that with such principles and behavior M. le duc d'Orléans was a liar to the point of bragging

---

[3] Louis the Debonair, also known as Louis the Pious (788-840) was the son of Charlemagne, but inherited none of his father's strength of character. His rule was marked by disorder, war, and partition.

about it and made a point of being the most skillfull of deceivers. . . .

M. le duc d'Orléans' curiosity, combined with a perverted concept of resoluteness and courage, had led him early in life to try to see the devil and make him talk. He seized on the most extravagant writings to convince himself there was no God, but believed in the devil to the point of wanting to see him and talk to him. This contrast is incomprehensible, and yet rather commonplace. He worked at it with all kinds of shady characters, and particularly Mirepoix, who died in 1699 as a second lieutenant in the Black Musketeers and was the uncle of the Mirepoix who is today a lieutenant general and Knight of the Order [of the Holy Ghost]. They would spend the night invoking the devil in the stone quarries of Vanves and Vaugirard. M. le duc d'Orléans confided to me that he had never seen or heard anything, and finally abandoned the folly. Then, first to oblige Mme. d'Argenton, and later because his curiosity had been whetted, he began to divine the present and the future in a glass of water. I have recounted elsewhere the things he said he saw, and he was no liar. . . .[4]

As for religion, it is impossible to say what he was; I can only say what he was not. But I cannot ignore his extreme uneasiness on this vital matter, and I am convinced that if he had fallen victim to a perilous and gnawing illness, he would have thrown himself in the arms of all the priests and friars he professed to despise. His great weakness was the pride he took in his godlessness and the efforts he made to surpass everyone in his boldness. I remember that one Christmas night at Versailles when he had accompanied the King to matins and the three midnight masses, he surprised the court by the concentration with which he was reading what looked like a prayer book. Mme. la duchesse d'Orléans' first lady in waiting, who had been with the family

[4] Saint-Simon says in the previous paragraph that Orléans was the worst liar at court. In this instance, he had a nine-year-old girl look into a glass of water in the presence of the soothsayer and asked her what she saw at the death of the King (nine years before Louis XIV died). She described the King's bedchamber and those attending it and omitted to mention Monseigneur, the duc de Bourgogne, and the duc de Berry, who were then in good health, but were to die before the King. When Orléans asked what was to become of him, the soothsayer showed him a portrait of himself on the wall, wearing a crown unlike any he had ever seen—a regent's crown.

a long time and used the old retainer's prerogative of familiarity, was filled with joy at the sight and complimented M. le duc d'Orléans the following day at a social gathering. He played along with her for a while, then said: "What a fool you are, Madame Imbert; do you know what I was reading? It was Rabelais, which I brought along so I would not be bored." One can judge the impression his reply made. It was only too true, and had been said from pure defiance.

Mme. la duchesse d'Orléans was another sort of person. She was tall and majestic in every way; her skin, bosom, arms, and eyes were admirable; her mouth was not bad, and her teeth were beautiful but a bit too long; wide and drooping cheeks spoiled her face but did not detract from her beauty; the most unattractive thing about her was her eyebrows, which were plucked and reddish, with very little hair; she had beautiful eyelashes and a good crop of chestnut hair. Without being hunchbacked or deformed, she had one shoulder higher than the other, which gave her a crablike walk. This defect was linked to another which inconvenienced her at court.[5]

MADAME DE MAINTENON (1715)

Françoise d'Aubigné, marquise de Maintenon (1635-1719), rose from dubious Caribbean origins to become the morganatic wife of Louis XIV. The success story of this seventeenth-century self-made woman could serve as a model for all arrivistes. *When she was seventeen, she married the elderly and crippled Paul Scarron, a writer of bad verse and boulevard comedies who, it was said, was generous enough to let his friends replace him when his vigor failed. Widowed nine years later, the young Mme. Scarron became governess of the King's bastards by Mme. de Montespan. The King took a strong initial dislike to her, but she was protected by Mme. de Montespan, who obtained important favors for her. How she replaced Mme. de Montespan in the King's affection remains mysterious. It seems that the King found her*

[5] She was probably suffering from scoliosis, a lateral curvature of the spine.

*understanding and compliant where Mme. de Montespan was hot-
headed and stubborn. Her influence over the King became so
great that she led him to the altar in 1684 and thereafter was a
discreet participant in the rule of France. Her later years were
marked by extreme piety, and she devoted herself to holy works
and the religious school for girls she had founded at Saint-Cyr.
She abandoned the King on his deathbed to retire to Saint-Cyr.
Saint-Simon distrusted her influence over the King and the harsh-
ness of his portrait has been criticized by historians.*

She was a woman of great wit whose knowledge of the world
had been refined and polished by the best people, who at first
tolerated her and then grew to enjoy her. Court practice had made
of her a most agreeable woman. The various positions she held
made her nature flattering, insinuating, complaisant, and obliging.
She had a gift, a taste, a habit, a need, for intrigue. It stemmed
from the many kinds of intrigues she had witnessed, and from
all those she had taken part in, as much for herself as to serve
others. Her grace was incomparable and her poise did not rule
out an air of reserve and respect, which had become natural
through long years of toadying. All this marvelously served her
talents, as did her manner of expression, which was soft, precise,
in good taste, and naturally eloquent without being long-winded.
In her prime, for she was three or four years older than the King,
she had been full of fine conversation and gallantry, with a great
fondness for the boudoir. She long retained these tastes. To her
prim and precious air, which was part of the style of the time,
was added the lacquer of self-importance, and later that of
piousness, which became her dominant trait and absorbed all the
others; piousness was essential to her influence over events and
to the maintenance of high position. This final characteristic
was her very being, to which all the rest was sacrificed without
prejudice. Her philosophy and her good fortune allowed for no
more than the outward signs of honesty and frankness. She was
not really a born hypocrite; necessity had long since made deceitfulness a habit, and her natural flightiness made her seem twice
as false as she was. She had no method in anything except through
constraint or self-discipline. She liked to flutter in knowledge,

amusements, and friends, except for a few friends of the old days, with whom she never wavered, and a few recently acquired friends, who had become necessary to her.

She could hardly vary her amusements after becoming queen. Her inconstancy then played with important matters, and she did great harm. She was easily and excessively infatuated, and just as easily lost interest and became disgusted, and both usually without cause or reason. She had lived so long in abjectness and misery that her mind had withered and her heart and feelings had been stained. Her thoughts and feelings were mean in all things, and she was always a little less than Mme. Scarron, wherever she was.

Nothing was more repulsive than the contrast between the baseness of her character and the radiance of her position; nothing was more dangerous, more detrimental to all worthwhile affairs, than the ease with which she changed friendships and the objects of her trust. She had another deceitful lure. If she was told something she liked at an audience, she replied with surprising candor which gave rise to the highest hopes; but a moment later, she would look annoyed and become abrupt and laconic. One searched one's mind to disentangle favor from disfavor, both of which had been so sudden, but it was a waste of time. The only cause was her flightiness, which was too great to imagine. There were a few who escaped her vacillations, but they were exceptions who confirmed the rule. Even their favor, no matter how great, came under a cloud after her marriage, when one could no longer approach her without caution and uncertainty. . . .

She had a veritable obsession for sponsoring all sorts of projects, which took up all her free time. Saint-Cyr made her waste an incredible amount of time. A thousand other convents cost her an incredible amount of money. She thought she was the universal abbess, particularly for spiritual matters, and undertook to rule on a wealth of diocesan details. These were her favorite occupations.

She thought of herself as a Mother of the Church. She investigated the worth of pastors, superiors in seminaries and monasteries, and mother superiors in convents. This gave her a wealth of frivolous, useless, exacting, and worthless tasks. She wrote an infinite number of letters, guided the souls of the Chosen, and threw herself into all sorts of puerile occupations which usually came to nothing. Sometimes the results were notable, but sometimes there were deplorable errors and poor choices.

THE DUC DE VENDÔME (1706)

Louis-Joseph, duc de Vendôme (1654-1712), was the illegitimate great-grandson of Henri IV by Gabrielle d'Estrées. He goes down as one of the most repulsive specimens of a libertine age, coarse, filthy for the sake of filth, violent for the sake of violence, and a monster of vanity. Thanks to his hunting skill and his gift for flattery, both of which pleased the King, he successively became commander in chief of the King's armies in Spain, Italy, and Flanders. He married Marie-Anne de Condé (Mlle. d'Enghien).

The duc de Vendôme was of average height, stout but vigorous, strong, and alert. He had a noble face and haughty air, natural grace in manner and speech, a great deal of native intelligence which he never cultivated, a natural eloquence, and great boldness which has since become the most brazen audacity. He was worldly, knew court life, and concealed a talent for using people under apparent indifference. He was an admirable courtier, who could draw profit from his greatest vices and was protected by the King's respect for his birth. He was polite when he had to be, rude when he thought he could get away with it, and affectedly familiar with the common people, concealing his vanity to win their affection. Under all this there was a pride that hungered for and devoured everything. As he rose in rank and in the King's favor, his haughtiness, rudeness, and stubbornness rose proportionately. He would not take advice, and made himself inaccessible to all save his valets and a small number of intimates. Praise, admiration, and finally adoration were the only paths by which this demigod could be approached, and his stupid remarks not only would not suffer contradiction, but demanded approval. More than anyone else, he shared and exploited the baseness of the French. He gradually accustomed his subordinates, and finally the whole army, to calling him Monseigneur and Your Highness. It did not take long for this gangrene to spread to the lieutenant generals and the most distinguished persons. They followed like sheep and not one dared address him in any other way. The custom became a privilege, and he would have considered himself insulted if anyone had called him anything else.

The King, who had been free with the ladies most of his life, and had devoted the rest of it to God, often at the expense of everyone else, had always been filled with a just but singular horror for all the inhabitants of Sodom and the least suspicion of perversion. The curious thing is that M. de Vendôme was all his life more publicly and deeply steeped in this filthy perversion than anyone else, treating it like any trivial and ordinary matter, and the King never criticized him for it, although he knew about it. Scandal followed him everywhere, at court, at his castle of Anet, and in the army. His valets and subordinate officers had to satisfy his horrible inclinations. They were chosen for this and were famous for it, and they were courted by M. de Vendôme's friends and anyone else who wished to approach him. We have already seen with what brazen effrontery he twice took the cure publicly,[1] daring to take a leave of absence from the army, and his state of health was much discussed at court. People wondered what strange weakness of the King had allowed Vendôme to do something which would have been forbidden to the royal princes.

His sloth was inconceivable. Several times he was almost captured, jeopardized victory and gave advantages to the enemy because he could not tear himself away from a comfortable lodging. He saw little of battle himself, and left that to his close companions, although he often refused to believe their reports. He could not do otherwise without changing his daily routine, which he was loath to do. His filth was extreme, and he bragged about it. Fools thought he was a simple man. His bed was always full of dogs and bitches who littered by his side. It never seemed to bother him. One of his principles was that everyone was as filthy as he was but did not have the honesty to admit it. He once argued this thesis with Mme. la princesse de Conti, one of the most meticulously clean persons in the world.

[1] The long and painful mercury cure for syphilis.

In the field, he usually rose late, mounted his *chaise percée,* and stayed on it to write dispatches and give the morning's orders. It was the time for generals and distinguished persons to come and see him. He had accustomed the army to this infamy. He had a huge breakfast served often with two or three friends, and relieved himself while eating, listening to the conversation, or giving orders; and there were always a great many bystanders. These shameful details must be given to describe the man. He relieved himself abundantly, and when the bowl was overflowing, it was taken out to be emptied under the noses of all those present; sometimes it had to be emptied more than once. When he shaved, he used the same bowl. He claimed that he observed a simplicity of manner worthy of the Romans, which showed up the sumptuousness and superfluities of others.

When all this was over, he dressed and played piquet or omber for high stakes; or, if he absolutely had to get on a horse for any reason, this was the time for it. When the orders had been given, he called it a day. His meals were taken with his companions. He was a hearty eater and an extraordinary glutton, although he knew nothing about food. He was very fond of fish, and the gamier and more rotten it was, the better he liked it. After the meal there would be discourses and arguments, but above all compliments, praise, and homage that continued all day from every quarter. He would never have forgiven the least criticism. He thought of himself as the greatest soldier of the century, and derided Prince Eugène[2] and all the others; the least contradiction of his views was a crime. Soldiers and low-ranking officers adored him for the familiarity he used to win their affection, which was matched by inordinate haughtiness with all those of high rank or birth including the most distinguished persons in Italy, who often had to deal with him.

This was the cause of the celebrated Alberoni's good fortune. The Duke of Parma had to deal with M. de Vendôme: He sent the bishop of Parma, who was startled at being received by M. de Vendôme on his *chaise percée,* and even more startled at seeing him get up in the middle of the conference and wipe his behind

---

[2] Euène de Savoie (1663-1736) was a celebrated general who entered the service of Leopold I, king of Bohemia and Hungary after being refused a commission by Louis XIV.

in front of him. He was so indignant that he left without saying a word or finishing what he had come for, and told his master that he would never go back again after what had happened. Alberoni was the son of a gardener who had cleverly donned an abbot's collar to go where he would never have been allowed in gardeners' overalls. He was a buffoon and pleased Monsieur de Parme in the manner of an amusing but base jester. Then, he found him intelligent, and saw that he could be put to better use. He did not think that M. de Vendôme's *chaise percée* required a more distinguished envoy, and sent Alberoni to finish what the bishop of Parma had begun. Alberoni, who had no self-respect to keep, and who knew what sort of man Vendôme was, resolved to please him at any price, for the success of his mission and his master's favor. M. de Vendôme was on his *chaise percée*, and Alberoni explained his business, making light of it with jokes that made the general laugh all the more because they had been preceded by praise and homage. Vendôme treated him as he had treated the bishop, and wiped his behind in front of him. At the sight, Alberoni cried: "O culo di angelo" ("Oh, ass of an angel"), and ran to kiss it. Nothing helped his success more than this infamous buffoonery.

The Grand Prieur (1706)

Philippe, at first chevalier de Vendôme, then Grand Prieur de France (1655-1727), was the brother of the duc de Vendôme and therefore the great-grandson of Henri IV. His designation as Grand Prieur means that he was the highest dignitary of the Knightly Order of Malta.

The Grand Prieur had all his brother's vices. In debauchery, he had an advantage over his brother in that he was fond of both fur and feather. Every night for the last thirty years he had been carried to bed dead drunk, and he was faithful to this custom until he died. He was a lackluster general and his well-known poltroonery was matched by a revolting audacity. He was more of a braggart than his brother, and was so insulting that no one would see him except obscure subordinates. He was dishonest to the marrow of his bones (which he had lost thanks to syphilis), a liar, a swindler, a knave, and even stole from his brother. He could be the perfect coxcomb, or extend base flattery to those he needed, and was ready to submit to anything for a three-franc piece. He was also the greatest and most careless squanderer in the world. He was very intelligent and had been perfectly handsome in his youth, with a strikingly beautiful face. On the whole, he was the vilest, most contemptible, and most dangerous creature imaginable.

MONSIEUR LE PRINCE (1709)

Henri-Jules de Bourbon, duc d'Enghien (1643-1709), was the son of "le grand Condé," one of the most famous generals under Louis XIV. The Condés were a collateral branch of the reigning house of Bourbon, and the eldest sons had the right to the title Monsieur le Prince or Monsieur le Duc. He married Anne of Bavaria, princess of the Palatinate.

Monsieur le Prince was a skinny, small-faced man, who impressed by the fire and audacity in his eyes and was one of the most complex personalities at court. No one had a wider range of intelligence and learning, as well as exquisite and all-embracing tastes. What he knew he knew well, even arts and sciences. No one had qualities more frank and natural, or a greater desire to please, which he did with discernment, grace, kindness, courtesy, nobility, and a hidden artfulness that seemed spontaneous. He gave all sorts of surprising and enchanting receptions, which were unequaled in magnificence, inventiveness, accomplishment, effort, and in the pleasure they gave. At the same time, never were genius and talents so wasted, and never was a powerful and lively imagination so completely directed toward self-destruction and malevolence; never were there so many pitfalls and dangers in a single personality, so much sordid avarice, so many base and shameful plots, injustices, depredations, brutalities; never was there such arrogance or so many secret pretensions, artfully managed, to introduce imperceptibly subtle usages and take advantage of them; never such outrageously bold and open enterprises to win what he sought; and never such a vile and overwhelming baseness in his most trivial needs and designs. It explains his toadying to magistrates, financiers, clerks, and valets, his servility to ministers, the refined abjection in his courting of the King, and his continual ups and downs with everyone else.

He was an unnatural son, cruel father, terrible husband, hateful master, and pernicious neighbor, incapable of friends or friendship. He was jealous, suspicious, perpetually apprehensive, extremely quick-minded, surprisingly penetrating, and spent his time devising stratagems to learn and discover everything. He lost his temper over nothings, made difficulties about everything, never found peace with himself, and kept his family terrorized.

In a word, avarice and passion held him in bondage. . . . He victimized Madame la Princesse, who was as ugly as he was, and virtuous and foolish besides. She was a hunchback with pungent armpits, whose trail could be picked up from a distance. All this did not prevent Monsieur le Prince from being furiously jealous. Until she died, the piety, untiring attentiveness, sweetness, and saintly submissiveness of Madame la Princesse were not enough to protect her from frequent insults, kicks, and blows. She did not dare make proposals or decisions in the slightest matters. When the fancy took him, he would summon her unexpectedly to go from one place to another. Often, when they were leaving in their carriage, he would make her get out, or walk down the street, and would do it again that afternoon or the next day. He once did it fifteen days in a row, when they were leaving for Fontainebleau. At other times he had her summoned in church and made her leave high mass, sometimes at the very moment when she was about to go to communion. She had to obey, and put off her communion for another time. It was not because he needed her, or feared she would decide something without him; it was an endless succession of whims. . . .

In the last fifteen or twenty years of his life, he was the victim of something more than angry outbursts. Curious aberrations were observed in public. The maréchale de Noailles told me that she received his visit one morning in her apartment while her bed was being made, with only the counterpane left to put on. He stopped in the doorway and said with rapture: "Ah, what a fine bed, what a fine bed!" He jumped on top of it, rolled and tumbled on it for a while in all directions, got off, and excused himself, saying that the bed had been so clean and well made he could not help himself. There had never been anything between them, the maréchale was above suspicion all her life, and was now at an age where none could arise. Her servants were stupefied, and she mastered her surprise and turned the incident into a jest with a great roar of laughter. It was whispered that there were times when he thought he was a dog, or some other animal, which he imitated. Reliable sources have assured me that once during the King's evening prayer, he stood near the kneeling-stool, threw his head back several times, and opened his mouth wide like a barking dog, but without making any sound. There were long periods during which no one saw him except an old valet who had some influence over him. In his last years, he personally weighed everything he swallowed against everything he evacuated, and wrote down the balance. There resulted dissertations that were a source of distress to his doctors.

Fever and gout attacked him repeatedly, and he made things worse with severe diet, a refusal to see anyone, even his immediate family, and an apprehensiveness that often led to fits of rage. Finot, his doctor and ours, and our friend besides, did not know what to do with him. He told us the most troublesome thing was that Monsieur le Prince claimed he was already dead and refused to eat, on the grounds that the dead did not eat. Yet if he had not eaten, he would have died for a fact. But he could never be persuaded that he was alive, and consequently, that he should eat. Finally Finot and another doctor who attended him decided to agree that he was dead, but to argue that some dead persons ate. They offered to show him some, and brought in several persons they could count on, and who said they were as dead as he was but still went on eating. This device did the trick, but he would only eat with the other "dead" and Finot. His appetite was good, although Finot despaired at the persistence of his fantasy. Finot would double up with laughter, however, when recounting the otherworldly conversations that took place at these meals.

MONSIEUR LE DUC (1710)

Louis III de Condé (1668-1710) was the son of Monsieur le Prince (Henri-Jules de Bourbon). Father and son were not among Saint-Simon's favorite people. Monsieur le Duc married Louise-Françoise de Bourbon, who gave him nine children.

Monsieur le Duc was considerably smaller than the smallest of men, and without being fat, was very bulky. His head was surprisingly large, and his face was frightening. You would have thought he was a dwarf belonging to Madame la Princesse. His complexion was a livid yellow, and it was hard to grow accustomed to his permanent expression of fury and haughtiness and his audacity. He had the remains of an excellent education, was intelligent and well-read, and could be polite and gracious when he wanted to; but he rarely wanted to. He did not inherit the avarice, inequity, and baseness of his forefathers, but did have their qualities and showed diligence and talent for military command. He also had their malevolence, all the wiles to increase his rank through subtle encroachments, and was even bolder and more heated in his forays. His perversity seemed to him a virtue, and he considered his strange and shameful vengeances a prerogative of his rank. His ferocity was extreme and apparent in all things. He was like a millstone that never stops turning, and his frightened friends fled before his outrageous insults, cruel jests, and devastating and unforgettable songs, which he made up as he went along. He was paid back in the same coin, and even more cruelly. He had no friends, only strange and obscure acquaintances, and he himself was as obscure as a man of his rank could be. Even his acquaintances fled him, and he chased after them seeking company. If he found them having a meal somewhere, he would fall on them as though down the proverbial chimney and berate them for having tried to hide from him. I sometimes saw M. de Metz, M. de Castries and others distressed by it. His savage nature led him to abuse everything, and the way he applauded his own abuses was intolerable. If the term can be used for a prince of the blood, it was this kind of insolence that made tyrants more hated than their tyranny. The difficulties of his family life, his continuous outbursts of furious jealousy and his anger at realizing their futility, the permanent contrast between conjugal love and rage, his father's preference for M. le prince de Conti,[1] the popularity of this same prince compared with his own alienation and unpopularity even with his own servants, and his fury at the rank of the bastards and M. le duc d'Orleans (despite his own usurpations): All these Furies tormented him ceaselessly and made him as dangerous as the beasts who seem to have been born to devour and make war on the human race. . . . Everyone was relieved at his death.

Le Nostre (1700)

André Le Nostre (1613-1700), Controller General of construction and gardens, designed the gardens and park of Versailles, which Saint-Simon considered a mixed blessing.

Le Nostre died after having lived for eighty-eight years in perfect health, with a sound mind and all the preciseness and good taste required by his duties. He was celebrated as the first to design the beautiful gardens that adorn France and have put to shame the reputation of Italian gardens, so that now the most famous Italian masters come here to learn and admire. Everyone respected and liked Le Nostre for his honesty, uprightness, and preciseness. He was always perfectly disinterested, and never tried to rise above his rank or appear to be more than he was. He worked for individuals as well as for the King, with the same application, trying only to improve on nature, and seeking true beauty as inexpensively as he could. His naïveté and frankness

---

[1] The second son in the Condé family carried the title of prince de Conti.

were charming. Once the Pope asked the King if he could borrow Le Nostre for several months. When he entered the Pope's chamber, instead of kneeling he ran up to him, threw his arms around him and kissed him on both cheeks, saying: "Hello there, Reverend Father, how well you look, and how pleased I am to see you in such good health!" The Pope, Clement X, laughed with all his heart and was so delighted by Le Nostre's bizarre welcome that he showed him great friendship.

On his return, the King took him through the gardens of Versailles and showed him what had been accomplished during his absence. When they reached the Colonnade he remained silent, but the King pressed him for an opinion. "Well, Sire," he said, "what would you have me say? You tried to make a gardener out of a mason [Mansart], and he has served you a dish according to his recipes." They both smiled, and the King said no more about it. It is true that this piece of architecture, which tries in vain to be a fountain, was completely out of place in a garden. The King, who liked to make him talk, took him into the gardens a month before his death and had him carried in a sedan chair next to his because of his age. And Le Nostre said: "Ah! My poor father, if you could see me now, a poor gardener, your son, being carried in a sedan chair alongside the greatest king in the world, my joy would be complete." As controller of buildings he lived in the Tuileries, whose garden he designed and was responsible for, as well as the palace garden. All his work is far superior to what has been done since, in spite of efforts to imitate him.

He used to say that flower beds were for nursemaids who could not leave the children and admired them from their windows. He excelled in them, as in all other parts of a garden, but did not hold them in high esteem. He was right, for people do not often walk by them any more.

MME. DE MAINTENON'S BROTHER (1697)

Mme. de Maintenon, despite the incredible elevation to which her base nature had miraculously arrived, was not without problems. Her brother's continuous outbursts were one of her major preoccupations. He was the comte d'Aubigné, and although he had never been more than an infantry captain, he bragged about his war days as though he deserved a better fate and had been cruelly wronged by not having been promoted marshal of France long ago. At other times, he would say with a wink that he had taken more than the worth of a marshal's stripes in loot. He would rail at Mme. de Maintenon for having done nothing to help make him a duke and a peer, and about everything else that came into his head. And yet he had been given nothing less than the governorships of Belfort, then Aigues-Mortes, then Cognac, which he kept with that of Berry after giving back Aigues-Mortes. On top of that, he was a knight of the Order. He chased the girls in the Tuileries and everywhere else, and always kept several, with whom he lived quite openly, taking in their families and friends, all of which cost a great deal of money.

Money burned a hole in the pockets of this lunatic, and yet he was amusing, with flashes of wit and a surprising gift for repartee. With all this, he was a gentleman, kind and polite, without any of the impertinence one might have expected because of his sister's position. In other matters he was marvelously impudent, and it was a pleasure to hear him describe his sister in the times of the Hôtel d'Albret and her marriage to Scarron, and sometimes in earlier days. He never held back on her romantic adventures and affairs, which he compared to her present piety, marveling at her prodigious good fortune. However diverting his remarks were, it could be very embarrassing to listen to him, for he could not be silenced, and instead of talking with two or three friends, would go on at table, in front of everyone, or on a bench in the Tuileries, or even in a gallery at Versailles, where he had the gall to call the King mockingly "my brother-in-law."

I heard him several times, particularly at my father's, where he would come for a visit or a meal more often than he was invited. My parents' embarrassment and annoyance made me laugh up my sleeve. A man of his temperament, so self-indulgent, and so free to mock without fear of reprisal or ridicule, was a great burden for Mme. de Maintenon.

A Singular Woman (1696)

Mme. de Castries was a pint-sized woman, a sort of half-baked lump of china. She was well made, but so tiny you could have strung her through an average-sized ring, for she had no buttocks, no bust, and no chin. She was very ugly and always looked painfully surprised, but her face shone with wit and lived up to its promise. She knew everything, history, philosophy, mathematics, and classical languages, although she never gave the impression of knowing anything other than her native tongue; her speech, even on the most trivial subjects, was precise, forceful, eloquent, and graceful, with a turn of phrase given only to the Mortemarts [her maiden name]. She was agreeable, amusing, gay, serious, everything to everyone, charming when she wished to please, but pleasing naturally and with a sensitivity that was not studied. She could also shame with ridicule that was not easily forgotten. Her thousands of trenchant complaints were a way of displaying her pride. She could be wickedly cruel, as well as an excellent friend, polite, gracious, and generally obliging. There was nothing frivolous about her, but she was open to wit, and loved a wit to her taste. She was a marvelous storyteller, and could invent a novel before your eyes, with surprising resourcefulness, variety, and geniality. With all her conceit, her devotion to her husband led her to believe she had married well; she was as conceited for him as for herself, and included him in everything. He paid her back with all sorts of considerations and respects.

A Ridiculous Woman (1701)

Mme. de Saint-Hérem was the strangest-looking and most singular woman imaginable. Once she burned her thigh while swimming in the middle of the Seine, near Fontainebleau. She thought the water was too cold and wanted to warm it, so she had some water boiled on the bank and poured around her. Before the water had cooled off in the river, she was burned so badly that she had to take to her bed. When it thundered, she crawled on all fours under a bed, and made her servants pile on top of it so that the lightning would strike them before it reached her. She and her husband had been wealthy, but she had lost everything through her foolishness. The amount she spent to have masses said for herself was unbelievable.

The best story about her, among thousands, is that of the lunatic who broke into her house on the Place Royale one afternoon when her servants were eating, and, finding her alone in her room, clasped her passionately in his arms. The good woman, who had been hideous at eighteen, and was now a widow of more than eighty, began to scream at the top of her lungs. Finally, her servants heard her and found her with her skirts raised, fighting off the madman. They seized him, had him arrested, and the story gave everyone a good laugh.

The Princesse d'Harcourt (1702)

The princesse d'Harcourt is a person worth describing, for she was typical of a court which had many odd specimens. She had once been very beautiful and passionate, but although she was not old, her grace and beauty had soured. She was a great, fat, energetic creature, with a complexion like milk soup, ugly blubber lips, and a towhead, with stringy hair that was always in disarray, as were her filthy and ill-fitting clothes. She was always intriguing, demanding, encroaching, and quarreling. Depending on those she had to deal with, she could be as low as grass or as lofty as a rainbow. She was a blond fury, and what is more, she had the effrontery, meanness, deceitfulness, violence, avarice, and avidity of a harpy. She was also a glutton, and those who invited her to meals despaired because she wanted to relieve herself as soon as she arose from table, but often did not have the time, so that she let fall behind her a train of filth. Madame du Maine's and Monsieur le Grand's servants cursed her with vehemence. She made no bones about it, she hiked up her skirts and went off, then came back saying she had been feeling ill; everyone was accustomed to it. She was quite a businesswoman, and would have run as far for a hundred francs as for a hundred thousand. Controller generals could never get rid of her, and she cheated businessmen as often as she could. She openly cheated at gambling, with inconceivable boldness. When she was caught, she reviled her accuser and pocketed her winnings. Since she always behaved this way, she was thought of as a fishwife with whom no one wanted to argue. She even made scenes at Marly, in the middle of a game of lansquenet, in front of Monseigneur and Mme. le duchesse de Bourgogne. At other games, like omber,[1] she was avoided, but it was not always easy. She stole as much as she could and said at the end of every game that if any mistake had been made, she was prepared to make restitution. She also decided whether mistakes had been made to her disadvantage. For she was very sanctimonious, and said she wanted to set her conscience at ease, "for in gambling, a mistake is always possible." She went to communion incessantly and to all the services, usually after gambling until four in the morning. Once, on a feast day at Fontainebleau, when the maréchal de Villeroy was on duty, she went to see his wife between vespers and evening service. The maréchale maliciously proposed a game to make her miss the service. She refused, and said finally that Mme. de Maintenon would be there.

The maréchale insisted, saying that Mme. de Maintenon could not possibly notice everyone who had or had not been at the service. They began to play. On her way back from the service, Mme. de Maintenon, who seldom went anywhere, decided to pay a visit to the maréchale de Villeroy. When she was announced, the princesse d'Harcourt had a fit. "I am lost," she screamed uncontrollably, "for she will see me gambling when I should be at the service!" She dropped her cards and slumped in her chair, completely at a loss. The prank's success made the maréchale laugh with all her heart. Mme. de Maintenon entered slowly and found them thus, with five or six others. The maréchale de Villeroy, whose wit was infinite, said that despite the honor of her presence, she was creating a disorder, and pointed to the

[1] A card game of Spanish origin.

disheveled princesse d'Harcourt. Mme. de Maintenon asked the princesse d'Harcourt, with a kind and majestic smile: "Madam, is this how you went to evening service today?" At that, the princesse d'Harcourt came out of her swoon with fury, said she was the butt of pranks and persecution, and that Mme. la maréchale de Villeroy must have known Mme. de Maintenon was coming and had tricked her into gambling so she would miss the service. "Persecuted!" replied the maréchale. "I could think of no better way to receive you than with a game of cards. It is true that for a moment you debated whether to go to the service, but your fondness for gambling was too strong. That, Madam," she said, addressing Mme. de Maintenon, "is the extent of my crime."

Monseigneur and Madame la duchesse de Bourgogne continually played practical jokes on the princesse d'Harcourt. One day they had firecrackers placed all along the avenue between Marly and the Perspective,[2] where she lived. She was horribly afraid of everything. Two porters were sent to offer to carry her when she was ready to go. Everyone was at the door to see the show. When she had reached the middle of the avenue, the firecrackers began to go off, and she screamed for help as the porters abandoned her. She screamed like a demon and struggled in her chair, almost knocking it over out of rage. The spectators ran up to get a closer look and to hear her rant at everyone in sight, including Monseigneur and Mme. la duchesse de Bourgogne. Another time the prince hid a large firecracker under her seat while she was playing piquet; as he was about to light it, a charitable soul warned him that the firecracker would probably cripple her, and he desisted. Sometimes they would send twenty Swiss guards into her room with drums, and she was awakened by the din. These scenes always took place at Marly. Another time, they stayed up very late until she had gone to sleep. She had rooms in the château, rather near the captain of the guards on duty, who was M. le maréchal de Lorge. There had been a heavy snowfall, and it was freezing: Mme. la duchesse de Bourgogne and her suite took snow from the first floor drawing-room terrace, on the same level as the princesse d'Harcourt's apartment; they woke up the guards to help them make snowballs; then, with the help of

---

[2] The Perspective was a wall painted with bucolic scenes that surrounded the buildings.

candles and a pass key, they softly slipped into her room, and abruptly drawing aside the curtains of her bed, they pelted her with snowballs. The sight of this filthy creature in her bed, rudely awakened, drowned in snow that covered even her ears, disheveled, yelling at the top of her voice, squirming like an eel, and not knowing where to turn, entertained those present for more than half an hour. The nymph was swimming in her bed with water dripping everywhere and beginning to fill the room. It was nearly enough to kill her. The next day she sulked and they made fun of her all the more.

NINON DE L'ENCLOS (1705)

Ninon, the famous courtesan known as Mlle. de l'Enclos since old age made her give up her profession, is another example of the triumph of vice coupled with wit, and amended by some degree of virtue. The commotion and disorder she caused among the highest-born and most brilliant young men strained the Queen Mother's well-known indulgence for ladies who devote themselves to the game of love. She decided to order Ninon to retire to a convent. When an officer brought the letter stamped with the King's seal, Ninon observed that no convent had been designated, and said without losing her composure: "Sir, since the Queen has been good enough to leave the choice of a religious refuge to me, pray tell her that I have picked the Franciscan friars of Paris." She handed the letter back with a fine curtsy, and the officer was too astounded by her effrontery to reply. The Queen Mother found her answer so amusing that she left her in peace.

Ninon never limited herself to one lover at a time. She had hordes of worshipers, and when she grew tired of one she told him so frankly and took another. The creature's hold over men was so great that none would ever have dared thrash it out with his successor, too glad to continue seeing her as a friend. Sometimes, when she was really taken by a lover, she kept him during an entire campaign. La Chastre, who was about to leave, claimed to be one of these happy few. Apparently Ninon's promise had not been very clear, and he was fool enough, and presumptuous enough, to demand a written note, which she gave him. He took it with him and often bragged about it. But the promise was badly kept, and every time she broke it, she exclaimed: "Oh! What a fine note La Chastre has got!" Finally, her new lover asked her what she meant. She told him, the story got around, and La Chastre was crushed by the ridicule.

Ninon had all sorts of illustrious friends, and wit enough to keep them and prevent them from quarreling among themselves. Everything she did had an outward respectability and decency which the highest-born princesses rarely attain. Thus, the most select and important members of the court were her friends, and it even became fashionable to be received by her, because of the people one could meet. There was never any gambling, boisterousness, quarreling, or talk about religion or the government; the conversation was witty and elevated in tone, with discussions of past and recent events, and love affairs (without opening the door to slander). . . .

She often lent money to her friends, and did important favors for them. She faithfully kept money and secrets entrusted to her. All this had given her a well-justified reputation and she was held in singular consideration. When Mme. de Maintenon had lived in Paris, they had been intimate friends. Now, Mme. de Maintenon did not like to have her mentioned, but did not dare disavow her. She kept writing her until her death, in a friendly way. L'Enclos, for Ninon had adopted this name ever since giving up the long-practiced profession of her youth, did not show equal reserve. On rare occasions, when she was particularly interested in someone or something, she wrote Mme. de Maintenon, who granted her requests with prompt efficiency; but after Mme. de Maintenon reached her zenith, they only saw each other, secretly, two or three times. L'Enclos had a marvelous gift for repartee, and among others two remarks to the late maréchal de Choiseul are unforgettable; one is a perfect squelch and the other a perfect caricature. Choiseul, one of her former lovers, had been a handsome ladies' man in his day. He deplored the fact that he was on bad terms with M. de Louvois, but the King included him in the promotion of 1688 for the Order, despite his minister. The promotion was unexpected, although he was well born and one of the best and oldest lieutenant generals. He was so pleased that he would admire himself in the mirror, adorned with his blue sash. L'Enclos caught him at it two or three times and finally told him with annoyance in front of everyone: "Monsieur le comte, if I catch you again, I will tell you who is being promoted along with you." There were certainly some sorry specimens in the lot, who were nonetheless better than those in the promotion of 1724 and others since then![1] The good marshal was virtue itself, but was neither intelligent nor amusing. After an overlong visit, L'Enclos yawned, stared at him, and cried out: "Lord, how many virtues you make me detest!" which is a line from some play or other.[2] One can judge what a scandal this created, and yet her sally did not lead to their falling out.

L'Enclos lived to be more than eighty, in health, popularity, and respectability. She devoted her last years to God, and her death was much lamented. The unusual nature of this person has led me to describe her in detail.

THE COMTE DE GRAMONT (1707)

Philibert, comte de Gramont (1621-1707), was banished from court by Louis XIV in 1662 because he was too attentive to a lady the King favored. He went to England, where he married Elizabeth Hamilton, whose brother, Count Anthony Hamilton, wrote the Memoirs of Count Gramont.

At the end of January, the comte de Gramont died in Paris, where he seldom went. He was more than eighty-six years old, had remained in perfect health until eighty-five, and kept his wit until the end. . . . He became attached to Monsieur le Prince,

[1] This bit of intelligence, the result of pillow talk from Ninon's lovers, was particularly funny to Saint-Simon, who had to wait until 1728 before becoming a Knight of the Order of the Holy Ghost. The "promotion of 1724" which he mentions is the one from which he was stricken by Monsieur le Duc. This scurviness on the part of a former friend was one of the reasons he quit the court entirely.
[2] The play is Corneille's *Pompée*.

whom he followed to Flanders. He spent some time in England and fell violently in love with Miss Hamilton. Her outraged brothers forced him to marry her, although he was already committed to another. He was a man of great intelligence, which he applied only to jokes, repartee, and a subtle and precise gift for finding the soft spots and weaknesses of everyone and describing them with devastating and unforgettable wit. The King's presence did not stop him, it rather seemed to encourage him, and no man or woman could intimidate him by their position, favor, greatness or merit. He had become accustomed to saying whatever he liked to the King, whom he amused and instructed with a thousand barbs, even about his ministers. He was a mad dog, and nothing escaped him. His well-known poltroonery sheltered him from all the consequences of his barbs. He was also an impudent swindler, and a shameless cheat at gambling; he gambled for high stakes all his life. Despite the King's generosity, he always played the beggar, and took money where he could find it. The King had given him the governorship of La Rochelle and the Aunis region when M. de Navailles died, and he sold it at a good price to Gacé, who has since become the maréchal de Matignon. The comte de Gramont had full access, and never left court. When he needed them, he could play the toady to the very persons he had tongue-lashed, and was ready to insult them again as soon as he obtained what he wanted. He never kept his word and had no sense of honor. He even told a thousand amusing stories about himself, in which he bragged of his turpitude, and he left to posterity memoirs of his life which even his worst enemies would not have published, and which are accessible to everyone.

He did everything he pleased, and it pleased him to do everything. He did not change with age. . . . He once met the archbishop of Reims leaving the King's study and looking very dejected after an audience concerning the monk of d'Hautvilliers' abbey: "Archbishop," he said loudly and insultingly, *"verba volant, scripta manent.* I am your servant." [1] The archbishop suffered the insult without a word. On another occasion, an envoy from a northern country came to pay the King his compli-

---

[1] "Words vanish; but writings remain." The archbishop was involved in the publication of a Jansenist and antiroyalist book printed in Holland and written by the monk of d'Hautvilliers.

ments, and did very poorly. When he had left, the King said he could not understand why someone so inept had been sent. "You will see, Sire," said the comte de Gramont, "he is the relative of a minister." He never let a day go by without attacking someone. He fell gravely ill when he was eighty-five, one year before his death, and his wife brought up the subject of God. He had completely neglected the subject all his life, and the accounts of the miracles surprised him very much: "Are you sure you're telling me the truth, Countess?" he asked. Then, as she was reciting the Our Father, he said: "Countess, that prayer is very beautiful. Who wrote it?" He did not have the least inkling of any religion. You could write volumes about his sayings and deeds, but they would be reprehensible once the effrontery, the sallies, and the frequent aspersions had been removed. Despite all these vices untouched by any virtue, he had submitted the court to his will, and it held him in fear and respect. When he died, the court felt itself delivered of a scourge which the King had all his life favored and honored. He was made a Knight of the Order in the promotion of 1688.

The Duc de Noailles (1711)

Adrien-Maurice, duc de Noailles (1678-1766), became president of the council of finances under the Regency, in 1715, thanks to Saint-Simon, who proposed him to the Regent. Saint-Simon hated the fatuous and erratic Noailles, but was determined to restore nobles to important government posts, even if it meant proposing his enemies. Despite his incompetence, lovingly described by Saint-Simon, Noailles became maréchal de France in 1734, minister of state in 1743, and abmassador to Spain in 1746.

He was born under a lucky star. He was rather tall, but thick-set, with a strong and heavy step, and wore only solid colors or his officer's uniform, for he wanted to affect natural simplicity. He also affected it with what one could call, for want of better expressions, offhandedness and good fellowship. It would have been hard to find a more versatile intelligence or more artfulness and flexibility in suiting his views to those of others and convincing them, when he profited by it, that he shared their goals and eagerness and was supremely preoccupied with their affairs. He was amiable when he wanted to be, gracious and affable, and seemed at ease even when he was most annoyed. He was jolly, amusing, and had a keen and tasteful wit that could not offend, full of prolific and charming sallies. He had a gift for music, and was a perfect guest, prompt to adopt the tastes of his hosts. He was even-tempered, and had a talent for declamation, so that he could speak all day and say nothing, even in the middle of the drawing room at Marly and during the saddest, most difficult and most embarrassing moments of his life. I saw and heard him many times, and, in my surprise, asked him how he did it. He had poise and graciousness, and was a facile conversationalist, for he knew something about everything and talked with elegant superficiality. He could spout platitudes on every subject, but as soon as the surface was scratched, it revealed him as a past master of gibberish. . . . However, he told charming stories, and had an effortless gift for making trifles amusing and finding laughter in the thorniest and most serious situations. We see here an impressive list of courtier's talents. He would have been a happy man if he had held himself to them. But he had others. His social graces and intelligence were lures, his friendship, respect, and trust were traps that concealed all the monsters the poets have found in the depths of hell: fathomless malevolence, unfailing falseness, natural perfidiousness that held nothing sacred, a blackness of soul that made one doubt that he had one and proved that he believed in nothing, contempt for the most elementary virtues, and, according to the fashions of the time, public debauchery and abandon or bald and sustained hypocrisy. He freely juggled all these crimes, and when caught, persevered instead of blushing; he was never at a loss for a lie or slander. When he was exposed and powerless, he coiled like a snake, preserving his venom through the most abject and repeated baseness, and tried to enlist your confidence with the determined aim of strangling you. He could betray anyone without a flicker of hate, anger or compunction, even his most trusted friends, whom he admitted had performed great favors for him and done him no wrong. The incentive for such unusual perversity was the most immoderate ambition, which made him hatch the blackest, most abysmal, most incredible plots to ruin all those who could obstruct his path or make it rougher and more uncertain. . . .

At the same time, with all his talents, intelligence, and learning, he was fundamentally incapable of assuming responsibilities of any kind. His overactive imagination and multiple views, the obliquity of the crisscrossing plans he had drawn up all at once, and his impatience to follow them up and untangle them, led to inextricable confusion. On the battlefield, this was the source of many useless, fruitless, and often harmful orders with which he harassed his troops. The marches and countermarches which no one could understand, the sending out of detachments without a reason, the six, eight, or ten counterorders that would come within an hour's time to the same troops, the orders to march or not to march that were given to the entire army, were the source of despair, contempt, and ruin. In political affairs, he would draw up a plan and work on it eight days, or sometimes fifteen or twenty days. He would live only for this plan, devote all his time to it and neglect everything else. But then another idea would take shape in his head, replace the first with the same ardor, be replaced by a third, and so on. He was a man of whims, caprices, and successive bursts of energy. He was capable of systematic planning only when constructing plots, cabals, traps, and when laying his mines which exploded under one's feet. . . .

His growing familiarity with me about future events led him to speak of the royal bastards with such violence that I will not repeat his remarks. One thing and another finally led him to propose, as though it were highly reasonable, a plan for the fortification of Paris. I could not conceal my surprise. "Paris!" I exclaimed. "And where would you get the building materials, and the money, and the years it would take to finish the work? And even if you could do it with the stroke of a magic wand, where would you get the garrison to defend it? Where would you get the munitions and supplies for the troops and inhabitants? Where would you get the artillery? And finally, even if its feasibility was as apparent as its absurdity, what would be the point?" He campaigned several days for this rare plan, and I did not oppose him, for it was obviously doomed to failure. When he saw he

could never convince me, he made another suggestion. He
wanted to bring all the public services, the courts and the schools,
to Versailles. I looked at him with surprise and asked where, when,
and with what money he would settle everyone in Versailles,
which nature had not favored, for it had neither a river, drinking
water, nor convenient watering places for horses, was built on
sand and mud, and nothing could grow there. I asked him moreover what could be the purpose of such a move, even if it were
possible, for it could only bring confusion and uneasiness to the
court, while it would leave Paris in a dangerous vacuum, and
ruin attorneys, magistrates, and the myrmidons of the courts and
universities. In a word, there was nothing practical or useful in
it. He said it would diminish the importance of Paris, which was
ruining the rest of the country, and cut the courts off from the
support of the people, thus preventing a dangerous alliance. He
finally agreed that Versailles was too inconvenient to accom-
modate them, declaimed against the immense establishment the
King had built there, praised Saint-Germain, and then proposed
casually that Versailles should be torn down and moved to Saint-
Germain, where with all its riches and materials, it could become
the most salubrious and admirable residence in Europe.

At this third proposal, words failed me. "This man is mad," I
said to myself, "and may at any moment attack me. What have
I done, and what will become of the country's finances?" [1] As I
went on talking to myself without moving my lips, he went on
discoursing, enchanted by the vision of Saint-Germain rising from
the remains of Versailles. Finally, noticing my silence, he asked
for my opinion. "Sir," I told him, "when you have fairy queens
with their magic wands at your disposal, I will agree with you.
For it is true that nothing could be more admirable, and I could
never understand how the cesspool of Versailles could have been
preferred to Saint-Germain; however, you need the intervention
of fairy queens for your proposal. Until you have them at your
beck and call, there is no point in prolonging this discussion."
He began to laugh, and insisted that it could be done, and was

[1] The conversation was taking place in 1715, after the duc de Noailles
learned that he had been named to head the financial council, thanks to
Saint-Simon.

not so impossible as I seemed to think. But of his three proposals, it was the one he insisted on least.

THE MARÉCHAL DE BOUFFLERS (1708)

The maréchal de Boufflers (1644-1711) was one of the few persons at court whom Saint-Simon really admired. He saw in this rough but virtuous soldier the prototype of what the nobility should be and had been until Louis XIV weakened its position by inventing the pleasant bondage of court life. This portrait is one of the rare occasions when Saint-Simon showed that he could praise as well as damn.

The strong points of the maréchal de Boufflers were order, exactness, and vigilance. His quality was clear, modest, natural, frank, and unemotional. In the heat of battle, he observed everything and gave orders as calmly as though in his drawing room. He was equal to himself in the most trying predicaments; nothing made him lose his head. His preventive measures and decisions left nothing to chance. Everyone was won by his kindness and politeness, which never deserted him. His equity, uprightness, willingness to seek advice and free discussion, and scrupulousness in giving credit for successful advice and deeds, won him affection and devotion. Soldiers and civilians adored him because of the care he took to make munitions and supplies last, his fairness in distributing bread, wine, meat, and other foods during sieges, and the attention he paid to hospitals and medical care. He turned green troops into veterans, for most of his garrison was made up of civilian conscripts and fugitives. He was accessible at all hours, attentive to everyone, and careful to avoid purposeless weariness and danger for others. He did everything himself, exposed himself to danger and exhausted himself for the general good. During battles, he slept with his clothes on, and from the start of a siege to the time the call for surrender was sounded, he would not go to bed more than three times. It is hard to understand how a man of his age, worn by war, could set his mind and body to such tasks, without ever losing his calm and composure. He was criticized for overexposing himself to dangers, but he did it so that he could observe everything and be ready for anything. He also did it to set an example and to make sure that his orders were being carried out. He was slightly wounded several times, which he tried to conceal as best he could, and which changed nothing in his daily routine. Once, when he was laid low by a wound in the head, he had to be carried home against his will. He refused to be bled for fear he would lose his strength, and wanted to get up.

His house was invested by soldiers who threatened to desert if they should see him in the field in less than twenty-four hours. He had to spend the day at home, submit to bleeding, and take a rest. When he made his reappearance, there was an explosion of joy.

THE DUC DE BEAUVILLIER (1714)

Paul, duc de Beauvillier (1648-1714), was tutor of the duc de Bourgogne and first gentleman of his household. Saint-Simon called him "the good duke," was one of his closest friends, and never decided anything without consulting him. Everyone respected him. Even the King said he was "one of the wisest men in my kingdom."

He was tall, very thin, with a long ruddy face, a very large aquiline nose, a sunken mouth, intelligent and piercing eyes, a pleasant smile, and a mild but usually serious and concentrated expression. He was born a lover of pleasure, lively, passionate, and hotheaded. He had natural intelligence, common sense, excellent judgment, but was sometimes too fastidious. He spoke pleasantly and easily, with a natural precision. He was apprehensive, discerning, wise, and had vast foresight that never led him astray. His simplicity and sagacity were extreme, and blended well. God touched him early, and I believe I can say that since that day, he never lost His presence. With his wisdom, his degree of piety can be well imagined. He was pleasant, modest, even-tempered, polite and distinguished, rather attentive, honest, and easily accessible to people of modest condition. He did not display his devotion, nor did he conceal it. He annoyed no one, although he watched over his servants a little too closely. He was so sincerely humble, although grateful to what he owed his rank, and so detached from worldly things, as we have already seen, that I do not think the saintliest monks could have done better. The extreme disorder of his father's affairs had nonetheless made him alert to the duty of managing his own. This did not keep him from being truly magnificent in everything, for he felt he owed it to his position.

Harlay (1707)

Achille III de Harlay (1639-1712), was First President of Parlement from 1689 to 1707. It was he who suggested to King Louis XIV that he could legitimize his children by the marquise de Montespan ("fruit of a double adultery" as Saint-Simon wrote) by not declaring the name of the mother. On this count and many others, Saint-Simon hated Harlay cordially.

Harlay was a short thin man with a diamond-shaped face, a long, aquiline nose, and vulture's eyes that seemed to see through walls and devour everything. He wore a collar and a pepper-and-salt wig, both as short as those worn by the clergy, a skullcap, and flat cuffs such as priests and the Chancellor wear. He always wore robes that were too tight for him. He spoke slowly, weighing his words and detaching each syllable. He had the old Gallic pronunciation, and often used archaic words. His manner was stiff, constrained, affected, false, and cynical. He let off an odor of hypocrisy, and his bows were deep and formal. When he walked, he always hugged the wall, and kept a respectful air that could not altogether conceal his arrogance and insolence. His remarks were always calculated and prideful, and when he dared, contemptuous and derisive. Even in the most casual conversation, he spouted sententious maxims. He was taciturn and tense, nor could anyone relax in his presence. He had a great deal of native intelligence, learning, and penetration, a keen knowledge of the world and the people with whom he dealt, a broad culture, a profound knowledge of the law and particularly common law (which has unfortunately become very rare), and he was well read and had a good memory. With a studied slowness of delivery, he had a surprisingly lively, accurate, prompt, and everpresent gift for repartee. In parliamentary tactics, he was far superior to the most subtle attorneys. He was the undisputed master of Parlement, and all the others, the judges and magistrates, were like schoolboys before him. He did what he wanted with them, and never curried their favor with familiarity. They usually did not even realize it, and when they did, were too meek to protest. On important occasions his vanity was magnificent, but this same vanity made him frugal in ordinary times, and even modest in his standard of living, because he wanted to imitate the great magistrates of ancient times.

It is most unfortunate that so many qualities and natural talents were devoid of virtue and devoted to evil, ambition, avarice, and crime. He was proud, venomous, malignant, a natural villain, humble, base, crawling when he had to, and false and hypocritical in his most trivial actions. He dealt out meticulous justice in unimportant cases to preserve his reputation, but otherwise practiced the cleverest, most persistent, and most consummate iniquity, favoring his interests, his passions, and the winds of court and fortune.

His perverse soul was tormented, not by remorse (which he never felt, or at least never showed), but by a kind of rage that was always on him, which made him the terror and scourge of all those who saw him. As it did not spare him, it spared no one else, and his sarcasms were frequent and piercing. His death was an occasion for public rejoicing, and Parlement, crushed under his terrible yoke, felt the deliverance more keenly than anyone. . . .

Once a husband and wife, both of whom were great talkers and quibblers, went to his tribunal. Their turn came and the husband tried to speak but his wife cut him off and began explaining the case. The First President listened for a while, then interrupted: "Sir," he asked the husband, "is this lady your wife?" "Yes, Sir," he replied, surprised by the question. "How I pity you," said the First President, shrugging his shoulders with an air of compassion and turning his back on them. . . .

Once the Jesuits and the Oratorians were about to bring a suit to trial, but the First President called them in to settle their differences peaceably. They discussed the matter, and as he saw them out, he said, turning to the Jesuits: "Good fathers, it is a pleasure to live with you," and to the Oratorians: "And a pleasure, good fathers, to die with you . . ."

Once the duchesse de la Ferté went to see him, and like everyone else, was victimized by his bad temper. As she was leaving, she complained to her notaire, and called the First President a dirty old dog. He was right behind her, but said nothing. Finally she noticed him, but hoped he had not heard, while he helped her into her carriage, as though nothing had happened. Not long after, her case was called, and she won it. She rushed to thank the First President, who received her with deep bows, modesty, and humility. Then, he said out loud in front of everyone: "Madam, I am delighted that a dirty old dog like me was able to help a dirty old bitch like you."

He treated ordinary people with total arrogance, and would tell a notaire or an attorney brought by distinguished persons to explain their case: "Be quiet, my good man! Who are you to talk to me? I am not addressing you." One can imagine, after such outbursts, how the rest of the case was handled. His treatment of certain counselors was no kinder. The Doublet brothers, both of whom were counselors (the eldest had merit and ability and was an estimable man), had brought the estates of Persan and Croÿ and taken their names. They went to the First President's audience. He knew them very well, of course, but asked who they were. On hearing the names of Croÿ and Persan he bowed very low. Then he straightened up and put on a look of surprise, as though he had just recognized them, and said: "I know you, you impostors," and turned his back on them. . . .

His few friends and his family suffered no less than others. He treated his son like a slave, and their life was a farce. They lived together and ate together, but never spoke to each other, except about the weather. When household and other matters came up, as they invariably did, they wrote each other sealed letters, which flew from one room to the other. The father's letters were pitiless, and the son's were almost as biting, for he gave as good as he got. The son never visited the father without asking for permission, and the father replied as though to a stranger. When the son entered, the father rose hat in hand, asked that a chair be brought for the gentleman, and only sat down when he did; when the son left, he rose and bowed. He was no more easygoing or familiar with his sister, Mme. de Moussy, although they lived in the same house. He so often railed at her during meals that she resigned herself to eating in her room.

CHAMILLART (1701)

Michel Chamillart (1652-1721) became minister in an unusual way. The King was a billiards enthusiast and learned that Chamillart wielded a wicked cue. Chamillart beat the King, but "with such modesty that the King was pleased." He became controller general, minister of state, and secretary of state for war before his disgrace. He was one of Saint-Simon's closest friends, although you would not know it from the following portrait, which shows him as a bumbling moron.

He was a very kind and honest man, with unsullied hands and the best intentions, polite, patient, obliging, an excellent friend and a harmless enemy. He loved the State, but above all he loved the King, and he was on excellent terms with him and with Mme. de Maintenon. Like all dull-witted persons, he was narrowminded and stubborn, pitied those who disagreed with him, and was incapable of hearing them out. As a result he was gulled in friendship, in business, and in everything, and was governed by worthless friends and those in whom he set great store, for various reasons. He was an incompetent who thought he knew everything. He had become that way from being promoted, which was all the more pitiful, for it was foolishness rather than presumption or vanity, since he did not have a trace of either. The curious thing is that the King's tender affection for him was prompted by his very incompetence. He admitted every blunder to the King, who enjoyed leading and instructing him, watched over his successes as over his own, and excused his failures. The court and everyone else also excused him, charmed by his accessibility and cheerful obligingness, the untiring patience with which he listened to complaints, and his gentle way of refusing as though it pained him. Despite the multitude of affairs he handled, he was able to remember everyone and everything clearly, so that those coming to see him were delighted that he had not forgotten their case, even though it was probably gathering dust.

THE ABBÉ DUBOIS (1715)

The abbé Dubois (1656-1723) became prime minister in 1722, under the Regency. He had been the duc d'Orléans' tutor, and Saint-Simon blamed him for the Regent's impiety and debauchery. Thanks to the Regent's weakness of character, Dubois wielded great power. One of the few matters on which he had no influence was the Regent's friendship with Saint-Simon. Dubois was made a cardinal in 1721.

The abbé Dubois was small, frail, and thin, with a clever and sly ferret-face. He wore a blond wig, and was the very image of what is called a "saker," [1] for want of a better word. Every vice known to man fought within him for the upper hand in a stormy and continuous struggle. Avarice, debauchery, and ambition were his gods; treachery, flattery and servility his means, and total impiety his natural medium. His only principle was that honesty and integrity are chimeras useful for adornment but which no one takes seriously, and it made him completely unscrupulous. He excelled in and thrived on base intrigues, and could not do without them. His every effort strained toward his goal with a pa-

[1] A bird of prey, the Southern European falcon.

tience that was exhausted only by success or repeated failure, unless he was able to find a better goal by piercing a new tunnel as he groped through the subterranean darkness. Thus, his life was spent in sapping. He could tell the boldest and most shamefaced lie with natural simplicity, uprightness, sincerity, and false humility. He would have been a graceful and facile speaker had not the wish to find out others and the fear of giving himself away made him develop an artificial stutter, which increased when he began to take part in important matters, and finally became intolerable and sometimes unintelligible. Without these uncontrollable devices and affectations, his conversation would have been pleasant. He was witty, very worldly, well versed in history and literature, and had an intense desire to please and insinuate himself everywhere. But all that was smudged by a smoke of hypocrisy which seeped from his every pore and made his very gaiety saddening. He was a traitor and an ingrate, capable of natural, premeditated, and reasoned malevolence, and an expert in devising the foulest crimes. He was unbelievably shameless when caught in the act. He envied everyone, coveted everything, and wanted all the spoils for himself.

You could write a book about Dubois' outbursts, particularly since he stopped trying to contain them after becoming master. I will limit myself to a few samples. Sometimes in the heat of passion he would run around a room, jumping on tables and chairs without once setting foot on the floor. M. le duc d'Orléans said he had often seen him at it. . . .

One day at Versailles after lunch, Mme. de Conflans went to see Dubois and came into a large study where eight or ten persons were waiting to speak to the cardinal. He was near the fireplace with a woman he was taking to task. Mme. de Conflans, who was very small, grew so frightened that she seemed to shrink even more. However, she came near as the other woman was leaving. The cardinal, seeing her approach, asked briskly what she wanted. "Your Eminence," she began. . . . "Ho, your Eminence, your Eminence," interrupted the cardinal, "whatever you want the answer is no, Madam." "But your Eminence," she went on. "By all the devils," he interrupted again, "let me repeat it: When I say no, I mean no." Mme. de Conflans tried to explain that she was seeking no favors, but the cardinal seized her shoulders, flung her around, and dug his fist in her back, saying: "Go to the devil and leave me in peace." She almost fell in a dead faint, and left in anger and in tears. . . .

The Easter Sunday after he had been named cardinal, he awakened at eight and almost broke the bells ringing for his servants. Heaping horrible and filthy curses and insults on them, he yelled that they had not awakened him in time to say mass, and that he was so busy he did not know where he could find the time. After all the shouting, his solution was not to say mass at all, and I wonder if he has said it once since his consecration. . . .

Every evening he ate alone, and his meal consisted of a chicken. For some reason, his servants forgot to bring it one evening. As he was going to bed, he remembered the chicken and began to ring and scream for his servants, who came running and listened to his outburst with great composure. He yelled all the louder, demanding why he was being served so late. He was most surprised when they replied tranquilly that he had already eaten the chicken but that if he wanted another they could put it on the spit at once. "What," he said, "I ate my chicken?" The cool boldness of his servants convinced him, and they had a good time mocking him.

There is no point in saying any more about him, for one could go on forever. This is enough to show what a monster he was. His death relieved all of Europe, great and small alike, and even his own brother whom he treated like a slave.

A PERFECT ENGLISHMAN (1721)

Colonel Stanhope,[1] the British ambassador to Spain, had served two long tours of duty there and has been mentioned often in these memoirs in connection with M. de Torcy. He was a perfect Englishman, a learned lover of books and the study of abstract sciences, well versed in history, and experienced in the interests of his nation and the details of British Parliament and

[1] William Stanhope, first Earl of Harrington (1690-1756).

court life. Although he had a gift for languages, he was taciturn and ponderous, and always kept his ears open. His knowledge of the court, commerce, and particular and general interests of the country in which he was serving was complete, and yet he was introverted, melancholy, thoughtful, and solitary. He maintained an honest establishment and set a fine table where distinguished guests were few and far between. There was something repellent in his cold and wooden politeness, and in the way he shifted from idle talk to worming out secrets. He indulged his private pleasures with great discretion in the gloomy depths of his apartment, and never went out unless he had to.

I had express and repeated orders to cultivate him in open confidence. Thanks to his special and solitary tastes I was able to see him just often enough to avoid blame; as for taking him into my confidence, I kept that at a minimum. He was an upright, intelligent, and sensible man, but everything was caged within him, and he did not know how to please. In any case, I was never crazy about England, and left such enthusiasms to Cardinal Dubois.

A Model Ambassador (1721)

After having put off, and discussed all the foreign ambassadors, we must finally come to M. de Maulévrier.[1] I never in my life saw him outside Madrid, or had anything to do concerning him directly or indirectly. The only member of his family I knew was his uncle the abbé de Maulévrier, the late King's chaplain, who is mentioned in these pages several times and with whom I had always been on good terms. I cannot fathom how I incurred the displeasure of a man totally unknown to me, who would not even have been named ambassador without my consent.[2] I was told in Paris that he was put out because I had been picked to

[1] Jean-Baptiste, marquis de Maulévrier, French ambassador to the court of Spain.
[2] Saint-Simon was then a member of the Council of Regency and could have vetoed Maulévrier's appointment.

go to Spain instead of the duc de Villeroy or the duc de la Feuillade. I resolved to ignore his impertinence and to pretend to like him. I found him very respectful, taciturn, and reserved, and soon realized that his thick skull contained nothing but sullenness, coarseness and foolishness. I could not imagine where the abbé Dubois had unearthed such a wild animal. . . .

Several days after my arrival, I paid him a formal visit. Either from ignorance or to trap me, he wanted to shake hands with my children, but I caught him in time. His stupidity had made him become fast friends with Grimaldo,[3] to whom he showed every dispatch he received from court. Nothing could have been more convenient for the Spanish minister. I alerted Cardinal Dubois, giving him the bare facts. He said he had found the remedy, which was never to write Maulévrier anything he did not wish Grimaldo to see. . . .

Maulévrier's vulgarity, ill-temper and stupidity had won him uncommon and general hatred. He saw no one, and told the lords of the palace openly that he would rather stay by himself than be with Spaniards. The accounts I was given of his repeated gruffness are inconceivable. He openly criticized Spanish habits, customs, and manners, saying that he found them all ridiculous. He took pleasure in saying how ugly he found the most beautiful buildings and festivities, and shamelessly added that he could not suffer Spain or Spaniards. Most of the lords of the palace ignored him and I found him isolated at court.

Although accounts of his brutishness reached me from all sides, I would have thought them exaggerated had I not been a blushing witness to one of the most outrageous. It was at Lerma on the eve of the wedding, and the first time I had been to see the King and Queen since my attack of smallpox. I was waiting in a small antechamber outside their apartments with Maulévrier and five or six Spanish grandees, with whom I was chatting.

In the same room there was a man on a ladder, hanging a tapestry. All of a sudden, Maulévrier began to scowl, and said: "Look at that clumsy animal up there; it's easy to see he's a Spaniard!" and continued to insult him. I was surprised as a duck in a thunderstorm, and all the grandees were staring at me.

[3] José Gutiérrez, marquis of Grimaldo, was president of the Spanish council of foreign affairs.

But that did not stop Maulévrier. "You bastard of a Spaniard," he said, "I would like to see you fall off that ladder and break your neck; you deserve it, and I would give two pistoles to see it." Truly, I was so shocked that I could not find a single word to change the subject. "Hey, you dumb bastard of a Spaniard!" he said. "You clumsy oaf! See how clumsy he is!" I listened to his words as though I did not realize what I was hearing or where I was. The grandees began to laugh and said: "M. le Marquis de Maulévrier overwhelms us with his praise." I wanted to sink through the floor. Even this did not stop Maulévrier, who kept up his attack. Finally I was summoned to see the King and Queen. I think that after I had left, the lords did not long remain in the company of such a model ambassador.

II

THE KING

INTRODUCTION

*S*AINT-SIMON *felt the glare but never the warmth of the Sun King's light. His passionate attachment to the quality of kingship led him paradoxically to become the King's bitterest critic. He wanted to venerate, but found reasons to criticize. He wanted to admire, but found grounds for contempt.*

Louis XIV, who lived from 1638 to 1715 and ruled for all but the first five years of his long life, was Europe's towering figure, envied and feared by other monarchs. He imposed the will of France through wars, alliances, and marriages. He ruled his subjects with harsh despotism and indifference to their needs. He made the nobility go through its paces like a troupe of trained seals. He had a vocation for greatness which has since become a model for other rulers, and yet he was not a great man. For this Saint-Simon could never forgive him.

The chapters on the King are the Götterdämmerung of the Memoirs, the most inspired, eloquent, and movingly sustained. And yet, after reading this exhaustive accumulation of detail, after following the King hour by hour from the lever to the coucher, after looking over his shoulder when he eats, being under the bed when he dallies with a mistress, feeling the joy of his smile and the terror of his frown, we are left with the final impression of a selfish, petty, recondite, and uninspired man, governed by his suspicions and weaknesses.

Suspicion of the nobility made him devise the court ritual, so that dissident barons and rebellious dukes could be turned into tractable courtiers always within sight and earshot. No one was a more devoted courtier than Saint-Simon, and yet he knew that the function of the nobles had been adulterated beyond repair. They no longer helped the King govern; they helped to keep him entertained.

Suspicion of Paris made him settle in Versailles. Caught up in the Fronde during his minority, he had to flee the rebellious nobles, leaving Paris in disguise. He never forgave the capital for being the cause of his fear and humiliation. He was like a man who has been frightened by a bull as a child and becomes a life-long vegetarian.

Pettiness made him prefer his bastards to his legitimate children. He begrudged the hereditary rights of his natural sons to the throne because they were not his to bestow or remove. But improving the rank of his bastards was a personal achievement, a measure of grandeur, tangible evidence of what the King could accomplish.

In his declining years, the King was under the sanctimonious and restricting influence of Mme. de Maintenon. With determined obliqueness, she picked his ministers and favorites, dictated the conduct of the court, and imposed her likes and dislikes—one of the latter being a rooted suspicion of Saint-Simon. She was also able to impose her piousness on a King who had reached the age when fear of death inspires an imitation of virtue. He married Mme. de Maintenon secretly, and secretly became a docile and complaisant husband. The court was shocked when he displayed his affection in public for the first time, not because of the liaison itself, but because the King was breaching his own severe rules and upsetting the highly artificial but authoritative order he had created. The backbone of the system was a code of behavior that governed the smallest details of the courtiers' daily routine: Louis XIV from his deathbed waved away his confessor so that he could prescribe the length of the coats to be worn at his funeral.

The King had manufactured a court that operated with the precise and tasteful cadence of a music box, protecting his ear from all dissonances. The courtiers were in the curious position of being in continuous attendance on him while hardly ever being able to talk to him. They watched him get out of bed in the morning, they marveled at his appetite at lunch, they followed at a respectful distance when he strolled through his gardens. But the moments in the day when they could address him privately were brief and strictly defined. Saint-Simon, during more than twenty years of court life under Louis XIV, only had three

audiences with the King and was ecstatic at being granted them.
Courtiers, according to the Versailles ground rules, were instru-
ments of the King's pleasure and beholders of his magnificence.

Louis XIV was heartless even toward the closest members of
his household. When the duchesse de Bourgogne miscarried, he
sulked because it interrupted the normal schedule of his day.
When he learned she might be unable to have any more chil-
dren, he perked up; at least she would then be the cause of no
more interruptions.

Saint-Simon's appraisal of the King leaves the reader to pick
up the broken pieces of his greatness. We may at least marvel
that the system worked at all. The elite of Europe's major power
were mesmerized into inanity by a King with modest gifts. In
some mysterious fashion, whatever talent and energy Louis XIV
did have rose to meet the challenge of his situation. He replaced
intellectual brilliance with an unwavering faith in the greatness
of his inherited crown and in himself as the incarnation of
France. His famous statement "L'état c'est moi" was no frivolous
boast—it was the cornerstone of his faith and identity.

Saint-Simon wanted to be taken in, but Louis' deficiencies
were too glaring; while thirsting for the King's favor, he did
everything to irritate him. To the monarch, Saint-Simon was an
annoying insect who buzzed about his person and could be dis-
missed with a wave of the hand. The King did not count on the
Memoirs, which cannot be dismissed as easily. And yet the pre-
vailing tone of the passages on the King is melancholy, for Saint-
Simon mourned his broken idols.

PORTRAIT OF THE KING (1715)

One can no more refuse this prince a great deal of goodness and
even greatness than one can overlook a greater amount of pettiness and meanness. It was impossible to distinguish between what
was genuine and what was false. In both cases, nothing is harder
to find than writers who knew him well and are capable of writing about him from their own experience, while remaining dis-

passionate enough to portray him without hate or obsequiousness, being guided in their praise or criticism only by the unadorned truth. As for knowing him, these memoirs may be counted on as reliable; as for objectivity, we can only try to achieve it honestly by suspending all our passions.

We must not speak here of his early years. He was crowned very young, but was stifled by the intrigues of a mother who wanted to govern, and even more by the ambition of a pernicious minister[1] who gambled with the State a thousand times to increase his personal glory. As long as the prime minister lived, the King was bent under his yoke, and we can strike those years from the monarch's reign. However, he learned to free himself. He fell in love; he discovered that idleness is glory's foe by leaning half-heartedly toward one and then the other; he had enough judgment to recognize Mazarin's death as a deliverance, even though he had not had the strength to deliver himself earlier. It was one of the finest moments of his life and eventually bore fruit in this maxim which he has held to implacably: To despise all prime ministers and all clergymen in his Council. At that time, he adopted another maxim, which he was unable to keep as firmly, for he did not always realize it slipped away from him: To govern alone, which was what he most prided himself on, what he was most praised and flattered for, and what he was least capable of.

He was born with a third-rate mind but one capable of improvement, cultivation, and refinement, and ready to borrow from others without imitation or embarrassment. He found infinite profit in being surrounded at court all his life by men and women of different types and ages, and of the highest and most varied wit.

If one must talk like this about a twenty-three-year-old king, one can say that he was fortunate in being surrounded by all kinds of distinguished minds as soon as he was introduced to society. His ministers at home and abroad were then the most powerful in Europe, his generals were the most famous, their seconds-in-command were the best and have since become the leading strategists. By unanimous consent, their reputations have survived his reign. The upheaval which had so furiously shaken the State at home and abroad since the death of Louis XIII gave birth

---

[1] Anne of Austria, and Mazarin.

to a court made up of a large number of illustrious and capable persons, and refined courtiers. . . .

It must be repeated: The King's mind was less than ordinary but capable of improvement. He loved glory; he aspired to order and discipline. He was born wise, moderate, secretive, and in perfect control of his language and gestures. Will anyone believe it? He was born good and just, and God endowed him with enough qualities to become a good king and perhaps even a great king. All his troubles came from elsewhere. His early education was negligible because no one dared approach him. He often spoke of those days with bitterness, and said he had been neglected to the point that one evening he fell into the pond in the Palais-Royal garden in Paris, where the court was then held. In the years that followed, he became extremely dependent. He barely learned to read and write. He remained so ignorant that he never knew anything about history, events, money, conduct, birth, or laws, which made him prey to the most patent absurdities, sometimes in public. . . .

Soon after he became master, his ministers, his generals, his mistresses and his courtiers noticed that he had a weakness for, rather than a love of, glory. They spoiled him with praise. Commendation and flattery pleased him to such a point that the most obvious compliments were received kindly and the most insidious were relished even more. It was the only way to approach him, and those who won his love knew it well and never tired of praising him. That is why his ministers were so powerful, for they had more opportunities to burn incense before him, attribute every success to him, and vow they had learned everything from him. The only way to please him was submissiveness, baseness, an air of admiring and crawling toadyism, and by giving the impression that he was the only source of wisdom.

Whoever strayed from that path strayed from favor, and that is what finished Louvois. The poison spread. It reached incredible proportions for an experienced and not unintelligent prince. Although he had no voice and no knowledge of music, he would hum to himself the overtures of operas which told of his greatness; you could see him swimming in self-praise, and sometimes at banquets, when violins were playing, you could hear him singing the music between his teeth when it concerned him.

This was the origin of his thirst for glory, which sometimes snatched him from his amorous dalliances. This is why it was so easy for Louvois to start wars in order to overthrow Colbert[2] or to maintain and increase his own power. At the same time Louvois insisted that no one could match the King as a military strategist or a field commander and that he was a better soldier than any of his generals. He convinced the King of this with the help of the generals, who were eager to please. This includes Condé, Turenne, and all those who succeeded them. He took credit for everything with admirable graciousness and complacency, and believed everything he was told. This was the origin of his love of parades, which he pushed to the point where his enemies called him the "parade king." His love of sieges was a cheap way to display his bravery and show off his ability, foresight, vigilance, and endurance. He insisted on staying at his command, and his admirably robust constitution was perfectly suited to protect him from hunger, thirst, cold, heat, rain, and bad weather. As he visited the camps, he enjoyed hearing murmurs of admiration about his splendor, his horsemanship, and his military achievements. His favorite topics of conversation with his mistresses and courtiers were his campaigns and his troops. He was eloquent, chose his words well, and with precision. He could describe an incident and tell a story better than any man alive. His most trivial remarks were never lacking in natural and manifest majesty.

He had a passion for detail. He was interested in everything that touched on his troops: Uniforms, arms, maneuvers, training, discipline, in a word, all sorts of vulgar details. He was just as interested in his construction projects, his household and his kitchens: He was always telling experts what they already knew, and they hung on his words like novices. This waste of time, which the King thought of as meritorious diligence, was the triumph of his ministers, who grew skilled in getting around him. They were delighted to see the King drowning in details, and were able to lead him according to their views and too often according to

[2] The two most celebrated ministers of Louis XIV were Jean-Baptiste Colbert (1619-1683), who reorganized the country's finances and made his influence felt in every sector of government; and his bitter enemy, Michel Le Tellier, marquis de Louvois (1641-1691), who engineered Colbert's disgrace and who as secretary of state for war urged the King to conduct adventurous campaigns to further his glory.

their interests by making him believe the ideas had originated with him. His increasing vanity and pride were continuously nourished, even by preachers from their pulpits. . . .

We have beheld a king who, as long as he had able ministers and captains, was great, rich, feared and admired as a conqueror and as the arbiter of Europe. Once they were gone, the machine kept rolling for some time on its own. But, inevitably, it came to a halt; faults and errors multiplied; decadence arrived with giant steps, but did not open the eyes of this jealous and despotic master who wanted to command and enact everything himself and who made up for the contempt in which he was held abroad by doubling the terror through which he ruled at home.

He was a fortunate prince in that he was a unique figure of his time, a pillar of strength, with almost uninterrupted good health. The age he lived in was so fertile and liberal in every way that it has been compared to the age of Augustus; he was fortunate also in having adoring subjects who gave their goods, their blood, their talent, sometimes their reputation and honor, and too often their religion and conscience, to serve him or only to please him. . . .

Little by little he reduced everyone to subjection, and brought to his court those very persons he cared least about. Whoever was old enough to serve did not dare demur. It was still another device to ruin the nobles by accustoming them to equality and forcing them to mingle with everyone indiscriminately. The idea was his and Louvois', who wanted to lord it over the nobility and make it dependent on him, so that those born to command found themselves commanding only in theory while removed from real responsibility. Using the pretext that all military service is honorable and that it is reasonable to learn to obey before one learns to command, the King made everyone except the princes of the blood begin as cadets in his guards or in the army, and even serve as simple soldiers, with guardroom duty winter and summer. He switched the scene of this purported basic training to the musketeers, after taking a fancy to that corps. It was no more of a school than the former, and there was nothing at all to be learned there except indolence and how to waste time; one also had to submit to being mixed with all sorts of people of every rank, which is what the King really wanted to obtain through this novitiate. One had to remain for an entire year in the exact observance of this useless and fiddling service. . . .

The court was another instrument of his despotic policy. We have just described the policies that divided, humiliated, and abashed the greatest of men, and the policies that elevated the authority and power of the ministers above everything, even the princes of the blood and people of the best quality, who found themselves diminished.

Now for the illustrations of these principles in other fields. The court left Paris for a permanent stay in the country for several reasons. The King had an aversion to the city, which had been the scene of great turbulence during his minority. He was convinced the danger of plots would be diminished by moving the court outside Paris, because of the distance from Paris to Versailles (however slight), and because it would be easy to notice the absence of courtiers. Paris had seen him shed tears at the time of Mme. de la Vallière's first retreat and had forced him to flee on the eve of Epiphany.[3] These things he could not forgive. Another reason for his aloofness was the fear of being accused of scandal by such a populous and diversified capital because he kept mistresses. Every time he entered or left Paris or appeared in its streets, his distaste for the importuning crowds, which he knew would cease bothering him if he left the city, was apparent.

As soon as these anxieties became known, the old Noailles, Lauzun, and other intimates among his guards exaggerated their vigilance and were said to have multiplied false emergencies so they could cast themselves in a good light and have the King to themselves more often. Another reason for leaving Paris was the King's fondness of hunting and walking, which made the country more convenient, since Paris was far from footpaths and forests. His growing fondness for building could not be satisfied in a city where he would constantly be a spectacle to the curious. Finally there was the belief that he would be more venerated by the multitudes if he stayed out of their sight and avoided overex-

[3] In 1649, the parliamentary Fronde broke out and the people of Paris took to the barricades. Louis XIV and the rest of the court were forced to flee unceremoniously from the capital. On another occasion, Mme. de La Vallière sought refuge in a convent, from which the King eventually retrieved her.

posure. All these considerations prompted the King to settle in Saint-Germain after the death of the Queen his mother. That is where he began to attract everyone with festivities and entertainments, and to make clear that he wanted an attentive court.

Because his love for Mme. de la Vallière was a secret, he took her for frequent walks in Versailles, which was then no more than a tiny card castle. It had been built for Louis XIII, who was annoyed (and his suite even more annoyed than him) at having to sleep in a wretched wagoner's inn or a windmill after the exhaustion of a long hunt in Saint-Léger forest or farther still. This was before the times reserved for his son when good roads, swift dogs, and large numbers of hired huntsmen and riders made hunts so comfortable and brief. Louis XIII seldom slept at Versailles, except to stay the night when he had to. The King his son used it to be alone with his mistresses, a pleasure which had never been tasted by Louis the Just, the worthy and heroic son of Saint Louis who had built the small Versailles. It was thanks to Louis XIV's assignations that little by little vast buildings went up at Versailles. They were very different from his lodgings at Saint-Germain, and convenient for a great number of courtiers, so that he moved there permanently just before the Queen's death.[4] He built numberless lodgings, and the courtiers asked if they could stay there, for at Saint-Germain almost everyone had to stay in town, and those who were given rooms at the castle were badly cramped.

To keep everyone assiduous and attentive, the King personally named the guests for each festivity, each stroll through Versailles, and each trip. These were his rewards and punishments. He knew there was little else he could distribute to keep everyone in line. He substituted ideal rewards for real ones and these operated through jealousy, the petty preferences he showed many times a day, and his artfulness in showing them. No one was more ingenious than he in nourishing the hopes and satisfactions to which these petty preferences and distinctions gave birth. He found Marly useful for this, and also Trianon; everyone was allowed to pay court at Trianon, but the ladies were allowed to eat with the King, and were chosen at each meal; there was also

[4] The move was made in 1682; the Infanta Marie-Thérèse died in 1683.

his candlestick, which he allowed to be held every night at bed-time by a courtier he wished to favor, and who was always chosen among the most distinguished present and was named by the King when he had finished his prayer.[5]

The royal jerkin[6] was another of these inventions: It was blue lined with red, and the cuffs, facings, collar, and vest were red; it was embroidered with gold and a little silver in a magnificent and unique design. Only a limited number of persons had a right to one, among them the King, his family, and princes of the blood; the latter had to wait for one to become vacant. The most distinguished persons in court had to ask the King for one as a favor or because of their rank, and it was a privilege to obtain one. The secretary of state in charge of the King's affairs would make out the royal warrant, but no secretary of state was entitled to one. The jerkins had been created for the small number of persons who had the right to accompany the King on his trips from Saint-Germain to Versailles without being expressly named. Since this is no longer done, the jerkins now convey no privileges other than the right to wear them during court or family mourning, if the mourning is minor or is nearing its end (particularly in the days when it was forbidden to wear gold and silver in mourning). I never saw one worn by the King, Monseigneur, or Monsieur, but Monseigneur's three sons often wore theirs, and so did all the other princes; as soon as one became available, the most distinguished persons in court fought to have it, and for a young lord to obtain it was a great distinction. This went on until the King's death. One could go on forever describing the King's devices for keeping the court intact, which he kept varying as he grew older and as the festivities at Versailles changed and declined.

He appreciated not only the continuous presence of distinguished persons but also the presence of persons of lesser rank. Upon rising, at bedtime, during meals, in his apartments, in the gardens of Versailles, everywhere the courtiers had a right to follow, he would glance right and left to see who was there; he saw and noted everyone; he missed no one, even those who were

[5] Saint-Simon was infrequently granted this honor.
[6] There were only sixty of these close-fitting jerkins, and they were not hereditary. They were given at the King's will and were considered a great honor, though they were not overly comfortable.

hoping they would not be seen; he always noted the absences of those who lived at court and the arrivals of those who came more or less often; he always found out the reasons for these absences, and never lost a chance to take whatever action was necessary. For the most distinguished persons, it was a demerit not to put in a regular appearance at court. It was just as bad for those of lesser rank to come but rarely, and certain disgrace for those who never, or almost never, came.

When their names came up, the King would say haughtily: "I know them not." As for those who were rarely present, he would say: "That is a man I never see." There was no appeal. It was also a crime not to ask for Fontainebleau, which he considered on the same footing as Versailles; for certain courtiers, it was a crime not to ask for Marly, either always or often, although this did not mean they would obtain it: Whoever was regularly invited to Marly needed a good excuse to get out of it.[7] Above all, the King could not tolerate people who liked Paris. He was more indulgent toward those who liked to live in the country, although one had to take precautions before leaving for an extended sojourn. This was true not only for the King's favorites, those with important duties, or those whose age and rank made their presence necessary. All courtiers were subject to the King's scrutiny whenever they took a trip. We have already seen the King's interest when I had to go to Rouen for legal proceedings. As young as I was, he had Pontchartrain write me to find out why I was leaving.

Louis XIV took great pains to inform himself on what was happening everywhere, in public places, private homes, and even on the international scene. He also wanted to know about family secrets and private relationships. Spies and informers of all kinds were numberless. Some did not know their information would ever reach his ears, while others knew. Some wrote him directly through special channels, and their letters took precedence over all other matters, while others came to see the King secretly in his cabinets. This secret network ruined countless persons of all kinds

[7] Few courtiers were invited to Marly because of its small size, and the selection was another means of granting privileges. Saint-Simon asked for but seldom "got" Marly, although Mme. de Saint-Simon was a frequent guest there. An invitation to the other residences such as Fontainebleau was easier to obtain, because they were larger.

root and branch, and they never knew how he had found them out. They were often unjustly accused, but the King never went back on a decision, or so rarely that nothing was rarer.

He had another failing which was dangerous for others and often for himself because it deprived him of loyal subjects. Although he had an excellent memory and was able to remember twenty years later a man he had seen once, and did not mix up what he knew, he was incapable of remembering all the countless things he was told daily. If he heard something unfavorable about someone and then forgot what it was, he retained the impression that there was something against the man, and that was enough to exclude him.

In cases like this, he never yielded to the explanations of a minister, a general, or even his own confessor. He replied that he could not remember what the man had done, but that it was better to choose another about whom he had heard nothing at all.

The malevolent office of police lieutenant was created as a direct result of the King's curiosity. The duties have since steadily increased. These lieutenants were more than feared, and were treated with greater consideration and as much respect as the ministers themselves, and even by the ministers themselves. Everyone in France, not excepting the princes of the blood, strove to remain on good terms with them. Besides the serious reports they sent him, the King wanted to hear all the Paris gossip and romantic intrigues.

But the King's most vicious method of securing information was opening letters. Through their ignorance and imprudence, a great many people continued to provide him with information for years, until the system was exposed. That is why the Pajots and the Rouilles,[8] who were responsible for the postal service, were so respected they could never be removed, or even promoted. The cause long remained a mystery, and they amassed enormous fortunes at the expense of the public and the King. The skill and efficiency of the letter-opening operation defies the imagination. The postmasters and the postmaster general sent the King extracts of all the letters that could interest him, and copies of entire letters when the content or the rank of the sender

[8] These two families long kept control of the postal system through intermarriage and nepotism.

warranted it. It took so little to condemn someone that those in charge of the postal system, from chiefs to clerks, were able to accuse whomever they wanted. They did not even have to rely on forgeries or prolonged investigations; one word of contempt for the King or his government, one jeer taken out of context and plausibly presented, sufficed to condemn without appeal or inquiry, and this means was always at their fingertips. The number of people who were rightly or wrongly condemned is inconceivable. The King's secret was never discovered, and nothing ever cost him less than to conceal it with profound silence.

He often stretched his gift for duplicity to the point of falsehood, although he never told an outright lie, and prided himself on keeping his word. That is why he almost never gave it. He kept other people's secrets as religiously as his own. He was flattered at receiving confessions and confidences, and no mistress, minister, or favorite could wrest the secret from him, even if it concerned them. One anecdote among many concerns a woman of quality, whose name no one ever found out: Her husband had been gone a year and she found herself pregnant just as he was returning from his military campaigns. At her wit's end, she asked the King for a secret audience to discuss her urgent problem, her request being kept confidential. She obtained the audience. In her extreme need, she told the King she would confide in him as though he were the most honest man in all his kingdom. The King advised her to take advantage of her great distress to lead a more sensible life in the future, and promised to keep her husband at the border for military reasons, and not to let him return under any pretext until all grounds for suspicion had vanished. In truth, the same day he ordered Louvois to give the husband command of a border post for the entire winter, and not to let him take any leaves, not even for a single day. It was a blow to Louvois, who was taken completely by surprise, and to the officer, who was distinguished and who had neither asked for nor wanted anything less than command of a border post through the winter. Still, they both had to obey to the letter, and without asking why. The King only told this story years later, when he was certain those concerned could not be identified. They never were, not even by the vaguest and most uncertain suspicions.

There was never a man who knew how to give so well, which

increased the value of his gifts; there was never a man who made better use of his words, his smile, even his glances. He made everything seem precious through quality and majesty, to which the concision and rareness of his remarks added a great deal. When he addressed or questioned anyone, the attention of all those present would be captured, even if the matter was trivial; to be addressed by the King was a distinction one could boast of, and which added to the consideration in which one was held. It was the same for the preferences he showed in all other sorts of attentions and distinctions. He never said a disobliging word to anyone.

On the rare occasions when he had to reprove, reprimand, or upbraid someone, he did it with a certain kindness, almost never curtly, and never angrily, with the unique exception of Courtenvaux,[9] which we have recounted elsewhere. However, he was not incapable of anger and sternness.

There was never a man so naturally polite, or whose politeness was so measured and so sure. In his attitudes, his replies, and when he said "I will see,"[10] there was never a man more alert to the distinctions of age, merit, and rank. He conveyed his attention to these distinctions with great precision in his greetings and acknowledgments. He was admirable when he acknowledged salutes at military reviews. But with women he was incomparable. He tipped his hat to every petticoat, even chambermaids (and he knew they were chambermaids), as was often the case at Marly. With ladies of quality, he removed his hat, but at a distance which varied according to their rank; with titled gentlemen, he half removed it, and held it in the air or over his ear in a manner more or less pronounced; with authentic lords, he restricted himself to snapping the brim; with princes of the blood, he removed it as he did with ladies; if he accosted a lady, he put on his hat only after having left her. All this went on out of doors, for indoors he never wore a hat. There was a matchless grace and

[9] Courtenvaux, the eldest son of Louvois, was captain of the "Hundred Swiss" King's guards. But the King had other special guards who were given the specific mission of spying on the courtiers at Versailles. The King's anger was provoked when Courtenvaux tried to obstruct the work of the rival guards, and he was threatened, in terms "that made everyone tremble," with removal from his command.

[10] The King's answer to requests was invariably "I will see."

majesty in his bows, which were light but more or less pronounced, and in his way of half rising from the table to greet every lady who had a right to sit during his meals;[11] he greeted none of the others, not even the princes of the blood; although he never gave it up, greeting the ladies tired him toward the end, and they avoided coming in after supper had begun. . . .

He was always patient throughout the long process of dressing. He was punctual at each of the day's events; there was a clear and laconic precision in his orders. If nasty winter weather prevented him from going out and he visited Mme. de Maintenon fifteen minutes earlier than usual (which he seldom did), and the captain of the guards on duty was not there, he would make a point of telling the captain that the King was guilty of not having warned he was coming earlier, and the captain was not at fault for having missed him. This unwavering punctuality was a great convenience for the courtiers, and also allowed the King to be served promptly.

He was fond of fresh air and exercise, which he kept up as long as he could. He had excelled in dancing, mall [pall-mall] and tennis. Even in later years he was an admirable horseman. He liked to see all these things done with grace and skill, and doing them well or badly was for him a merit or demerit. He said that since these things were not essential, one should not do them at all if one could not do them well. He liked to shoot, and there was no better or more graceful marksman. He required the best setter bitches; he always had seven or eight in his apartments, and enjoyed feeding them so they could get to know him. He was also very fond of hunting the stag, but since breaking his arm while hunting at Fontainebleau soon after the Queen's death, he followed in a carriage. He rode alone in a sort of small calash, with four horses that were changed half a dozen times during the hunt. He drove it himself at full speed, with a skill and accuracy that the finest coachmen could not match, and with the same grace with which he did everything. His postilions were children from nine to fifteen years old, and he himself directed them.

[11] At the King's meals, the princesses of the blood, foreign princesses, and duchesses were given a stool, and to "have the stool" was the greatest single distinction that a woman at the court of Louis XIV could boast. All others had to stand.

He loved splendor, magnificence and profusion in everything. He found it useful to make his tastes the law dominating the entire court. Courtiers spent extravagant sums on furniture, clothes, carriages, houses, and gambling, to please and entertain him.

The heart of the matter was that he managed to exhaust everyone's means by making luxury a matter of honor. Many were cleaned out, and everyone was reduced little by little to complete dependence on the King's bounty. He took pride in the grandeur of his court and in the mingling which served to annihilate natural distinctions. It was a spreading affliction, a cancer that gnawed at everyone. From the court it spread to Paris, the provinces, and the army, and since that unhappy precedent, everyone is judged according to the extent of his luxury and magnificence. This is a great strain on most individuals, and tempts them to commit graft and theft in order to bear the expense.

The King's Passion for Building (1715)

Who can count the buildings he erected? At the same time, who will not deplore their bad taste, and his whims and arrogance in building them? He abandoned Saint-Germain, and never built anything useful or decorative in Paris except the Pont Royal because he had to, which is why Paris is so inferior to other cities throughout Europe, in spite of its size. When the Place Vendôme was built, it was meant to be square. M. de Louvois supervised the construction of the four corners. His plan was to make it the site of the King's library, the treasury, the mint, all the academies, and the high council, which still holds its sessions in a rented room on the square. The first thing the King did on the day of Louvois' death was to stop the work in progress and order the corners cut to make the square smaller, so that only private houses could be built there, which is the way it can be seen today.

Saint-Germain was unique because of its marvelous view, adjacent forest, the beauty of its trees, its grounds, its location, and the advantage of its mineral waters, the admirable amenity of its gardens, its heights, and its terraces, and the charms and pleasures of the Seine. In a word, it was a self-contained city, which had only to be kept up. The King gave it up for Versailles, the most mournful and unpleasant place possible, without a view, without a forest, without mineral water, and without grounds or fresh air because it was all quicksand and swamp.

He took pleasure in tyrannizing nature and subduing it with works of art and precious objects. He built one thing after the other, pell-mell; he mixed the beautiful with the ugly, the spacious with the cramped. The apartments of the King and Queen were among the most badly placed, with a view that was dark, confined, and offensive. The gardens were startlingly magnificent but unpleasant for strolling and equally lacking in taste. One can only reach the shade of the trees by crossing a vast torrid zone that leads to a rise; and the gardens end after this short hill. The gravel burns the feet, but without it one would sink into quicksand and black mire. One cannot help being repelled and disgusted by the outrages committed everywhere against nature. The abundant waters brought and channeled from all over become green, thick, and muddy; they emanate an uncomfortable and unwholesome dampness, and a smell that is even worse. However, the fountains are incomparable, although they must be used sparingly; as an over-all impression, one admires the gardens but shuns them. On the side facing the courtyard, the closeness is suffocating, and the vast wings of the building spread out as though unattached. On the side facing the gardens, one can relish the beauty of the general view, but the palace looks as though it had burned down and was still missing a top floor and a roof. The top-heavy chapel (Mansart built it to try to get the King to add another floor), looks from every angle like the mournful replica of a huge catafalque. The craftsmanship is exquisite, but the arrangement is worthless; everything in the chapel focuses on the balcony, because that is where the King always sat, and the side aisles are inaccessible through the small passageways built to reach them. One could go on forever describing the monstrous defects of such a tremendous and tremendously expensive palace[1] and its vast dependencies: orangeries, vegetable gardens, kennels, small and large

[1] The cost came, historians say, to 65,651,257 pounds (French pounds, worth then about the same in dollars of today).

stables, a prodigious commons, in fact an entire city where once there had only been a miserable inn, a windmill, and the tiny card castle Louis XIII had built so he would not have to sleep in the hay. It could have fitted in Versailles' Marble Courtyard, and its principal building had only two small wings. My father knew it well, and slept there often. And again, this Versailles of Louis XIV, this masterpiece of extravagance and bad taste, whose fountains and groves cost their weight in gold, was never completed; among so many rooms there is no banquet hall, no theatre,[2] no ballroom, and there remains a great deal to be done both in front and in back. The seedlings planted in the parks and lanes have not yet grown. Game must endlessly be brought to the parks; the numberless irrigation channels are four or five leagues long, and the vast circumference of the walls surrounds Versailles as though it were a small province of the saddest and ugliest country in the world.

Trianon was in the park and at the gateway to Versailles. It had first been a porcelain pavilion[3] where one went for snacks, then it was expanded to provide overnight accommodations, and finally it became a palace of marble, jasper, and porphyry, with delightful gardens; facing it across the Versailles canal was the zoo, full of exquisite nothings, and garnished with all sorts of the rarest bipeds and quadrupeds; finally, there was Clagny, built for Mme. de Maintenon and left to the duc du Maine. It was a superb castle on the outskirts of Versailles, with its own fountains, gardens, and park; its aqueducts were in every way worthy of the Romans and neither Asia nor antiquity have anything to offer as vast, as varied, as well wrought, as superb, as filled with the rarest monuments of all ages, with the most exquisite marbles, bronzes, paintings, and accomplished sculptures.

But nothing could be done to remedy the shortage of water, and the artistic fountains were and are still running dry, in spite of the ocean-sized reservoirs that had been brought just in case over the quicksand and the mire at a cost of many millions. Who would believe it? The shortage of water became the ruin of the infantry. Mme. de Maintenon then reigned supreme; we will dis-

[2] A theatre was built after Saint-Simon's death.
[3] The first Trianon built by Louis XIV was a small castle "à la Chinoise" with porcelain walls in floral designs.

cuss her when her turn comes. M. de Louvois was on the best of terms with her; we were at peace. It was he who thought of diverting the course of the Eure between Chartres and Maintenon and bringing it to Versailles. Who can say how much this stubborn attempt cost in gold and men during the several years that it went on?

In the camp set up for this purpose, it was forbidden under threat of punishment to talk about the sick and the dead who had fallen victim to this harsh labor and to the effluvium that rose from the ground. How many others took years to recover from disease! How many never regained their health! In spite of this, none of the officers on duty at the camp, not even the colonels, brigadiers, and generals, had the right to leave or absent themselves from the work for even a quarter of an hour. War finally interrupted the scheme in 1688, and it was never resumed; some shapeless monuments are all that remain of this cruel folly.

The King finally grew weary of crowds and magnificence, and decided he wanted something small and intimate. He looked around the Versailles area for a site that would satisfy this new taste. He visited several; he scoured the slopes that lead to Saint-Germain and the valley where the Seine meanders after leaving Paris and irrigates so much rich land. He was urged to stop at Luciennes, where Cavoye has since built a house with an enchanting view; but he replied that he only wanted a cottage, and thus a site that would not tempt him, while that lovely place would ruin him.

Behind Luciennes, he discovered a deep and narrow valley with steep sides. It had no view and was surrounded by swamps and hills, with a miserable village called Marly on the side of one hill. This enclosure without any possible view was just what he wanted; the narrowness of the valley also pleased him because it was constricting. He picked the site as he would have picked a minister, a favorite, or a general. The valley served as a sewer for the entire area, and it was a mighty task to dry it up and bring land to cover it. The hermitage was built. It was only intended to be slept in three nights a week, from Wednesday to Saturday, two or three times a year, by the King and a dozen of his most indispensable courtiers. But bit by bit, the hermitage grew.

The hills were razed to build annexes and give an imperfect

patch of view. Finally, Marly became what can still be seen today, abandoned since the King's death: buildings, fountains, aqueducts, the curious Marly machine,[4] parks, an ornate forest, statues, and priceless furniture. The thick and cultivated forests contained trees brought from Compiègne and even farther, three fourths of which died and were replaced; vast woods and dark paths were turned into immense canals where one rode in gondolas, then turned again into forests that never saw the light of day; I saw these changes take place in a six-week period; the designs of fountains and waterfalls were changed as soon as they were finished, and this happened over and over; the prodigious machine we have already mentioned, with its enormous aqueducts, pipes, and reservoirs, served only for Marly and never brought water to Versailles; it is not enough to say that Marly did not cost as much as Versailles. If one adds the cost of the frequent trips to Marly, where at the end of his life the King spent as much time as at Versailles, the total cost of Marly can be counted in billions. Such was the destiny of this lair of serpents, toads, frogs, and carrion, chosen for one reason: That it would not be costly. Such was the King's bad taste in all things, and his prideful pleasure in forcing nature, which neither war nor piety could ever dull.

THE KING'S LOVE LIFE (1715)

From such unfortunate excesses of power, we must now move on to other excesses which were more natural, but even more pernicious in their way: The King's love life. Its scandal spread through Europe, confounded France, unsettled the state, bore evils that almost toppled him from the throne, and reduced his legitimate posterity to a single strain. These mishaps have grown into disasters that will long make themselves felt. In his youth, Louis XIV was more powerfully attracted to women than any of his subjects, but he grew weary of passing fancies and fixed his atten-

[4] The Marly machine, famous throughout Europe, was a complicated hydraulic contraption designed to bring water to Versailles.

tions on La Vallière. The progress and the fruit of that attachment are well known.[1]

But even during the reign of Mme. de La Vallière, he was touched by the rare beauty of Mme. de Montespan. When she noticed it, she vainly pressed her husband to take her to Guyenne; he was too sure of himself and of her to listen. She had warned him in good faith. Finally she succumbed to the King, who took her away from her husband with an uproar that resounded horribly throughout Europe and gave the world the unprecedented spectacle of a King with two mistresses at the same time. When he visited his borders, military camps, and regiments, both of them followed in the Queen's carriage. People came from miles around to see the three queens, and it became a topic of conversation. Finally Mme. de Montespan triumphed, and held sway over the master and his court with a brilliance she no longer had to veil; to add to the public scandal, M. de Montespan was jailed in the Bastille and then exiled to Guyenne when he protested. . . .

Mme. de Montespan was mean, capricious, and temperamental. Not even the King was spared her arrogance. It was said that to pay her court was to be court-martialed, and the saying became a proverb. It is true that she spared no one, and often her only aim was to amuse the King. Since she was infinitely witty, nothing was more dangerous than to be the butt of her ridicule. She loved her parents and her family, and was faithful to her friends. The duchesse de La Vallière won the Queen's love through a constant show of consideration and respect, while Mme. de Montespan's arrogance became almost intolerable, and the Queen often said of her: "That whore will be the death of me." We have seen elsewhere the retreat, austere penitence, and pious end of Mme. de Montespan. . . .[2]

We must now move on to a new kind of love, just as shocking as the others to the world at large and which the King carried to his grave. These few words are enough for everyone to recognize the celebrated Françoise d'Aubigné, marquise de Maintenon,

[1] The Duchesse de La Vallière gave birth to a son and a daughter sired by the King, and ended her days in a Carmelite convent.
[2] The marquise de Montespan retired to a convent after giving the King seven children and after having been replaced in his affections by Mme. de Maintenon.

whose permanent reign lasted no less than 32 years. She was born in the islands of America,[3] where her father, who may have been a gentleman, had gone with her mother to earn a living. Obscurity enveloped the family whom she left to come to France. She landed at La Rochelle, where Mme. de Neuillan, the mother of the maréchale-duchesse de Navailles, took her in out of pity. Through this old woman's poverty and avarice, she was reduced to keeping the keys of her attic and measuring the horses' daily ration of oats. After that, she came to Paris without means and without family, but young, shrewd, witty, and beautiful. She had the good luck to meet the famous Scarron. He found her agreeable, and his friends even more so. She felt it was a great and unexpected boon to marry this jolly and learned cripple.[4] Others who perhaps had a greater desire for her than he did convinced him that he should save this unhappy waif from her misery by marrying her. The marriage took place and the young wife became a favorite with Scarron's wide and varied circle of friends; it became fashionable to go to his home since he was unable to go out, and the best and most distinguished men of intellect, of the court, and of the city gathered there, drawn by the charm of his wit, learning, imagination, incomparable gaiety in the face of adversity, fertile mind, and tasteful sense of humor. Mme. Scarron met all sorts of people, which did not prevent her from being reduced to the charity of Saint-Eustache Parish at the death of her husband.

The respectfulness, desire to please, wit and attractiveness of Mme. Scarron took the fancy of Mme. de Montespan. They became friends, and when Mme. de Montespan bore the King M. du Maine and Madame la Duchesse, the children were entrusted to Mme. Scarron, who was given a house in the Marais where she could bring them up in secret. In the years that followed, the children were brought to Mme. de Montespan, shown to the King, and eventually recognized.

Their governess pleased Mme. de Montespan more and more and she tried several times to introduce Mme. Scarron to the

[3] Her family had settled in Martinique.
[4] Paul Scarron (1610-1660) was an author of burlesque comedies who was bedridden with paralysis most of his life. He was 25 years older than Mme. de Maintenon.

King. The King could not stand her and the little attention he paid her was only to be obliging, and was marked by a distaste he did not attempt to conceal. The Maintenon property near Versailles was up for sale, and Mme. de Montespan was tempted to buy it for Mme. Scarron. She would not give the King a moment's rest until he had promised to give her the money for the governess, who soon afterward adopted the name of Maintenon. Mme. de Montespan also pressed the King for enough money to renovate the castle and replant the garden; for M. d'Angennes, the former proprietor, had left everything in disrepair. The King at first turned a deaf ear, then refused. Finally, exasperated by Mme. de Montespan's stubborn insistence, he grew angry. He said he had already done too much for that creature, that he could not understand Mme. de Montespan's fancy for her or her obstinacy in wanting to keep her on after he had so often asked her to get rid of her. He added that he did not mind admitting he could not abide her, but that he would agree to give the money, even though he felt he had already given far too much to a creature of her kind, on the condition that he would never have to see her or speak to her again. M. le maréchal de Lorge, who was present, never forgot these words, and repeated them to me and to others with great accuracy. He was struck by them then, and even more so since so many startling and contradictory events have taken place. Mme. de Montespan did not dare say another word, and was upset at having pushed the King too far.

M. du Maine had a very bad limp; it was said that he had been dropped by a nurse as a child. All efforts to heal him had failed and it was decided to send him to various specialists in Flanders and other parts of the kingdom and to the waters at Barèges. Accounts of the trip which his governess sent Mme. de Montespan were shown to the King; he found them well written and enjoyable, and found they made his son's absence less painful.

Mme. de Montespan's temperament did the rest. She indulged her every mood and the King was victimized more than anyone else. He was still in love, but he was suffering. Mme. de Maintenon reproached Mme. de Montespan for her moodiness, which helped her obtain the King's favor. He was told by several persons about her efforts to appease his mistress, and he began to discuss his problems with Mme. de Maintenon and to tell her how she should proceed with Mme. de Montespan. Little by little, she was admitted by the King into that most intimate circle consisting of the lover and the mistress. She was shrewd enough to take advantage of the situation and was so successful that she gradually took the place of Mme. de Montespan, who realized too late that the governess had become necessary to the King. Having reached this point, Mme. de Maintenon told the King he should no longer tolerate such a difficult mistress and they both complained so often about her that she replaced Mme. de Montespan completely and was able to maintain her new position. Fortune, not to say Providence, which was preparing the deepest, most public, most permanent, and most extraordinary humiliation for this most vainglorious of Kings, continued to fortify his fancy for that expert and capable woman. Mme. de Montespan's continuous jealous scenes and frequent outbursts of bitter recrimination with which she abused the King helped to reinforce his affection for Mme. de Maintenon. . . .

During his most vigorous years, no illness could excuse his mistresses from traveling with him in full regalia (even the most privileged women had to be dressed formally for carriage rides before the brief trips to Marly eased this practice).

Whether they were pregnant, sick, less than six weeks over lying-in, or in other difficult situations, they had to be formally dressed, adorned, squeezed into their corsets, and ready to go to Flanders or even farther, to dance, stay up late, attend every festivity, eat, display gaiety and liveliness, gad about, and never show fear of discomfort because of the cold, the air or the dust. And all this had to be done on the appointed day at the appointed hour, without a minute's delay.

The King always traveled with his carriage full of women: His mistresses, his bastard daughters, his daughters-in-law, sometimes Madame,[5] and the other ladies of the court when there was room. This was the case for hunts, and trips to Fontainebleau, Chantilly, Compiègne, and the like. When he went shooting or strolling, or when he went to Marly or Meudon for the night, he traveled alone in a calash. He did not want his ministers in the carriage with him because they might take advantage of the situation to

[5] Madame was the wife of the King's brother.

ask him for something. It was said that old Charost,[6] more than forty years ago, had used this method, which had made the King wary. . . . In his carriage during these trips there was always an abundance and variety of things to eat: meats, pastries, and fruit. Before the carriage had gone a quarter league the King would ask who was hungry. He never ate between meals, not even a fruit, but he enjoyed watching others stuff themselves. It was mandatory to eat, with appetite and good grace, and to be gay; otherwise, he showed his displeasure by telling the guilty party she was putting on airs and trying to be coy. The same ladies or princesses who had eaten that day at the King's table were obliged to eat again as though they were weak from hunger. What is more, the women were forbidden to mention their personal needs, which in any case they could not have relieved without embarrassment, since there were guards and members of the King's household in front and in back of the carriage, and officers and equerries riding alongside the doors. The dust they kicked up choked everyone in the carriage, but the King, who loved fresh air, insisted that all the windows remain open. He would have been extremely displeased if one of the ladies had pulled a curtain to protect herself from the sun, the wind, or the cold.

He pretended not to notice his passengers' discomfort, and always traveled very fast, with the usual number of relays. Sickness in the carriage was a demerit which ruled out further invitations. I heard the duchesse de Chevreuse tell that once while traveling in the King's carriage from Versailles to Fontainebleau, she was seized after about two leagues by the kind of urgent need one feels incapable of resisting. She was a favorite of the King's, and he always wanted her along on his trips. The trip continued without interruption, and the King stopped along the road for lunch in the carriage. Her needs, although more and more pressing, did not make themselves felt during lunch, when she could have gotten out and gone to a house on the other side of the road for a moment; but the meal, while she had eaten little, redoubled the extremity of her case. Although she was almost forced to give in and ask for the carriage to stop, although she

---

[6] The duc de Charost had been a lieutenant general and governor of Picardy.

nearly lost consciousness, her courage sustained her until Fontainebleau, where she could wait no longer. She saw the duc de Beauvillier, who had arrived the day before with the King's children, at the door of the carriage. Instead of following the King, she took the duc by the arm and told him she would die unless she relieved herself. They crossed part of the Oval Court and reached the chapel, which was fortunately open, and where mass is said every day. Necessity has no laws; Mme. de Chevreuse relieved herself fully in the chapel, behind the duc de Beauvillier, who stood guard at the door. I only report this painful incident to show the daily embarrassment even the most favored courtiers were exposed to when they approached the King; for Mme. de Chevreuse was then in her zenith. Such incidents, which seem trivial, and are trivial, are too characteristic to be omitted. When the King had to relieve himself he did not hesitate to stop the carriage and get out; but the ladies were not allowed to budge.

The King's Day (1715)

At eight o'clock, the valet on duty, who had slept in the King's room and was already up, wakened the King. The chief doctor, the chief surgeon and his nurse (as long as she was alive), all came in together. The nurse kissed him; the others rubbed him down, and often changed his shirt, for he perspired heavily. The grand chamberlain, or in his absence the first lord of the chamber for that year, was summoned at eight fifteen with all those who had full access. Someone would draw open the bed curtains and present holy water from the bedside stoup. The lords hovered around the bed, and if one had something to tell the King, the others turned away; when no one had anything to say, which was usual, they only stayed a few minutes. The one who had opened the curtains and presented the holy water now presented the missal of the office of the Holy Ghost, after which everyone waited in the council chambers. The King called them back after saying his short prayer. While the person who had given him holy water handed him his dressing gown, other lords and those who had business with the King entered; then came the valets of the King's chambers, and all distinguished persons on hand; then everyone else came in while the King was putting on his shoes; he did almost everything himself, with grace and skill. He shaved every other day, and had a short wig. He never appeared without it in public, not even when receiving in bed or on the days he took medication. He often spoke of hunting, and sometimes had a word for one of those present. There was no dressing table, and a valet held a mirror before him.

As soon as he was dressed, the King prayed in the alcove by his bed, and all the clergymen present got down on their knees, the cardinals without their kneeling cloths.[1] The others remained standing, and the captain of the guards came to the altar rail during the King's prayer, to show him into his study. All those who had a right to accompany him into his study did so. He gave the necessary orders so that everyone knew, in less than ten minutes, what his activities would be that day.

Then everyone left the study except the bastards, M. de Montchevreuil and M. d'O,[2] who had been the bastards' governors, Mansart and (after succeeding him) d'Antin, and the interior valets, all of whom had come into the study through a back door. This was a time for relaxed and easy talk, and there was a good deal of discussion about plans for gardens and buildings, which lasted until the King's business for the day began. All the court was waiting in the gallery for the King to go to mass. When he was ready, he summoned the captain of the guards, who was sitting outside the study. . . .

The intervals were used for audiences, when the King granted them, or for speaking to someone, or for holding secret meetings with foreign ministers in the presence of Torcy. . . . The King then attended high mass, and the music was always a motet. He sat in the gallery except on ceremonies and feast days. Anyone who wished could talk to him on the way to and from mass, although if they were not distinguished they had to ask the captain of the guards for permission. He left the chapel gallery by a side door. The ministers were alerted during mass and gathered in the King's chamber, where distinguished persons

---

[1] Cardinals had a right to kneel on small cloth squares.
[2] One of the most illustrious and certainly the shortest of French names.

could go and chat with them. The King wasted no time on returning from mass, and began his Council meeting almost immediately. Thus ended the morning. . . . On Fridays after mass the King saw his confessor, which could last until lunch. . . . Often, on days when there was no Council meeting, lunch was served early to leave more time for hunting or walking. The usual time was one o'clock; if the Council was still meeting, lunch was delayed without advising the king. . . .

The King always ate lunch alone in his room, at a square table across from the middle window. The abundance of food varied with the orders he gave in the morning; but there were always a great many dishes and at least three courses not counting fruit. Once the table was set, the principal courtiers and most distinguished people came in, and the first lord of the chamber notified the King that lunch was ready.[3] If the grand chamberlain was absent, he served the King.

I sometimes saw the King's sons standing while he was having lunch, and he did not offer them a seat. I often saw princes of the blood and cardinals in the same posture. I also saw Monsieur, who had come from Saint-Cloud to see the King, or who had just left a foreign affairs council, the only sort he attended: He presented the King his napkin, and remained standing. A little later, the King noticed he was still there and asked him if he did not wish to sit down; Monsieur bowed and the King ordered that a seat be brought. A few moments later, the King said: "My brother, why don't you sit down?" Monsieur bowed, and sat until the end of lunch, at which time he handed the King his napkin again. On other occasions, when Monsieur arrived from Saint-Cloud, the King asked if he wished to eat and ordered that a place be set. If he refused, he left a moment later without the matter of a seat having been brought up; if he accepted, the King asked that food be brought. . . . When Monsieur attended the King's lunch, he brightened up the conversation considerably. Although he was at table, he handed the King his napkin at the beginning and the end of the meal, and cleaned his own hands on it before returning it to the grand chamberlain. The King usually did not say much

[3] The courtiers stood around and watched the King eat. Louis XVI was much admired because he could knock off the top of a soft-boiled egg with one blow of the fork.

during lunch, just a few words here and there. He spoke more freely if one of the lords he knew best was present. . . .

It was extremely unusual for the King to have guests at lunch: It was only done for certain great feasts, or sometimes at Fontainebleau, or when the queen of England was visiting. No women attended the King's lunch. On very rare occasions I saw the maréchale de la Motte who, as their governess, brought the King's children. When she appeared, a seat was brought, and she sat down; for she was a duchess by royal warrant.[4]

After lunch, the King went into his study. It was one of the moments of the day when distinguished persons could speak with him. He stopped for a moment at the door to listen; then he went in, and few dared ask for permission to follow him. Those who did and were permitted to, stood with him in the embrasure of the window closest to the shut door. The man speaking to the King reopened the door to leave when he was through. . . .

At this point the King's usual diversion was to spend some time with his setters and feed them himself. Then he called for his wardrobe attendants, changed before the few distinguished persons who had been introduced, and left by the small stairs that led into the Marble Court, where he climbed into his carriage; from the bottom of the stairs to the carriage, and vice versa, anyone who wanted to could talk to him.

The King had an extreme fondness of fresh air, and lack of it gave him headaches and dizzy spells. This was because he had long been addicted to perfumes, until finally they all disgusted him except orange blossom, and anyone approaching him had to be careful not to be wearing any. He was not very sensitive to cold, heat, or rain, and only extreme bad weather prevented him from going out every day. He went out for three reasons: To hunt the stag once or several times a week at Marly and Fontainebleau with hounds; to shoot in his parks, and no man in France was such an accurate, adroit, and graceful marksman; and to walk. Once or twice a week, and especially on Sundays and holidays, there were no hunts and all the workmen were off; the

[4] There were different kinds of titles. The two main categories were by "warrant," which was given as a favor for some special service much like British knighthood today and was not hereditary, and hereditary titles, which are ruled by primogeniture. Saint-Simon's title was hereditary, but only second-generation.

other days he liked to watch them at work and he walked among his gardens and buildings; sometimes he took walks with the ladies in the forest of Marly or Fontainebleau, and joined them for snacks; at Fontainebleau, walks were a magnificent spectacle, with the entire court spread out around the canal, and some of the courtiers on horseback. At Marly, there was a special privilege which existed nowhere else: On leaving the castle, the King said out loud: "Sirs, your hats"; at this all the courtiers, officers of the guard, and building superintendents put on their hats, whether they were standing in front, behind, or beside him. He would have been displeased had anyone kept his hat off or delayed in putting it on. This lasted throughout the walk, that is to say sometimes four or five hours in the summer or other seasons. Sometimes the King ate early at Versailles in order to spend the afternoon strolling at Marly.

Hunting the stag was the privilege of a greater number of courtiers. Whoever wished to hunt at Fontainebleau could; elsewhere, only those who had been given permission once and for all and those who had obtained the jerkin could go; the jerkin was blue with red lining, and one silver braid between two gold.

The King wanted a goodly number of hunters, but too many importuned him and troubled the hunt. He was pleased with those who enjoyed the hunt, and did not want anyone to go unless he truly enjoyed it; he thought going out of duty was ridiculous, and never held it against those who never went. He was the same way about gambling. He wanted heavy gambling to go on continuously in the drawing rooms of Marly, and many tables were set up for lansquenet and other games. At Fontainebleau when the weather was bad he liked to watch the best tennis players (he had once been an excellent player himself). At Marly he often looked in on a game of mall, which he had also played skillfully in his prime.

After lunch in the summer, the minister with whom he had work to do arrived. When the work was done, he would spend all afternoon strolling with the ladies, playing games with them, and sometimes holding a lottery in which black tickets won, and every ticket was black; it was a gallant and spontaneous way of giving, with a nod to chance, useful presents such as bolts of

cloth, silverware, or jewels which were more or less precious.
Mme. de Maintenon joined in the lottery, and almost always
gave away what she won. The King never joined, and sometimes
there were several tickets for only one gift. Apart from these
afternoons, lotteries were also held when the King lunched with
Mme. de Maintenon. He began having lunch with her late in
life, at first rarely, and finally about once a week, with music
and games, and the ladies who knew Mme. de Maintenon
best. . . .

When the King returned from his outings, anyone who wished
could talk to him as he went from his carriage to the small stairway. He changed his clothes and went into his study. It was the
best time for the bastards and the officers of his household to
visit him. There were three such intervals a day, when they could
give their reports orally or in writing, and when the King took
care of his own correspondence. He stayed in his study for an
hour or more, then went to visit Mme. de Maintenon. Anyone
who met him on the way could speak to him. At ten o'clock,
supper was served. The major-domo, bearing his staff, alerted
the captain of the guards in Mme. de Maintenon's anteroom,
where he had just arrived, having himself been alerted by one
of his men. . . .

The captain of the guards told the King supper was ready and
returned to the anteroom. Fifteen minutes later the King came
to supper, which was always formal, and anyone could speak with
him as he went from Mme. de Maintenon's anteroom to his table.
The King's children and grandchildren were there, and a great
many courtiers and ladies, both seated and standing. On the eve
of a trip to Marly all those who wanted to go were present;
this was called "asking for Marly." The men asked in the morning of the same day, saying to the King: "Sire, Marly." In his
final years, the King grew weary of this; a blue boy took the
names of those who wanted to go, but ladies continued to ask
for Marly in person.

After supper, the King stood several moments at the foot of
his bed, surrounded by all the court. Then he went into his study,
and called for those he wished to see. He spent a little less than
an hour with his legitimate and bastard children and grand-

children, and their husbands and wives. The King was in one armchair, and Monsieur, who accepted the prerogatives of a brother within the family circle, was in another. Monseigneur and all the other princes stood, and the princesses sat on stools. . . . The conversation usually dealt with hunting or some equally trivial matter. When the King was ready to retire, he said good night, left his study, fed his dogs, knelt at the railing of his bed to say his prayers, and undressed. He said good night with a nod, and, as his family left, stood in front of the fireplace and gave his orders to the colonel of the guards; then those who had full or secondary access and those with business warrants were allowed to enter; the ceremony was brief. Everyone left as the King got into bed. It was a good time to talk to the King. When one began to address him, the others withdrew.

THE KING'S DIET (1715)

The King's persistent attacks of gout had led Fagon to swaddle him every night, so to speak, in piles of feather pillows. They made him sweat so that every morning he had to be rubbed and changed before the grand chamberlain and the first lords of the chamber were allowed to see him. In his early life he had drunk only the best Champagne wine, then for many years held himself to a watered-down Burgundy past its prime. He would laughingly say that foreign lords had sometimes regretted having wanted to taste wine at his table. He had never drunk undiluted wine, nor any kind of liquor, tea, coffee, or chocolate. For breakfast, instead of a little bread, wine, and water, he had long been in the habit of drinking two cups of sage and veronica. At meals, between meals, before retiring, and even on the days he took medicine, he usually drank a pint of iced water with a little orange-blossom extract. He never ate anything between meals, except a cinnamon drop which he would slip into his pocket with a great many biscuits for his setter bitches when the fruit was served. In the last year of his life he had become more and more constipated, so that Fagon made him begin his meal with a large variety of iced fruit: Blackberries, melons and figs, so ripe they were almost rotten. With dessert he ate more fruit and a quantity of sweets that was always surprising. At dinner, year round, he consumed a prodigious quantity of salad. Every morning and evening he ate several very thick and pungent soups, taking each in quantity without prejudice to the rest. Everything he ate was at least twice as highly spiced and pungent as is customary. Fagon was against sweets and spices and when he saw the King eat them he made very amusing faces. Yet he dared not say anything except from time to time to Livry and Benoist[1] who replied it was their job to feed the King and his job to purge him. He ate all sorts of meats and fish, without exception, save for venison and waterfowl, and always respected fast days, although for the last twenty years his Lent had only lasted several days. That summer[2] he doubled his diet of fruit and drink.

At last, the fruit taken after his soup bloated his stomach, dulled his digestion, and took the edge off his appetite for the first time in his life. He had never known hunger; however, late circumstances sometimes delayed his dinner. I heard him say several times that his appetite was whetted with the first spoonfuls of soup, and he ate so prodigiously, so substantially, and so equably morning and evening that one never tired of watching him. Such quantities of water and fruit, unrelieved by spirits, turned his blood to gangrene by diluting it. It was further thinned by his nightly sweating, and this was recognized as the cause of death at his autopsy. His organs were all so beautiful and healthy that it can safely be said he could have passed the century mark. Most surprising of all were his stomach and his bowels, which were twice the length and volume of an ordinary man's. That is the reason he was such a hearty eater at all times. . . .

All his life he ate little bread, and only the crumb since losing his teeth. He continued to eat large quantities of soup, light minces, and eggs; but his appetite was gone.

[1] The King's first headwaiter and taster (free translation of the French term *controlleur de la bouche*), respectively.
[2] 1715, the year of his death.

THE KING'S DRESS (1715)

The King always wore plain brown, sometimes set off by a gold button or a bit of black velvet. He wore an open vest of embroidered cloth or satin, either blue or red. He shunned rings and wore jewels only on his shoe buckles, his garters, and his hat, which was trimmed in Spanish needlepoint and decorated with a white plume. Except for weddings and other holidays, he wore his Order of the Holy Ghost under his coat. It was very long and studded with eight or ten million francs' worth of precious stones.

THE KING AT CHURCH (1715)

The King was very strict at church. During mass, everyone had to kneel at the Sanctus and remain kneeling until the priest's communion. He was annoyed if he saw someone talking or if he heard the least noise. He rarely missed the evening service on Sunday, always attended on Thursday, and stayed through the whole Blessed Sacrament octave. He went to communion five times a year, and wore his ceremonial dress and the necklace of the Order; on Holy Saturday he went to the parish and on the other days he went to his chapel. These days were Pentecost Eve, Assumption Day (followed by a high mass), All Saints' Eve and Christmas Eve. On his communion days there was a low mass without music, and he blessed the sick. He also went to vespers on communion days, and after vespers he organized the distribution of various charities with his confessor in his study; it was extremely rare for him to take interest in charities on other occasions; on the day after communion he went to high mass and vespers. He went to matins and to three midnight masses with music, which was an admirable sight in the chapel; the next day he went to high mass, vespers, and evening service. On Maundy

Thursday he waited on the poor at dinner, and then went to chapel to adore the Blessed Sacrament before retiring. At mass he told his beads (he did not know enough to do more) and knelt except during the Gospel. At high mass, he sat in his armchair at the proper times. At jubilees, he visited the churches on foot. And on fast days, including Lent, he ate lightly.

OPPOSITION TO THE KING (1709)

M. de La Rochefoucauld, who had retired to Chenil, received an atrocious anonymous letter attacking the King, which said specifically that Ravaillacs[1] could still be found and compounded this folly with praise of Brutus. The duc rushed to Marly in great excitement and had the King informed in the middle of a Council meeting that he had something urgent to communicate. The sudden apparition of a blind man, retired from court, and his urgent need to talk to the King made courtiers wonder what was up. Once the Council was over, M. de La Rochefoucauld gave the King the letter with great emphasis. He was very badly received. Since everything is eventually found out at court, we knew what M. de La Rochefoucauld had come for. The ducs de Bouillon and de Beauvillier had received the same letters, had brought them to the King, and had been better received because they had acted with greater simplicity. The King's grief over the letters lasted several days; but after mulling it over he realized that people who threaten and warn are less intent on committing a crime than on arousing anxiety. What annoyed the King far more was a profusion of bold and extravagant placards against his person, his conduct, and his government, which kept appearing at the gates of Paris, and in front of churches and public places. At night, his statues[2] were defiled in various ways that were dis-

---

[1] François Ravaillac assassinated Henri IV in 1610.
[2] There were statues of Louis XIV at the Place Vendôme and the Place des Victoires.

covered in the morning, and the inscriptions were erased. There was also a multitude of poems and songs in which the King was not spared.

NEWS OF BATTLE IS WITHHELD
FROM THE KING (1708)

The King did not learn of the battle of l'Escaut[1] for several days. It would have been kept from him longer had it not been for the duc de La Trémoille, whose only son had distinguished himself in action, and who was vexed because the King made no mention of it. He brought the matter up while serving the King at lunch, and said his son had suffered greatly while crossing the Escaut with his regiment. "How 'suffered'?" said the King. "Nothing happened." "There was heavy fighting," replied La Trémoille, who proceeded to describe the battle. The King listened attentively, even questioned him, and admitted to everyone present that he had not heard about it. One can imagine his surprise, and the surprise that he caused. It happened that shortly after lunch, Chamillart unexpectedly entered the King's study. The King finished the little work he had and then asked Chamillart the significance of the battle, of which he had not been informed. The minister replied uneasily that it was nothing at all. The King insisted, mentioned details, and cited the regiment of the prince de Tarente.[2] Chamillart admitted that the crossing of the river had been unpleasant in itself and that the battle had been just as unpleasant, but that the former was unimportant and the latter unavoidable. He said Mme. de Maintenon had not wanted the King bothered with the news, and they had agreed to keep it from him. At this singular reply, the King stopped short, and added not a word.

[1] In 1708, the Duke of Marlborough pushed the French troops back across the Escant River in Flanders in a major action of the War of the Spanish Succession.
[2] Son of the duc de la Trémoille.

The Heartlessness of the King (1707)

Mme. la duchesse de Bourgogne was with child, which greatly inconvenienced her. The King had declared that he wanted to go to Fontainebleau at the start of spring, which was not his habit. In the meantime, he wanted his trips to Marly. He could not do without his granddaughter, whom he found most amusing, but traveling was not advisable in her condition. Mme. de Maintenon was anxious for her, and Fagon[1] tactfully gave the King his opinion: The King was annoyed, for he was accustomed to have his way in all things, and had been spoiled by his mistresses who had traveled in full dress while pregnant or just after their lying-in. Requests that his granddaughter be excused from Marly irritated the King without swaying him. He would only agree to twice delay the trip scheduled for the day after Quasimodo.[2] He left on Wednesday of the following week, despite everything that had been done to prevent him or to have him agree to leave the princess at Versailles. The following Saturday, the King was strolling between the castle and the Perspective and amusing himself at the carp basin. There were no ladies with the King, which was rare in the morning, and suddenly he saw the duchesse de Ludes walking toward him. He realized she had something urgent to tell him and met her halfway; we stopped to let him join her alone. The tête-à-tête was brief. She left the King, who returned to us near the carp basin, without saying a word. He looked over everyone there, and said with annoyance to no one in particular: "The duchesse de Bourgogne has had a miscarriage." M. de Bouillon, the duc de Tresmes, and the maréchal de Boufflers whispered to each other, and the duc de La Rochefoucauld exclaimed loudly that it was the greatest misfortune in the world, for since she had already had several miscarriages, she might never again be able to conceive. "So what?" interrupted the King

[1] The King's surgeon, Guy Fagon (1638-1718).
[2] The first Sunday after Easter, when neophytes wore white robes at church and heard the first words of the Introit at mass: *Quasi modo.*

angrily. "What is that to me? Doesn't she have a son already? And even if he dies, isn't the duc de Berry old enough to marry and sire one? And what do I care whether one or the other succeeds me? Are they not all my grandchildren?"

And he added impetuously: "Thank God she is wounded, if she had to be, for now I will not be opposed by matrons and doctors when I want to take a trip or do other things. I will come and go as I please and be left in peace." This tirade was followed by such silence you could have heard an ant walk: We lowered our eyes and hardly dared breathe. Everyone remained stupefied and even the workers and gardeners did not move. The silence lasted a good quarter of an hour. The King broke it to lean over the railing and talk about a carp. No one replied. He then discussed the carps with some of the workers, who did not hold up their end of the conversation; only the carp were discussed. Everyone was listless, and the King left soon afterward. As soon as he had gone and we dared look at one another, our eyes met in silent understanding, in expression of awe and grief, and we shrugged our shoulders. I can see it now. M. de La Rochefoucauld was furious and, for once, had a right to be; the first equerry was faint from fear. I examined everyone with my eyes and ears and congratulated myself for having realized long ago that the King loved and was concerned with no one but himself, and that he was an end unto himself.

How to Handle the King (1715)

Le Tellier,[1] in the old days before he became chancellor of France, knew how to handle the King. One of his best friends (and he had many because he knew how to keep them) had asked him to put in a good word for him with the King. Le Tellier promised to do his best. The friend replied that in his place and position, he should be able to do even more. "You are not familiar with the terrain," replied Le Tellier. "Of twenty pro-

---

[1] Michel Le Tellier (1603-1685) held various government posts before becoming chancellor in 1677. He was the father of Louvois.

posals we bring the King, we are certain he will agree to nine-teen and refuse the twentieth. We never know which one will be refused, but it is usually the one we hold most dear. The King reserves the right to say No to show us that he is the master and rules the land. On the rare occasions when we match his stub-bornness, either because the matter is vital in itself or because we are eager to have our way, you can be almost sure that he will throw a fit of temper; however, once the King has had his way and exhausted his anger, he becomes more tractable. He is pleased to have exposed our impotence and sorry to have disappointed us, and that is the moment when we can obtain what we like."

This was, in effect, the way the King behaved with his ministers all his life. The youngest, least able, and least respected among them was able to govern him completely, although he was con-stantly on his guard against them, and was convinced that he was having his way. He behaved the same way with Mme. de Maintenon, and congratulated himself for upbraiding her from time to time. Sometimes he would make her cry and keep her on tenterhooks for several days. . . . Sometimes she faked illness after these scenes, and that was usually how she got the most out of them.

Not that these devices, or even the most obvious reality, could ever constrain the King in any matter. He was interested only in himself, and his interest in others, no matter who they were, was only in relation to himself. In this, his callousness was extreme.

THE KING BERATES A LACKEY (1695)

The King, usually so even-tempered and so completely in control of his slightest gestures even in the most sensitive situations, lost his temper on this one occasion: Rising from table at Marly, with all the courtiers and ladies, he noticed a pantry boy slip a biscuit into his pocket as he was removing the dessert plates from the table. The King had just been handed his hat and his cane, and forgetting his dignity, he ran after the startled valet, hit him, insulted him and broke his cane over his back before the equally startled onlookers: In truth it was a reed cane and not very resistant. Then, brandishing the cane stump like a man out of his wits and continuing to insult the valet, who had long since fled, he crossed the small drawing room and an anteroom to visit Mme. de Maintenon. He stayed with her nearly an hour, as he often did in the afternoon at Marly. On his way back to his own apartments, he ran into Père de La Chaise among a group of courtiers, and said in a very loud voice: "Father, I gave a good drubbing to a rascal and broke my cane over his back; but I do not believe I have offended God"; and immediately he proceeded to recount his supposed crime. Everyone on hand was already trembling from what they had seen or heard from eyewitnesses. Their fear increased when they heard him: The King's familiars criticized the valet in low tones; the poor Father, speaking between his teeth, pretended to agree with the King, so as not to add to his anger in front of everyone. One can judge how quickly news of the King's temper spread, and how terrified everyone was. Everyone understood that the valet had been a pretext, and no one could guess the real cause.

THE KING CUTS A BANKER'S PURSE STRINGS (1708)

Samuel Bernard was the richest banker in Europe, and made the biggest and safest financial deals; he was aware of his importance and demanded treatment in proportion to it. The controllers general, who needed him more often than he needed them, treated him with great respect and consideration. One day at Marly the King told Desmaretz[1] he was pleased to see that M. Bernard was with him, and added to the latter: "I will wager that you have never seen Marly. Come let me show it to you and then I will return you to Desmaretz." Bernard followed and, for the duration of the stroll, the King conversed only with Bergeyck[2] and with him, and as often with him as with the other. He took them

[1] Nicolas Desmaretz was minister of finance several times under Louis XIV.

[2] The comte de Bergeyck was controller general of the armed forces.

everywhere and showed them everything with the kind of charm he knew how to deploy so well when he was bent on favoring someone. The King was normally very miserly with his words, and I was not alone in admiring the way he was catering to a man of Bernard's kind. I soon discovered the reason and was filled with wonder at the expediencies to which the greatest of kings are reduced. Although Desmaretz had left no stone unturned, the coffers were drained and there was a great want. He had been to Paris and knocked at every door: So many pledges had been forgotten and so many promises broken that he found only excuses and refusals. Like the others, Bernard did not want to advance any money, for he was owed a great deal. In vain, Desmaretz brought up the enormous profits the King had allowed him to pile up and the urgency of current needs; Bernard remained implacable. The King and his minister were cruelly inconvenienced. Desmaretz told the King that, all things considered, only Bernard could save them, for he had the greatest and most widespread capital, and it was only a matter of breaking his will and a stubbornness which sometimes bordered on insolence. He pointed out that Bernard was vain to the point of folly and would open his purse if the King deigned to flatter him. The King was in such dire straits that he agreed, and Desmaretz proposed the method I have just recounted to enlist Bernard's help with discretion and without risk of refusal. Bernard was completely taken in: He was so delighted by his stroll with the King that the first thing he told Desmaretz was that he would rather risk ruin than see a prince who had so favored him in difficulty.

He praised the King to the skies. Desmaretz seized the advantage and got much more than he had hoped for.

War Games at Compiègne (1698)

The King decided to hold war games and Compiègne was besieged according to an abridged version of military regulations: Lines, trenches, artillery, tunnels, etc. Crenan[1] was defending

[1]Marquis de Crenan, director of the infantry.

the city. . . . Saturday, September 13, was chosen for the attack: The weather was fine, and the King mounted his rampart, followed by all the ladies; the courtiers were out in strength and there were many distinguished foreigners. From the rampart you could see the entire plain and the position of all the troops. I was standing in a semicircle, only three steps away from the King, with no one in front of me. It was the most beautiful sight imaginable: There was the entire army, and a prodigious number of spectators of all sorts, on horseback and on foot, who kept their distance from the troops so as not to get in their way; then there was the game between attackers and defenders, which was in full view since it was all for show. The only precaution taken was to insure the precision of the deployments. But there was also another sort of spectacle, one that made such a lasting impression on me that I could describe it as well in forty years as I can today: That was the spectacle to which the King lent himself from the top of his rampart and which was seen by his entire army and by the numberless and varied crowds on the rampart and in the plain.

Mme. de Maintenon was facing the plain and the troops in her three-windowed sedan chair, which the porters had left on the rampart. Mme. la duchesse de Bourgogne was sitting on the front left bar; standing behind her in a semicircle were Mme. la Duchesse, Mme. la princesse de Conti and all the ladies, and behind them all the men. The King was standing near the right-hand window of the sedan chair, in a semicircle of the most distinguished men. The King was almost always bareheaded, and he often leaned toward the window to explain the maneuvers to Mme. de Maintenon. Each time he did so, she was kind enough to open her window, but never more than a few inches; I admit I watched them more carefully than I did the troops.

Sometimes she opened it to ask the King a question; but most of the time it was he, without waiting for her to ask, who leaned toward the window to tell her something; sometimes, when she had not noticed, he tapped on the window so she would open it. He spoke only to her, except to give brief and infrequent orders and answer Mme. la duchesse de Bourgogne, who tried to engage him in conversation; occasionally the young princess would yell something at Mme. de Maintenon, who replied in sign language, without opening the front window. I studied everyone's expression: They all showed a surprise and shame which they could barely conceal, and everyone behind the sedan chair and in the semicircles was more concerned with Mme. de Maintenon than with the army, but remained respectful out of fear and embarrassment.[2] The King often placed his hat on top of the sedan chair so that he could get close to the window, and this oft-repeated exercise must have strained his back considerably. Monseigneur le duc de Bourgogne was with the maréchal de Boufflers, serving with the rank of general, as he did for all the army's deployments. It was about five in the afternoon, and the weather was the finest one could have hoped for.

Across from the sedan chair there was a steep path which led to the plain through an opening in the rampart wall, and which was used to communicate the King's orders to the troops. At one point Crenan sent Canillac, a colonel in the Rouerge regiment, to pick up one of the King's orders. Canillac climbed up the path and reached the top of the rampart; I can see him now just as clearly as I did then. As he climbed to our level, he saw the sedan chair, the King, and all the courtiers, which he had not noticed from the plain because his position was at the foot of the rampart. The scene stunned him so that he stopped short and gaped open-mouthed, a look of frozen astonishment on his face. Everyone noticed it, and the King said heatedly: "Well then, Canillac; come up here." Canillac did not move; the King repeated: "Come up here; what's the matter with you?" He went up to the King with halting steps, gazing distractedly right and left. I have already explained that I was only three steps away from the King; Canillac passed in front of me and muttered something inaudible.

"What's that you're saying?" asked the King. "Speak up!" But Canillac could not pull himself together. He said as much as he was able to; the King could not understand much of it, and seeing he would get no more, replied as best he could, adding in a grieved tone: "You may go, Sir." Canillac did not have to be told twice, and disappeared down the path. As soon as he had

[2] A morganatic marriage between King Louis XIV and Mme. de Maintenon had been celebrated secretly in 1685. The war games at Compiègne were held fourteen years later, and marked the first time that the King openly displayed affection and deference for Mme. de Maintenon. This was why Saint-Simon was so shocked.

gone, the King looked around him and said: "I don't know what's got into Canillac, but he has lost his head, and could not even remember what he had to tell me." No one replied.

When the moment of capitulation had come, Mme. de Maintenon apparently asked permission to leave. "Madame's porters!" the King shouted. They came and carried her off. Less than fifteen minutes later, the King left, followed by Mme. la duchesse de Bourgogne and almost everyone present. There were many winks, nods, and whispers: Everyone was shaken by what he had seen. It was the same for all those who had been in the plain; even the soldiers wondered what the King had been doing hunched over a sedan chair all the time; the officers did not know what to tell the soldiers. One can judge the effects of such a spectacle on foreigners. It was the talk of Europe, and became as famous as the Compiègne camp, with its pomp and prodigious splendor. After that, Mme. de Maintenon seldom visited the camp, and when she did it was in her carriage with her three or four lady friends.

England Bets on the Death of a King (1714)

Although it is not time yet to speak of the King's health, it was in perceptible decline. His appetite, which had always been prodigious, was failing. Despite general concern at court he had not altered in the slightest detail the arrangement of his life or daily routine, which remained as varied as ever. Foreign countries were no less concerned and scarcely less well informed. Bets were made in England on whether he would survive the 1st of September, only three months away. Although the King wanted to be kept up on everything, no one was eager to give him the news from London. He usually had Torcy read him the newspapers from Holland after the Council of State. One day when Torcy was reading a newspaper he had not yet scanned he came upon an article from London about the bets; he stumbled, mumbled, and skipped over it. The King, noticing his confusion, asked its cause;

Torcy blushed to the whites of his eyes, hunted for the right words, and finally said the article was an impertinence unworthy of being read. The King insisted, but Torcy was so embarrassed he refused to read it; finally, he could not refuse repeated commands and he read the article from beginning to end. The King pretended not to be moved by it; but he was, deeply, to the point that having sat down at table just afterward, he could not refrain from talking about it to those present, without mentioning the newspaper. This happened at Marly, where I sometimes went to pay court at the start of the meal, and by chance I was there that day. The King looked at me along with the others, but as though he was expecting some reply. I took care to keep my mouth shut, and lowered my eyes.

THE KING'S DEATH (1715)

On Monday, August 26, after the two cardinals had gone, the King dined in bed in front of all those who were admitted to his room. As the dishes were being cleared, he asked them to draw near and said these words, which were promptly noted: "Sirs, I beg your pardon for the bad example I have given you. I must thank you for the manner in which you have served me and for the attachment and loyalty you have always shown me. I am extremely sorry not to have done for you what I should have done. These difficult times are the reason. I wish to ask for my great-grandson the same diligence and loyalty with which you have served me. He will probably have to suffer many setbacks. Let your example serve for all my other subjects. Follow my nephew's[1] orders. He will govern the kingdom; I hope he will govern it well; I hope also that you will all contribute to its unity and help draw back those who stray. I feel I am growing sentimental, and I see that you are too; please forgive me. Sirs, farewell: I hope that sometimes you will think of me."

Soon after everyone had left, the King sent for the maréchal de

[1] Philippe d'Orléans, who automatically became Regent at the death of Louis XIV, since the Dauphin's father was dead.

Villeroy, and told him the following, which Villeroy has since disclosed: "Monsieur le maréchal, I wish to give you from my deathbed a new mark of friendship and trust. I name you governor of the Dauphin, the most important employment I may grant. You will know from my will what course to follow with the duc du Maine. I have no doubt that you will serve me after my death as faithfully as you have during my life. I hope my nephew, a man whom I have always loved, will receive the necessary confidence and respect. Farewell, Monsieur le maréchal; I hope that sometimes you will think of me . . ."

Some time later, he asked the duchesse de Ventadour to bring the Dauphin to him. He had him draw near and said before Mme. de Maintenon, the very few most intimately privileged, and the necessary servants, who noted his words: "My child, you will be a great king. Do not imitate the passion I had for building and war; try, on the contrary, to keep peace with your neighbors. Render unto God His due; recognize your obligations to Him and require your subjects to honor Him. Always follow wise counsel; try to relieve the suffering of your people, which unhappily I was unable to do. Never forget the gratitude you owe Mme. de Ventadour. Madame (addressing her), let me embrace him"; and embracing him, he said: "My dear child, here is my blessing with all my heart." They removed the little prince from the King's bed, but he had him brought back and embraced him again. Lifting his hands and eyes to heaven, he blessed him once more. The sight was very moving. . . .

Some time later, the King told Mme. de Maintenon that he had heard it was difficult to accustom oneself to death; but that although he was approaching the fearful moment, he did not find it such a painful resolution. She replied that it was very painful for those who were attached to the creatures of the earth, bore hate in their hearts, or had restitutions to make. "Ah!" replied the King, "as for restitutions, I owe nothing to any man; and as for my debt to the kingdom, I trust in God's mercy." The following night, the King was very restless. He clasped and unclasped his hands, repeated his accustomed prayers, and beat his breast when he recited the Confiteor.

On Wednesday, August 28, the King paid a compliment to Mme. de Maintenon which she did not appreciate, and to which she did not reply. He said that his only comfort in departing from her was the hope that, because of her age, she would soon join him. At seven in the morning he summoned Father Tellier, and as they spoke of God, the King saw in the mirror above his fireplace two young lackeys sitting at the foot of his bed and crying. He said: "Why do you cry? Did you think I was immortal? For my part, I never thought I was, and considering my age you should expect to lose me."

A coarse Provençal peasant learned while traveling from Marseilles to Paris that the King was on his deathbed, and arrived that morning at Versailles with what he said was a cure for gangrene. The King was so ill and his doctors so helpless that they consented without protest in front of Mme. de Maintenon and the duc du Maine. Fagon tried to get a word in, but the peasant, whose name was le Brun, heaped abuse on him; Fagon, used to abusing others and having them tremble with respect at the sight of him, was dumfounded. At eleven in the morning, the King was given ten drops of the peasant's elixir in Alicanta wine. Soon afterward he regained strength; when his pulse slowed and weakened at four o'clock he was given more and told it would bring him back to life. He took the glass and replied: "To life or to death, whatever pleases God . . ."

He continued to take le Brun's remedy, and the peasant was always there to see it administered. When the King was offered a broth, he replied that he should no longer be addressed as a living man, and that it was not a broth he needed, but his confessor, who was summoned. One day when he was wakening from a coma, he asked Father Tellier for general absolution of his sins. The confessor asked if he was suffering greatly: "No, replied the King, and that is what bothers me. I would like to suffer more for the expiation of my sins." . . .

The promise of the day was not fulfilled. He had been visited by the parish priest of Versailles, who told him that prayers were being said for his recovery. The King replied that there was no longer any question of recovery, and that the prayers should be said for his salvation. The same day, while giving orders, he called the Dauphin "the young King" in a slip of the tongue. He heard a murmur rise from those at his bedside, and said: "Why do you protest? I am not sad."

At eight o'clock in the evening he took some more of the Provençal peasant's elixir. His mind appeared clouded and he said himself he felt very bad. At about eleven o'clock in the evening the doctors looked at his leg. The gangrene had spread from his foot and knee to his thigh, which was very swollen. He lost consciousness during the examination. He had noticed with sadness the absence of Mme. de Maintenon, who had planned not to return to his bedside. She was summoned several times during the day, and it could not be concealed from the King that she had gone to Saint-Cyr; he had her summoned and she returned that evening.

The day of Friday, August 30, was as disastrous as the previous night: The King was failing fast, and his mind remained cloudy. From time to time he took a little meat jelly and clear water, for he could no longer stand wine. In his room there were only the most indispensable valets, the physicians, Mme. de Maintenon, and Father Tellier, who made infrequent appearances, summoned by Blouin or Mareschal. . . . At five o'clock that afternoon, Mme. de Maintenon went to her apartment, gave her furniture to her maid, and went back to Saint-Cyr, from where she never again emerged.

On Saturday, August 31, the night and the day were horrible; the King was only conscious during rare and brief instants. The gangrene had risen above the knee and contaminated his entire thigh. He was given some of the late Father Aignan's[2] excellent remedy for smallpox, which the duchesse du Maine had offered. The doctors were willing to try anything, for they had lost all hope. Toward eleven in the evening they found him failing so rapidly that they made him say the prayers for the dying. The prayers brought him back to consciousness and he recited them in such a strong voice that he could be heard above all the gathered clergy. At the end of the prayers, he recognized Cardinal de Rohan and said: "These are the Church's last blessings." Rohan was the last man to whom he spoke. Several times he repeated, "*Nunc et in hora mortis*," then said: "Oh my God, help me; make haste to save me." Those were his last words. He did not regain consciousness during the night, and his long agony ended on Sun-

---

[2] François Aignan was a Capuchin friar who had brought back exotic remedies from a trip to the Orient.

day, September first, 1715, at eight fifteen in the morning, three days short of his seventy-seventh birthday, in the seventy-second year of his reign.

He signed the celebrated peace of the Pyrénées in 1659 and married a year later, at the age of twenty-two. He was twenty-three when death delivered France of Cardinal de Mazarin; twenty-seven when he lost the Queen his mother, in 1666. He was a widower at forty-four, in 1683, lost Monsieur when he was sixty-three, in 1701, and survived all his sons and grandsons, except his successor,[3] the king of Spain and the children of that prince. Europe never knew so long a reign, nor France a king so long-lived.

REACTIONS TO THE KING'S DEATH (1715)

There were two sorts of persons at court: Those who rejoiced at the end of a reign which held no promise for them and now could set their sights on better positions and those who, wearied by the heavy and oppressive rule of the King and his ministers, felt a delighted freedom. Everyone in general felt delivered from the inconvenience of a court requiring continuous novelty. Paris, weary of its subjugation, found relief in the hope of liberation and in the joy of witnessing the demise of those who had abused their authority. The provinces, which had despaired because of their devastation, now breathed easy and quivered with delight. Parliaments and judges, crushed by edicts and rulings, now had hope of new license and authority. The people, ruined, abused, despairing, now thanked God for a deliverance which answered their most ardent desires. Foreign nations, although delighted to be rid of a monarch who for so many years had imposed his law, and who had always miraculously escaped their efforts to bring him to task, behaved with greater propriety than the French. The marvels of the first three quarters of his seventy-year reign, and the personal magnanimity of a fortunate king whom fortune abandoned in the last quarter, had understandably dazzled them.

[3] Actually, Louis XV was a great-grandson.

As a matter of honor, they granted him after his death what they had constantly refused him during his life. Not a single foreign court exulted; all took pains to praise and honor his memory. The Emperor went into mourning as though for his own father; and in Vienna, the prohibition of all entertainments was strictly enforced, even though the carnival was due four or five months after the King's death.

VI

SAINT-SIMON:
HIS LIFE AND CAREER
AT COURT

INTRODUCTION

*I*f Louis de Rouvroy, duc de Saint-Simon, had lived to see the
French Revolution, he would have been astonished to find
that he was one of its heroes. Pirated editions of his Memoirs began to appear in 1781, and were hailed for their courageous con-
demnation of the court of Louis XIV. Passages dealing with social
injustice, a halfhearted attempt to repeal the salt tax, and graft
among the ruling classes were praised as progressive political tracts
predicting the breakdown of French monarchy.

This is somewhat akin to making Karl Marx the hero of the in-
dustrial revolution. Saint-Simon had indeed seen the flaws in the
system, but was devoted to restoring the feudal powers of the nobility under the King, not to doing away with the monarchy in
favor of the people. Although his compassion for suffering and injustice was sincere, so was his deep mistrust of the common man.
For him, a decent man was one who never tried to rise above his
station or abuse the God-given birthrights of others. Saint-Simon
liked Le Nostre, possibly the greatest landscape architect who
ever lived, because Le Nostre never thought of himself as more
than a gardener. He had a certain distaste for Voltaire, whose
father was the Saint-Simon family notaire, because the author of
"Le Siècle de Louis XIV" had gained a degree of social acceptance along with literary fame.

Saint-Simon's life was devoted to a sometimes absurd and
maniacal crusade to re-establish the rights of the peers, based on
their original sacred dignity. Originally, the peers crowned the
monarch, and this symbolic gesture indicated the source of his

mandate. Saint-Simon never forgot that at the crowning of Charlemagne the peers had held the diadem over the emperor's head. He compared this summit of ducal privilege with the position of the peers under Louis XIV—diverted from government posts and army commands, assailed by newly named nobles trying to consolidate their titles, and threatened by the King's bastards, who had their eye on the crown.

Saint-Simon became the self-appointed caretaker of ducal rank, the inquisitor of minute infractions in court etiquette, continuously tilting at windmills of imagined abuses. His own peerage was only second-generation; his father had been a page of Louis XIII who came to the monarch's attention because he did not drool into his hunting horn and devised a way for the king to change horses without dismounting. The recentness of his own ducal title led him to make exaggerated claims that he was descended from Charlemagne through the female line "with a certainty that may not be contested."

His life at court was a series of disputes or "affairs" in which he was always the outraged party trying to expose the "perversity" and "monstrous usurpations" of others. Matters of rank had vast importance at court, and no one took them lightly. But Saint-Simon's claims were so exorbitant that other courtiers finally grew to consider him a dangerous crank.

If a prince held the King's napkin at communion, Saint-Simon saw a plot to create a precedent. Because members of Parlement removed their bonnets for princes but not for dukes he devoted a campaign of many years to correct this "enormous usurpation." He conducted a tireless one-man siege against seventeenth-century status seekers and exposed their cleverest schemes, some so clever that they existed only in his imagination. He finally had to face the discouraging fact that the King did not sympathize with his vigilance. Though disapproving of the way the King had stultified the nobility, Saint-Simon desperately wanted his approval. His few private audiences with the King were the apex of his court career. The first meeting took place in 1691, when he was presented by his father as a volunteer for the musketeers. Eleven years later he quit the army in a fit of pique because he had been overlooked in a list of promotions. From the time he was pre-

sented, to the time the King died in 1715, he was granted only three private audiences. Each time, Saint-Simon came to the King trembling with emotion and bursting with explanations of how calumnied and misunderstood he was. The King listened with polite attention, and gave Saint-Simon his blessing and a word of sobering advice: If you don't want to be talked about, stay out of trouble. At his last audience, in 1710, Saint-Simon fawned over the King in an embarrassing manner, finally pleading for an apartment at Versailles. The King refused, and the memoirist, forced to salvage something from the audience, noted that it was unusually long and that the King seemed most interested. There is something unwholesome and infantile in this subject-king relationship. One feels at times that Saint-Simon is like a child being wicked to draw attention from his parents.

In all personal matters, he was completely virtuous. Since he was constantly condemning the behavior of others, his own had to be above reproach. Sometimes he implies that the observation of self-indulgence and dishonesty in others had cured him of both. It goes much deeper than that. In Saint-Simon there is an atrophy of all the senses but one, sight. Food and wine held far less interest for him than the gestures which surrounded them. He was not attentive to the quality of the wine, but to the reverence with which it was served. He thought of sexual passion as a trap invented by the devil for the abasement of man and as a means for women of gaining political power. It was the marvel of the court that he had sired two children. He often referred to Paris as "the sewer of Europe" and to sex as though it was a disease, "spreading combustion through the world." He was probably the only man at court who was faithful to his wife, although lack of interest in other women was not the only reason for his devotion. His unwavering conjugal love is one of his most redeeming qualities, and comes out unexpectedly in the Memoirs. On the day of her death, he was working at his writing table as usual, but his quill pen stopped halfway down the page to draw a line of tear-shaped marks followed by a cross. The next entry was dated six months later. He asked in his will that "wherever I am, I want my body to be buried in the tomb of the parish church in La Ferté next to that of my very dear wife. I want our two coffins to be riveted to each other with iron bars, hooks, and rings, so that it is impossible to separate them without breaking both." The coffins were separated during one of the jacqueries of the French Revolution, when local rabble disinterred the remains and threw them to the winds.

Saint-Simon's virtue is part vanity, a satisfaction in abnegation. It is clear that he enjoys refusing to take part in Law's "Mississippi" project far more than he would enjoy the quick profits he might reap. Untarnished virtue was also a prerequisite for his role as conscience of the Regent. He derived much the same satisfaction from lecturing the Regent as the Regent did from his debauchery. At other moments, Saint-Simon shows that even he could contain the seed of lasciviousness. Each sense has a corresponding set of vices, and to Saint-Simon's only operating sense corresponds voyeurism. Thanks to the Memoirs, we can view the voyeur: Quivering with exultation as he hides behind a tree to spy on the visiting Czar, dissects the surprise and anger of members of Parlement, or notes the discomposed expressions of courtiers learning the death of Monsieur.

After the King died, the court went out of focus for Saint-Simon, losing much of its mysterious enchantment. And yet, under the regency of his close friend Philippe d'Orléans, he could have made a superb political comeback. He might have become prime minister, instead of remaining a crotchety and barely tolerated court malcontent. He persuaded the Regent to experiment with a system of government by council, in which the nobility would be heavily represented. To show his good faith, he suggested the names of his worst enemies, so he could pack the councils with dukes. Government by council produced no startling improvements, and real power still lay in the hands of a single man, this time the prime minister, who took advantage of the Regent's indolence. Saint-Simon was too affected by the style of the court, its inner mechanism and magnification of triviality, to be an effective politician.

He was too accustomed to backstage maneuvering and acting through intermediaries to assume a position of direct responsibility. Perhaps he realized that his Memoirs would suffer if he accepted an important post, which would not leave enough time for the observation of others. Whatever the reasons, he refused to meet the needs of the Regent for a forceful and unscrupulous prime minister. He kept trying to influence his old friend with long and sanctimonious tirades, warning him against debauchery and dangerous companions. But the Regent listened with an increasingly distracted ear and Saint-Simon's star fell once again. The Regency, which should have marked his political fulfillment, led to his retirement from court, for when the Regent died in 1723 he was completely discredited.

Saint-Simon may have considered himself the theoretician of the Regency, the political thinker who elaborated a vast canvas of renewal that would repair the damage done to France by Louis XIV. Actually, instead of a comprehensive political theory, he could provide only a patchwork stitched together out of a number of unrelated obsessions.

He felt the nobles had been sent out to pasture in favor of the professional classes summoned by Louis XIV. He called the secretaries of state "the five kings." He wanted a decentralized and corporate system of government.

He thought the third estate should be kept reasonably content. Starving men revolt; decently fed men stay in their place.

His views on foreign policy were dictated by suspicion of England and the need for alliance with Spain. In religion, he was a Gallican liberal, calling for a national church to counter the abuses of papal domination.

Invective was his natural tone in political affairs, and he reserved the flower of his hatred for the royal bastards. The crime of the bastards was accepting privileges to which they had no legitimate right. Only one, the duc du Maine, ever actively plotted to take the throne, and Saint-Simon made his demise a matter of personal vengeance. He devoted years to convincing the Regent to act against the duc du Maine and set up the parliamentary machinery to strip him of his rank. Victory came in two battles, the parliamentary session of 1715 over the will of Louis XIV and the Bed of Justice three years later. The substance of the victory was slight. It consisted in the successful repudiation of a contested claim which would never be more than a footnote to the history of the period. And yet it was the summit of his achievement. If we were to judge Saint-Simon on the basis of his court career, he could be dismissed as a pathetic victim of its artificial values who expended himself on matters of little consequence.

In this sense, the Memoirs *constitute an inadvertent bid for rehabilitation. Saint-Simon is like a general who has lost most of his battles but leaves posterity a definitive history of his wars. What he did was not great, or even very successful; but the telling of it is. The three thousand copybook pages covered with his small and precise handwriting are credentials that free him from the sterility of the court he described.*

SAINT-SIMON'S FATHER (1692)

High birth and wealth do not always go together. The fortunes of war and family mishaps had ruined our branch and left my forefathers too poor for brilliant military careers. My grandfather, who had served in every war of his time as a passionate royalist, had retired to his estate. His penury forced him to offer his two eldest sons as pages to Louis XIII, a fashion followed by some of the best families.

The King loved to hunt, and in those days there were none of the conveniences introduced by the King his son, such as trails, and an abundance of dogs, huntsmen, and relays. Noticing the King's impatience when he changed horses, my father devised a method of bringing a fresh horse head-to-hindquarters alongside the horse the King was on. Thanks to this method, the King, who was athletic, was able to jump in a moment from one horse to the other without setting foot on the ground. The King was pleased: He always asked for the same page when he changed horses, inquired about his origins, and grew to like him. He finally dismissed Baradat, the First Equerry, whose arrogance and hauteur had become intolerable, and gave the position to my father. When Blainville died, my father became first lord of the King's chambers.

My father became the King's favorite, protected only by his kindness. He never curried favor with any minister, not even Cardinal Richelieu, and that was one of the things Louis XIII liked about him. My father told me that when the King decided to promote him, he secretly informed himself about my father's birth and character (which he had not bothered to learn about before), to see if he was worthy of bearing the weight of high position without falling to pieces. . . . The King liked people of quality and sought them out so that he could honor them. . . .

If the King knew how to love my father, he also knew how to reprimand him. . . . The King was truly in love with Mlle. d'Hautefort. It was usually to see her that he visited the Queen, and he often spoke with her.[1] He continually discussed her with my father, who saw clearly how strong his passion was. My father, who was young and gallant, could not understand a king at once so much in love, so unable to hide it, and so incapable of pursuing it. He thought it was shyness on the King's part. One day, when the King was passionately discussing the young woman, my father expressed his surprise, offered to act on the King's behalf, and promised swift success. The King let him speak, but then said severely: "It is true that I am in love with her, that I feel it, that I seek her out, that I speak of her eagerly and think of her even more; it is also true that I cannot prevent this weakness, because I am a man; but the more my quality of kingship can give me easier satisfaction, the more I must guard against scandal and sin. I forgive you this time because of your youth, but if you want me to go on loving you, never bring this matter up again." My father was so astonished the scales fell from his eyes. He saw that what he had taken for shyness was pure and triumphant virtue.

[1] She was a lady in waiting to Anne of Austria, the wife of Louis XIII.

SAINT-SIMON'S BIRTH AND EARLY LIFE (1691)

I was born during the night of the 15th to the 16th of January, 1675, the son of Claude, duc de Saint-Simon and peer of France, and his second wife, Charlotte de l'Aubespine, and was the only child of that bed. I bore the title of Vidame of Chartres[1] and was brought up with great care and application. My mother, who was very virtuous and had a great deal of common sense and a methodical mind, took continuous pains to shape my mind and body. She feared that I would become one of those young men who think their fortune is made and who are their own masters too soon. My father, who was born in 1606, could not have lived long enough to prevent such a mishap. My mother endlessly repeated the urgent need for a young man to prove his true value when he entered the world alone and on his own. This was especially true for a young man who was the son of a favorite of Louis XIII, all of whose friends were dead or unable to help, and of a mother who had been brought up by the old duchesse d'Angoulême and who had never had friends her own age. The flaws she found in all my relatives, uncles, aunts, and cousins, left me to myself and increased my desire to do well without help or favoritism. . . .

At the same time, she undertook to boost my morale and make me realize that I would be able to overcome these difficult handicaps. She succeeded in giving me a great desire to do so. My lack of inclination for study and for sciences did not help. But my hostility toward studies was balanced by a taste for reading and history, so that I wished to make something of myself through the imitation of historical examples. I have often thought that if I had wasted less time on other subjects and been allowed to study history more seriously I could have done something with it.

[1] A Vidame (vice-domini) was a secular assistant to the bishop. His main job was to administer the bishop's lands but it soon became an honorary title.

This reading of history which I undertook, especially of the memoirs which have appeared since the death of Francis I, led to the ambition to write my own memoirs about events I would witness and perhaps take part in, so that I could inform myself on the affairs of my time.

I immediately recognized the drawbacks of such a project; but I felt that a firm resolution to keep the whole thing secret was a sufficient remedy. Thus I began my memoirs in July 1694 when I was camp master of a cavalry regiment that bore my name. It was the Gimsheim camp on the Old Rhine, and the army was commanded by the maréchal duc de Lorge.

In 1691 I was in my last year of secondary school and had also begun to go to the Mesmon and Rochefort riding academy. I was getting very bored with studies and teachers, and wanted to enter military service. The King himself had organized the siege of Mons on the first day of spring, and almost all the young men of my age had gone there for their first campaign. What piqued me most was that M. le duc de Chartres[2] was already there. Although I was eight months his junior we had been brought up together and friendship united us, if the expression may be used to describe a bond between two young men of such unequal rank. Thus I resolved to pull myself from childhood, and will not mention the ruses I used to succeed. I went to my mother but saw that she did not take me seriously; I appealed to my father, and convinced him that the King would rest next year after laying an important siege this year. I outwitted my mother, who only discovered my scheme as I was about to leave and I had made my father promise not to let himself be influenced by her.

The King had stiffened recruitment conditions so that only princes of the blood and royal bastards were exempt from spending the first year of service in one of his two companies of musketeers. In the company of their choice, recruits learned to obey. Then they could command a company of cavalry or become junior officers in the King's infantry regiment, which he liked and respected above all the others, before being granted permission to purchase their own cavalry or infantry regiment. My father took me to Versailles, which he had not visited since

[2] Later to become Philippe d'Orléans and Regent after the death of Louis XIV. He was the son of Monsieur, the King's brother.

his great sickness at Blaye. . . . He bowed to the King and said
I was a volunteer for the musketeers. It was on the feast day of
Saint-Simon Saint Jude, at half past twelve, as the King was leav-
ing his Council.

His Majesty honored my father by embracing him three times.
They discussed me, and the King, finding me small and frail, said
I seemed awfully young. My father rejoined that I would serve
him all the longer. . . .

Rainstorms were the most serious misfortune of the siege.
Trenches lined with brushwood were the only way of passing
between the King's tents but they had to be dug every day because they washed out. The trenches were full of water and mud,
and the camps and quarters were inaccessible. Sometimes it took
three days to move a cannon from one battery to the other. Carts
were useless, and bombs and cannonballs had to be carried on the
backs of horses and mules, without which all transportation
would have been impossible. The lack of paths also prevented the
army of M. de Luxembourg from using its carriages. His army
was perishing because it had no grain. The only remedy that could
be found was an order from the King to his household to send
a daily detachment of men carrying bags of grain to a village
where they could be picked up and counted by M. de Luxembourg's men. This task was given the King's household even
though it had had no rest during the siege, had carried brushwood, mounted the guard, and performed other services. The
cavalry also was in continuous service and was reduced to using
leaves for fodder.

But the example of the cavalry did not inspire the King's household, which was accustomed to all kinds of distinctions. There
were bitter complaints. The King insisted and said he would be
obeyed. It had to be done. The first day, a detachment of foot
guards and light cavalry arrived at the grain depot early in the
morning. They began to grumble, grew more and more excited,
and finally threw down the bags and refused to carry them. Cres-
nay, in whose brigade I was serving, had asked me very courte-
ously if I would agree to go along with the grain detachment, or
if I would rather carry out other duties. I chose the grain, because
it was being talked about and I felt I could further my interests.

I arrived with a detachment of musketeers in the midst of the red troops' refusal.[3]

I picked up a bag of grain and loaded it in front of them. Marin, a cavalry brigadier and a lieutenant of the King's guards who was there to supervise the loading, saw me. Angered by the disobedience of his troops, he pointed me out, gave my name, and shouted that since I did not feel the task was beneath me, soldiers and horsemen would be neither sullied nor dishonored by imitating me. His words and his severe mien had such prompt results that, without a word of protest, the men vied with each other to load the bags; and from that day, the matter caused not the slightest difficulty. After he had supervised the loading, Marin reported the incident and the effect of my example to the King. Thanks to this, the King addressed several obliging remarks to me and, during the rest of the siege, he went out of his way to say something nice every time he saw me. I was all the more grateful to Marin, since I did not know him at all. . . .

Two days after the enemy garrison had left the siege, the King joined the ladies at Dinant and returned with them to Versailles. I had been hoping that Monseigneur would continue the campaign and that I could join the detachment of musketeers that was to remain with him. It was not without regret that I started on the road to Paris with everyone else. The court made a stop over at Marienbourg, protected by the musketeers. I had struck up a close friendship with the comte de Coëtquen, who was in my company. He was infinitely cultivated and charming, and his great wit and kindness made his company most agreeable. However, he was rather peculiar and very lazy. His father was dead, and he was very rich through his mother, who was from Saint-Malo. That evening at Marienbourg he invited several of us to supper. I arrived at his tent early and found him lying on his bed. I playfully chased him from the bed, and lay down in his place, in front of several other guests and officers. He jokingly took his rifle, which he thought was unloaded, and aimed it at me. Imagine the surprise when it fired! Luckily for me, I was at that moment lying flat on the bed. Three bullets passed an inch over my head, and as the rifle had been aimed a bit high, these same

[3] The King's guards wore red uniforms.

bullets whistled by two governors who were strolling behind the tent.

The thought of what could have happened made Coëtquen ill. It was all we could do to bring him around and it took him several days to get over it. The moral of the story is that one should never play with firearms.

THE MARRIAGE OF SAINT-SIMON (1695)

My wedding day was approaching. The year before, the maréchal de Lorge's eldest daughter had been under consideration by me. The matter had been dropped almost instantly, but on both sides there was a strong wish to renew conversations. . . . The kindness and integrity of the maréchal de Lorges, so genuine but so rare, gave me an extreme desire to marry into his family, where I felt I could find everything I lacked to lead and sustain me and where I could live agreeably among many illustrious members of a lovable family. . . .

They had an only son, who was twelve years old and whom they loved to distraction, and five daughters. The two eldest, who had spent their childhood with the Benedictine sisters in Conflans (where the sister of their grandmother Mme. Frémont was prioress), had for the last two or three years been brought up with their grandmother, whose house communicated with that of the rest of the de Lorge family. The eldest was seventeen, the other fifteen, and their grandmother never lost sight of them. . . .

The maréchal and the grandparents secretly preferred Mlle. de Lorge; the maréchale's preferences went to Mlle. de Quintin, the younger daughter, and if she had had her way she would have sent the elder to the convent to give her favorite a better chance for marriage. The latter was dark, with beautiful eyes; the other was blond, with a perfect complexion and figure, a very agreeable face, an extremely noble and modest air, and something majestic that stemmed from virtue and natural sweetness. As soon as I had seen them both, that was the one I liked best, and the one I hoped would make my life's happiness. There was no comparison in my mind, and she has since been the complete and only source of my happiness. As she has become my wife, I will abstain from saying further here, except that she has gone infinitely beyond all that I had been promised and hoped for.

Things were still secret but had advanced to the point where I felt I could confide in Phelypeaux, who displayed apparent friendship and curiosity and was Bignon's[1] nephew.

As soon as he learned my secret he ran to Paris to tell the duchesse de Bracciano. I went to see her upon arriving and was surprised to find her trying to wheedle the news of my marriage out of me by every conceivable means. I parried her questions with banter, but she finally named names to show me that she knew. I realized I had been betrayed, but I held fast, neither confirming nor denying. I fell back on the argument that she was doing such a good job of marrying me that I could only hope it was true. She and her two nieces reproached me for my lack of confidence in them, and she took me aside two or three times, the better to get it out of me. I saw that she was maneuvering to break off the marriage, either by having me give away the secret, which the maréchal was bent on keeping, or by having me formally deny it, a lie which could have caused trouble.

However, I did not give her satisfaction, and she could get nothing out of me. I ended this painful visit outraged at Phelypeaux. Asking for an explanation or blaming his treason would have been going too far with a man of his profession and condition. I decided to forget the matter and hold my tongue, but to consider him henceforth with the reserve that treason merits. I later had the pleasure of hearing Mme. de Bracciano admit her foolish hope, and we had a good laugh over it.

Everything being agreed and arranged, the maréchal de Lorge went to the King for both of us, so we would not attract attention. The King was kind enough to tell him he could not do better, and spoke very obligingly of me. . . . On the Thursday before Palm Sunday, we signed the marriage articles at the Hôtel de Lorge and brought the contract to the King two days later. I was spending all my evenings at the Hôtel de Lorge, but the marriage was broken off abruptly because of something in the

[1] Bignon had served as counsel for the financial details of the marriage.

contract that had been badly explained and which each side insisted on interpreting in its own way. Fortunately, as we were stubbornly confronting positions, d'Auneuil returned from a trip to the country and straightened things out at his own expense. He was president of the court of appeals and the only brother of the maréchal de Lorge. I must pay him the compliment of saying that I have remained profoundly grateful. Thus, God uses unexpected means to bring about his will. Very little leaked out concerning this misadventure, and the marriage took place at the Hôtel de Lorge on April 8, which I consider the happiest day of my life, and with good reason.

My mother behaved like the best mother in the world. On the Thursday before Low Sunday, we went to the Hôtel de Lorge at seven in the evening and signed the contract. A great feast was served for close relatives of both families, and at midnight the parish priest of Saint-Roch said mass and married us in the Lorge's private chapel. The day before, my mother had sent 40,000 pounds' worth of gems to Mlle. de Lorge and I had sent 600 louis in a basket brimming with all the presents one gives on these occasions.

We slept in the main apartment of the Hôtel de Lorge. The following day, M. d'Auneuil, who was staying across from us, gave a great dinner in our honor. After that the bride received all of France at her bedside, where duty and curiosity attracted the crowds; and the first to come was the duchesse de Bracciano with her two nieces. My mother was still in her second mourning and her apartment was done in black and gray, so that we preferred to receive at the Hôtel de Lorge. After these visits, to which we devoted a day, we went to Versailles. That evening, the King deigned to visit the bride in Mme. de Maintenon's quarters, where my mother and hers did the presentations. On the way there, the King bantered with me, and he was kind enough to receive them with a great deal of praise and distinction. From there, they went to supper, where the new duchesse took her stool.[2] Arriving at table, the King told her: "Madam, will you please sit down." The King's napkin was unfolded, and when he saw all the duchesses and princesses still standing, he rose in his

---

[2] Duchesses had the right to sit on a stool in the presence of the King. It was a jealously guarded distinction.

chair and told Mme. de Saint-Simon: "Madam, I have already asked you to sit." And all those who had the right sat down, with Mme. de Saint-Simon between my mother and hers. The next day she received all the court at her bedside in the apartment of the princesse d'Arpajon, which was more convenient because it was on the ground floor. M. le maréchal de Lorge and I only went there for royal visits. The following day they went to Saint-Germain and Paris, where I received the entire party for a great evening banquet. The next day I gave a small supper for those of my father's friends who were still alive. I had taken care to tell them about my marriage before it was made public, and I carefully kept up my friendship with them until their deaths.

Saint-Simon Unearths a Plot (1698)

Having gone one morning to pay my court to the King at Meudon, where courtiers were free to go, I chanced after the King's rising to take a seat in a room called Madame's chamber, which the King crossed on his way to mass. It happened that hanging in that room was the tapestry of an audience dealing with the Pisa treaty, representing those who had attended. I noticed that the comte de Soissons and the comte d'Harcourt were represented wearing hats. I cried out at this mistake: Chamlay, who was sitting near me, said that M. de Savoie and de Lorraine always wore hats at audiences. I agreed, but explained the difference.[1] I knew I was dealing either with the foolishness of those who had designed the tapestry or with the ruse of princes, who were setting a precedent with the help of a tapestry. I mentioned this to the duc de Chaulnes (who was still in good health), the duc de Chevreuse, the duc de Coislin, and others who had been at the

---

[1] The comte de Soissons was member of a collateral branch of the princely Condé-Bourbon family, while the comte d'Harcourt was on a lower rung of the equally princely Lorraines. Saint-Simon interpreted the error in the tapestry as another conspiracy of the princes, who were forever trying to lift themselves above the peers by usurping details of rank. By having themselves represented in the tapestry with their heads covered before a Papal Legate, they were creating a precedent full of dangers to Saint-Simon.

audience. M. de Luxembourg, who was still alive and who had been very active at the audience, was also told about the mistake in the tapestry. They went to see Sainctot, who had been master of ceremonies when the audience was held. Sainctot agreed that only the Papal Legate had worn a hat at the audience and that the two counts had been bareheaded. They suggested that Sainctot should note the lie in the tapestry in his register. He tried to dismiss the matter and convince them there was no need to note it, and we shall see why later. But when he saw them getting angry, and threatening to take the matter to the King, he dared resist no longer. They all went to see Desgranges, the master of ceremonies. He showed them the register, which did not have a word on who was or was not wearing a hat. The inference was that the two counts had worn hats as they usually did, for otherwise it would have been important enough to mention. The lords could not help telling Sainctot how strongly they were moved by his treachery. He was ashamed and apologized for such a misrepresentation. He was told what to write about the tapestry in the margin of the register, and signed it.

But this was not enough for the lords, each of whom asked Sainctot for a written certificate about the lie in the tapestry, the omission in the register, the facts of the audience, and the notes in the margin. He furnished it to them the following day with many compliments and was delighted that no more was said about the matter. All this is to show that problems of rank are in the hands of worthless persons who think they can do as they please, for whomever they wish to please, at the expense of truth and justice.

SAINT-SIMON IS RECEIVED BY PARLEMENT (1702)

That same winter I was received by Parlement. The King, when obtaining privileges for his bastards, had always begun with a de facto arrangement, followed by royal warrants, letters of patent, declarations and decrees. Thus the King, who had long since established that no peer could be received by Parlement without his permission (which he never refused), began to discourage the presentation of peers under twenty-five. Through this usage which he could later validate by decree, he created an age difference between the presentation of his bastards and the peers. I knew this, and had feigned neglience to put off my reception for more than a year after my twenty-fifth birthday. Finally I went to see the royal princes, the bastards, and Harlay, the First President, who overwhelmed me with compliments. M. du Maine asked for the date of my reception several times; then, with an expression of joy contained by courtesy and modesty, he said: "I would hate to miss it; it will be a great honor for me to attend, and I am too touched that you are willing to have me to miss it." And with a thousand compliments he saw me to the garden (it was at Marly, during one of the trips on which I was invited). The answers of the comte de Toulouse and M. de Vendôme were plainer, but they seemed no less pleased, nor less courteous or attentive to their duties than M. du Maine. Since the cardinal de Noailles had received the purple, he no longer came to Parlement, where he had to sit according to the seniority of his peerage. I asked him to come during one of his public audiences. "But you know I no longer have a seat," he said. "And I, sir," I replied, "who know you have a very fine seat, beg you to use it during my reception." He began to smile, and so did I: We got along nicely together. Then he saw me to the head of the stairs, with both of us passing side by side through the wide-open doors.[1]

Dongois, who was Parlement's chief clerk, was very well known and often sought out because of his knowledge and capacities in parliamentary affairs. I knew him well, and discussed the procedural details of my reception with him. He was a fine and obliging man, but this did not prevent him from setting three traps for me; I should not have expected less from a clerk. But I saw through all three and was able to avoid them. He told me I should dress all in black without gold braid out of respect for the Parlement; that my coat should not be longer than my jerkin out of respect for the princes of the blood, who wore short coats; and that out of respect for the First President, I should pay him a thank-you visit on the morning after my reception, in parlia-

[1] It was a great honor for a duke to have both panels of a cardinal's doors opened for him.

mentary dress. He did not tell me outright to do these three things, but dropped a great many hints. I held my tongue, and did exactly the opposite. Through my own experience, I was able to warn those who were received after me, and they also avoided the traps. Let me add in passing that tricks such as these have done great harm to the dukes, and that such repeated deviousness is more than surprising.

SAINT-SIMON QUITS THE ARMY (1702)

There were sweeping but very strange reforms after the Peace of Ryswick. The King left Barbezieux[1] in command despite his youth and impetuousness, and disregarded the merit of the royal regiments (particularly the cavalry) and the quality of his officers. I did not know him at all. My regiment was disbanded, and what was left of it was given to Duras' royal regiment, which was normal procedure. My company was incorporated in the company of Duras' brother-in-law, the comte d'Uzés, whom Duras sought to please. My lot was that of many others, but I never got over it. The colonels of disbanded companies were sent to other regiments and I wound up in Saint-Mauris' regiment. He was a gentleman from Franche-Comté whom I had never seen before in my life and whose brother was a highly respected lieutenant general. Soon after, a priggish rule which had nothing to do with the realities of military service established two months a year of duty in the field with one's regiment. It seemed most uncivilized to me, but nonetheless I was prepared to obey. However, I had fallen victim to various ailments and had been advised to try the soapstone mineral waters at Plombières, so I requested permission to go there. For three years, I spent my two-month periods there, in exile from a regiment where I knew no one, where I had no troops, and where there was nothing for me to do.

[1] Louis-François Le Tellier, marquis de Barbezieux and son of Louvois (1668-1701), was secretary of state for war. The Peace of Ryswick, ending the Augsburg coalition, took place in 1697.

This did not appear to annoy the King. I often went to Marly and he sometimes spoke to me, which was a very deliberate and calculated sign. In a word, he treated me well, and better than others of my age and rank. Several colonels who were my juniors were given commands, which seemed only reasonable, considering their time of service. Rumors of a general promotion did not stir me, for these were times when dignity and birth counted for nothing and special promotions were granted only for actions in the field.

I did not have enough seniority to dream of becoming a brigadier. My aim was to serve at the head of a regiment, since war was about to begin, and it would be humiliating to start it as aide-de-camp to Saint-Mauris, and without any troops to command. After all, on returning from the Neerwinden campaign, I had been picked to command a regiment, I had put it into shape, and I dare say I commanded it with commendable diligence during the four campaigns which ended that war. When the new promotions were made public, their large number surprised everyone. There had never been a list like it, not by a long shot. I avidly went down the list of cavalry brigadiers to see whether my turn might come soon. I was startled to find that five of my juniors had been named brigadiers. Their names have remained engraved on my memory: They were d'Ourches, Vendeuil, Streiff, the comte d'Ayen, and Ruffey. It is difficult to feel more put out than I did. The confused equalitarianism in the order of promotions was humiliating enough. But I found the favoritism for the comte d'Ayen (despite the nepotism involved in his case)[2] and the four others unbearable. I held my tongue, not wanting to act out of anger. M. le maréchal de Lorge[3] was outraged for himself and for me; his brother, the maréchal de Duras, was no less outraged, for it was an affront to them both, and he had become my friend (he was a friendly sort). Both of them suggested that I quit the army. My resentment gave me a great desire to do so. But I was forcefully held back by the thought of my youth, the war about to start, the rewards of a military career, the fear of idleness, the pain of hearing others talk of war each summer, the departures, and the promotions granted to distinguished soldiers who rise in

---

[2] The comte d'Ayen was a nephew of Mme. de Maintenon by marriage.
[3] Saint-Simon's father-in-law.

the ranks and make a reputation for themselves. I spent two months in this quandary, determined to leave the army each morning, but unable to keep my resolve through the day. . . .

Finally I made up my mind, and when the time came for action, I followed the advice of my friends: I did not let a single word of discontent escape my lips, allowing public discussion of my omission (particularly among military men) to speak for me. The King's anger was inevitable and I was expecting it. Dare I say that I was not indifferent to it? He was offended when one ceased to serve him, particularly if one was of distinguished birth: He called it quitting. But to leave his service as the result of an injustice stung him to the quick, and he always found a way to get even. The persons who advised me did not compare the consequences of leaving his service, which at my age could not last forever, and the shame and disgust of continuing to serve. They believed however that respect and caution should inspire me to every consideration I could devise. I wrote a brief letter to the King in which there were no complaints, not the slightest mention of the promotion list or the regiment, and not a word about discontent. I expressed my distress at being forced to leave his service because of bad health and added that only my assiduous presence at his side and the honor of seeing him and attending his court continuously would console me. My letter was approved and I presented it to him myself at the door of his study as he was returning from mass on the Tuesday of Holy Week. Then I went to see Chamillart,[4] whom I had never met. He was on his way to the Council, and I repeated the substance of my letter to him, without adding anything that could smack of ill feeling. Then I left for Paris. I had asked some of my friends to try and find out the King's reaction to my letter. I stayed eight days in Paris and waited until Easter Tuesday to return to Versailles. I learned from the Chancellor[5] that after the Council had been called on Holy Tuesday, he went into the King's study and saw the King reading my letter. The King called over Chamillart and spoke to him in an aside. I know that he told Chamillart heatedly: "Well,

[4] Michel Chamillart was then secretary of war.
[5] Louis II Phelypeaux, comte de Pontchartrain, was Chancellor from 1699 to 1714.

sir, here is another quitter!" He then read every word of the letter to Chamillart. Apart from that, I was not told of any other mention of my letter.

It was on Easter Tuesday, after his supper, that I appeared before the King for the first time since my letter. I would hesitate to repeat the following trifle were it not characteristic of the King in these circumstances. Although the room where he undressed was well lit, the chaplain of the day held a lighted candlestick during the evening prayer, then gave it to the first valet of the chamber, who carried it before the King. The King glanced all around him and called the name of one of those present, to whom the first valet of the chamber handed the candlestick. This was a highly regarded favor and distinction, for the King knew how to give value to nothings. He only gave the candlestick to the most distinguished persons in dignity and birth, and extremely rarely to those whose age or function made up for their lesser birth. He often gave it to me, and seldom to ambassadors, except for the Nuncio and, in later years, the Spanish ambassador. One removed one's glove, advanced, and held the candlestick while the King got into bed, which did not take long. The candlestick was then returned to the first valet of the chamber, who gave it to someone else of his own choice who was allowed to remain with the King. I had purposely drawn back, and everyone including myself was very surprised when I was named. Since then, I have had it almost as often as before. There were others distinguished enough to receive the candlestick, but the King was so vexed at my behavior he did not want to show it. For the next three years, that was all I got from him. He used the most minor incidents, not to mention more important occasions, to make me feel his disfavor. He never spoke to me any more. His glance fell on me only by accident.

SAINT-SIMON'S FIRST AUDIENCE
WITH THE KING [1] (1699)

I went to see M. de La Rochefaucauld, who urged me to speak
to the King at his bedtime. "I know him well," he told me. "Speak
fearlessly, but respectfully, and touch only on your affair, do not
discuss the dukes, and leave the Rohan matter to M. de Rohan.[2]
Believe me, people like you should speak for themselves. Your
openness and modesty will please the King; he will like your
attitude." I demurred, and he insisted. I wanted to see whether
his advice came from the heart, and I suggested we immediately
go see M. le maréchal de Lorge, whom I would ask to speak for
me. "Once again, don't do it," replied the duke, "for it will do
you no good; speak for yourself. If I get a chance at his bedtime,
I will put in a word for you." This last remark persuaded me.

I went to the King's apartments, and wanted to go in with the
duc de Noailles, who had just taken the King's orders for the
morrow. He said it would be better if we did not go in together,
and suggested that I try at the King's bedtime. After being informed by Noailles, Boufflers agreed to the plan and promised
not to go in to take the orders until I had spoken. I stood near
the sitting-room fireplace, and followed the King when he went
to get undressed. As he stood with his back to the hearth, saying
good night as usual to all those who did not have full access, and

---

[1] Saint-Simon saw the King privately only three times in his life. This
was the first, briefest, and most impromptu occasion. Saint-Simon found
out that Monsieur le Grand (Louis de Lorraine) had complained to the
King that Mme. de Saint-Simon had taken the place of his wife, the comtesse d'Armagnac, at an audience given by the duchesse de Bourgogne for
the Earl of Jersey. The truth was that Mme. de Saint-Simon was pregnant
and sat at the first empty place she could find because she was feeling
uncomfortable. She willingly gave up the seat to the comtesse d'Armagnac
when the latter arrived. Saint-Simon resolved to see the King that same
day to explain the situation and absolve himself of "the Lorraines' base
slander."

[2] M. de Rohan's wife had been bodily unlodged from her rightful seat
by the princesse d'Harcourt at the same audience.

waiting to give his orders, I went up to him, and he stooped to listen while staring at me fixedly.[8]

I told him I had just learned that M. le Grand had complained to him about Mme. de Saint-Simon, that nothing meant more to me than his respect and approval, and that I begged him to allow me to tell him the facts. I immediately began to give him the details, without omitting a single one. Following the advice of M. de La Rochefoucauld, I held myself to a simple and true report of the event, which constituted a complete denial, without adding any complaints about the Lorraines or M. le Grand. The King did not interrupt me once all the time I was speaking. When I had finished, he said with a gracious and contented air: "That is fine, Sir, there is nothing in it," and smiled and nodded as I was about to leave. But after a few steps I came near the King in a lively way and assured him that every last word I had told him was true; I received the same reply.

The hour I had chosen to talk to the King was so unusual, and the spectators had found my discourse so long, so animated, and so well received, that they were most curious to learn what had prompted it, although most of them guessed it had to do with what had happened that morning. There were a great many courtiers waiting in the antechambers.

THE OFFERTORY (1703)

An affair in which I had a prominent part ended the year. On the several important holidays when the King went to high mass and vespers, a lady of the court would take up a collection for the poor. The Queen, or the Dauphine if there was no queen, appointed someone for each occasion. In the interval between dauphines, the duty fell to Mme. de Maintenon. The maids of honor of the Queen or the Dauphine were always chosen, but after these posts were done away with, young ladies of the court were assigned, as I have just explained.

[8] The King was five feet four inches tall, and this stooping does not say much for Saint-Simon's height.

The house of Lorraine, whose rank goes back to the time of the League[1] and has been sustained and increased by constant industry and attention, imperceptibly avoided collection duty to create a distinction. By claiming exemption, they sought assimilation with the princes of the blood, as they did also through marriage. Their example was imitated by other houses to whom the King had granted equal rank.[2] For a long time, no one paid attention to the maneuver. Finally, it was noticed by the duchesse de Noailles, her daughter the duchesse de Guiche, the maréchale de Boufflers, and several others, who discussed it among themselves and with me. On the day of the Immaculate Conception, when there was no high mass, Mme. de Saint-Simon attended the King's vespers. Mme. la duchesse de Bourgogne had forgotten to name anyone for offertory and threw the collection bag at Mme. de Saint-Simon at the last minute. She agreed, for we did not yet realize that the princesses were trying to gain some advantage. After I had been advised, I promised myself that the duchesses would become just as devious as the princesses in this matter until something was done to restore equality. The duchesse de Noailles discussed the matter with the duchesse du Lude,[3] who was spineless and frightened of her own shadow and who shrugged the whole thing off. There was always some new, ignorant, or base duchesse to be found from time to time for the offertory. Finally, egged on by the duchesse de Noailles, the duchesse du Lude mentioned the matter to the duchesse de Bourgogne, who decided to test the princesses. On the next holiday, she notified Mme. de Montbazon that she had been picked. She was the young and beautiful daughter of M. de Bouillon, attended court assiduously, and was a good choice to prepare the way for the others. She was in Paris, where the ladies customarily went before holidays. She excused herself on account of illness, took to her bed half a day, then resumed her normal occupations. This was proof of the princesses' plot. Neither the duchesse du Lude nor the duchesse de Bourgogne dared act, although the latter felt annoyed. But the result was that no duchesse now wanted or

[1] The Holy League, founded in 1576 to suppress Protestantism in France.
[2] The house of Lorraine and several others had the rank of foreign princes.
[3] The duchesse du Lude was a lady in waiting of the duchesse de Bourgogne.

dared to take the collection bag. This soon became apparent to all ladies of real quality. They sensed that soon the offertory would be left to them, and began to avoid it. The collection bag fell into all sorts of hands, and sometimes no one could be found to take it. Things went so far that the King grew angry and almost made Mme. la duchesse de Bourgogne take the bag herself. I was warned by the ladies of the palace, who tried to keep me from leaving for Paris for the holiday, saying that I was still in the King's disfavor for having left his service and that storm clouds were gathering over my head. I was still in the situation I have described, I was never invited at Marly, and these ladies tried to flatter me into staying by telling me I could improve my position. I agreed on condition that my wife would not be named to take the bag, but since I could not obtain this guarantee, we left for Paris.

The maréchale de Coeuvres refused collection duty because she was a Spanish grandee. In her place, the duchesse de Noailles, her mother, offered her daughter-in-law, the comtesse d'Ayen. On another holiday, Chamillart's two daughters, the duchesses de La Feuillade and de Quintin-Lorge, who happened to be at Versailles, both refused when they were notified. After that, the bubble burst. Weary of these maneuvers, the King personally ordered Monsieur le Grand to have his daughter pass the bag on New Year's Day, 1704. Monsieur le Grand, who had never forgiven me the apology demanded of the princesse d'Harcourt to the duchesse de Rohan, used the incident to his advantage and at my expense.

I was given an early warning the next day by the comtesse de Roucy, who had been told the following by Mme. la duchesse de Bourgogne, an eyewitness: The King had told Mme. de Maintenon in an angry voice that he was very displeased with the dukes, whom he found less obedient than the princes, and that while all the duchesses refused the collection, he had only to propose it to M. le Grand for his daughter and she accepted. He added that there were two or three dukes he particularly had in mind. Mme. la duchesse de Bourgogne would not give her any names, but she did whisper the names to Mme. de Dangeau, who a moment later warned me to be careful because a storm was about to break over my head. I was with the Chancellor when I was given this advice, and neither of us had any doubt that I was one of the three mentioned by the King. I explained what had happened and asked for his advice. He told me to wait so that I would not act heedlessly. That evening, Mme. Chamillart told me the King had spoken to her husband about the matter in bitter terms. I had kept them informed of the affair from the beginning, and it was they who had prevailed on their daughters the duchesses to refuse the bag. I saw Chamillart early the next morning. He told me that the night before in Mme. de Maintenon's rooms, the King had not even given him a chance to open his satchel, but had angrily asked him what he thought of the dukes who were less obedient than the princes. The King also said that Mlle. d'Armagnac had accepted collection duty. Chamillart replied that he had only learned of all this the day before, since such matters seldom reached his cabinet. He added that the dukes were most unhappy at being condemned for something they would have been eager to do had they been asked, while the princes were most happy that the request had gone to Monsieur le Grand. The King muttered that it was very strange that since I had left his service, my only concern seemed to be to study rank and make charges against everyone. He said I was the originator of this affair and that if he had his way he would send me so far away it would be a long time before I would ever bother him again. Chamillart replied that the reason I inspected things more closely than others was that I had greater capacities and knowledge than others, and that since a peer's dignity came from the king's, His Majesty should be grateful to me for upholding it.

Then he added with a soothing smile that everyone knew he could send people wherever he pleased, but that it was hardly worth using his power when a word was enough to get what he wanted, and if he did not already have it, it was only because the word had not been uttered. The King was not appeased and replied that what annoyed him most was the refusal of Chamillart's sons-in-laws and daughters, and particularly the youngest,[4] apparently at my instigation. Chamillart replied that one of his sons-in-law had been absent at the time, and that the other had only asked his wife to conform to what the others were doing. The King was not convinced, and continued to grumble angrily

4 The duchesse de Quintin-Lorge.

before getting back to work. I thanked Chamillart for having spoken so well of the dukes in general and of me in particular. He advised me to have a word with the King at the earliest opportunity about the dukes, the collection, and myself, since the King was displeased. . . . It was no small thing at my age, and being on such bad terms with the King, to seek him out for an audience. I was unaccustomed to acting without the advice of the duc de Beauvillier. But Mme. de Saint-Simon was against my consulting him, for she was sure he would advise me to write to the King instead of talking to him, which would be less graceful and less forceful. She added that a letter cannot conduct a conversation, and that any advice contrary to that I had already received would serve only to perplex me. I agreed, and went to wait for the King to finish lunch and go into his study, when I asked if I could follow him inside. He silently beckoned me in, and sat in the embrasure of the window. As I was about to speak, Fagon and other members of the household passed by. I waited until I was alone with the King. Then I told him I had heard he was displeased with me because of the offertory, but that I had so great a desire to please him that I could not but beg him to allow me to explain my behavior. At this introductory plea, he assumed a severe air, but did not reply. "It is true, Sire," I continued, "that since the princesses have refused the bag, I have avoided it for Mme. de Saint-Simon. I wanted the duchesses to avoid it too, and I kept some of them from accepting because I did not think it was in the best interests of Your Majesty."

"But to refuse the duchesse de Bourgogne," replied the King in an angry and masterful tone, "is a lack of respect. It is like refusing me."

I replied that I did not think Mme. la duchesse de Bourgogne had anything to do with naming the ladies for the offertory and that the duchesse du Lude or the first lady of the palace did the choosing. "But, Sir," interrupted the King again, and with the same haughty and irascible air, "you have held discourses." "No, Sire," I said, "I have held none." "What? You have held none? . . ." he continued with the same haughty air. At this point, I dared to interrupt him, and drowning out his voice, I said: "No, Sire, I tell you, and if I had held discourses I would admit it to Your Majesty just as I have admitted that I made my wife refuse the bag and prevented other duchesses from accepting it. I have always had reason to believe that since Your Majesty did not comment on the matter, you ignored what was happening, or that knowing, you did not care. I urgently beg you to believe that had the dukes and particularly myself detected in Your Majesty the slightest wish to have the duchesses accept the collection, they would have accepted eagerly on every holiday, and especially Mme. de Saint-Simon. And if that had not been sufficient demonstration of my desire to please you, I would have taken up the collection myself with a dish like a village churchwarden. But, Sire," I continued, "can Your Majesty imagine that we would consider any duty in your presence as beneath us, and particularly a duty that duchesses and princesses fulfill daily and gladly in the parishes and convents of Paris? Yet it is true, Sire, that the princes are so busy turning everything to their advantage that they have made us suspicious, particularly since they refused the bag." "But they did not refuse it," the King said in a softer tone, "they were not picked for it." "They refused it, Sire," I repeated with emphasis, "not the Lorraines but the others (and I named Mme. de Montbazon). The duchesse du Lude must have mentioned it to Your Majesty, and as a result we took our stand. But since we know how much Your Majesty dislikes all discussions and decisions, we thought we could keep the princes in their place by avoiding collection duty. As I have already had the honor of informing Your Majesty, we were convinced that Your Majesty either did not know or did not care about the matter, for you had not commented on it." "Oh well! Sir," replied the King in a soft and low voice, "this will not recur, for I have asked Monsieur le Grand to appoint his daughter for the New Year's Day collection, and I am pleased that she will give the good example, because of my friendship for her father." Looking the King straight in the eye, I begged him again in my name and in the name of all the dukes to believe that there were none more dutiful or more convinced (and myself more than anyone else) that our dignities came from his and that our persons were showered with his blessings. I added that as king and benefactor of us all, he was the absolute ruler of our dignities, which he could increase or diminish as something entirely his own. Then, with a gracious, kind, and familiar air, the King said that was the way to think and speak, that he was pleased with me, and other such sincere amiabilities. I seized the opportunity to tell him I could not disguise my pain at seeing that while I only wanted to serve him I was the constant victim of evil misrepresentations. I added that I could not forgive those responsible and that I could not help suspecting Monsieur le Grand. "He has never forgiven me the affair of the princesse d'Harcourt," I added, "which Your Majesty remembers and which I will not repeat so as not to bore you; Your Majesty realized that my report was accurate and that Monsieur le Grand's was not." From the soft, thoughtful, and open way in which the King replied that he remembered the affair, I believe he would have listened patiently to a retelling. But I did not feel it was a good idea to keep him so long. I ended by pleading that he have me warned or tell me himself if he heard anything displeasing about me, a favor that would be immediately returned by my explanation, my confession, or my request for forgiveness. After I had finished speaking he remained beside me as if waiting to see whether I had anything else to say. He left with a gracious little bow after repeating that everything was fine and that he was pleased with me.

SAINT-SIMON IS ALMOST NAMED AMBASSADOR TO ROME (1706)

The King, weary of fending off office seekers bent on a dukedom, cut Torcy short as he was about to read the dispatches from Rome. He told the ministers they should choose an ambassador to Rome, that he wanted a duke, and that they should go down the list to see who was suitable. He read the names from a little almanac, starting with M. d'Uzès.[1] He soon reached my name, without having stopped at any other. At my name, he paused and said: "What do you think of this one? He is young,[2] but he is worthy, etc." Monseigneur, who favored d'Antin, did not say a word; Msgr. le duc de Bourgogne, the Chancellor,

---

[1] The dukes were listed by seniority in title, not alphabetically.
[2] Saint-Simon was then thirty-one years old.

and M. de Beauvillier supported me; Torcy said there was merit in their advice but proposed they should continue down the list; Chamillart opined that no better candidate could be found. The King shut his almanach and said there was no point in looking further, since he was picking me, but that he wanted the secret kept for several days until he had a chance to tell me. The matter was no more controversial or drawn out than that.

Beauvillier and Chamillart separately examined my debts and revenue (along with Mme. de Saint-Simon, who showed them my records), and estimated what the expenses and allowance of an ambassador would be. Both advised me to accept; Beauvillier, because it happened that I could accept the embassy without ruin and that if I refused it the King would never forgive me, particularly since I had left his service. He would look upon me as a sluggard who refuses to do anything, he would make his displeasure felt through every manner of disdain, he would turn me down whenever I made a request, and he would thus ruin my present and future affairs far more effectively than ever could my failure as an ambassador. . . .

Defeated by their arguments, I finally accepted, that is, I made the resolution to accept, and I admit that I did it with pleasure. Mme. de Saint-Simon, wiser and more cautious, let herself be persuaded, but was grieved at having to leave her family. I cannot refuse myself the pleasure of repeating here what these three ministers[3] told me separately and without any prompting about a woman who was then twenty-seven but was known to them because they often advised us on matters of family and court (including this one).

All three advised me strongly never to keep secrets from her in my embassy affairs, always to have her at my side while reading or drafting dispatches, and to consult her with deference on everything. Rarely have I been so receptive to advice, and I can state that I was worthy of it. My life continued afterward as though nothing had been said, although she knew of our conversations. I had no occasion to follow the advice in Rome, since I did not go there; but I had long been faithful to it and I con-

[3] The three, among Saint-Simon's most steadfast friends, were: the duc de Beauvillier, first gentleman of the King's wardrobe; Michel Chamillart, secretary of state for war; and the Chancellor, the comte de Pontchartrain.

tinued all my life to tell her everything. I must also be allowed to say this: I never found counsel so wise, so judicious, and so useful, and I admit with pleasure that she kept me from many mishaps, great and small. I took her help without reserve in all things, and found in it an infinite advantage in the conduct of my affairs, which were not unimportant in the King's late years and all through the Regency. What a sweet and rare contrast to the useless and incompetent women whom ambassadors are discouraged from taking with them or confiding in, and whose preoccupations are extravagance and rank; what an even greater contrast to the rare capable women who throw their weight around: She was blessed with perfection of judgment, exquisite and just in all things, but pleasant and reserved, unself-conscious instead of vainglorious, and with unfaltering modesty, good humor, and virtue. . . .

Finally I learned that my choice as ambassador would be decided at the next Council. We were at Marly, in the same pavilion as Chamillart. I asked him to come and see me before retiring when he returned from the Council, so I would know what was to become of me. He arrived in Mme. de Saint-Simon's room, where we had been waiting anxiously. "You are going to be very relieved," he told me, "but I am very disappointed; the King is not sending an ambassador to Rome. The Pope has finally agreed to make the abbé de La Trémoille a cardinal, a promotion long delayed by his reluctance, and the new cardinal will be in charge of the King's affairs, in place of an ambassador." Mme. de Saint-Simon was delighted; it was as though she had foreseen the strange discredit into which the King's affairs were about to fall in Italy, the difficulties and disorder these mishaps would create for his finances, and the cruel situation to which he would inevitably have been reduced in Rome. The time I had used for reflection was an easy consolation for the loss of a flattering assignment; but I had no illusions about the harm that had been done.

D'Antin and Dangeau had been infuriated by my nomination. So had the maréchal d'Huxelles who wanted to be begged for his acceptance of my nomination so that he could get a dukedom in exchange and who was now left empty-handed. Since there was no other way to take the wind out of the sails of a young man whose station was rising at their expense, and since they knew how suspicious the King was of knowledge and intelligence, they began to praise me excessively and applaud the King's choice, which had finally become a matter of public knowledge. M. and Mme. du Maine had never forgiven me for not going to Sceaux* and for having resisted their numerous advances, as I have explained before. I did not hide my feelings about the way the bastards had usurped their rank. They feared and resented my good fortune, and I can only attribute Mme. de Maintenon's strange aversion to me (which I only discovered much later) to M. du Maine, who was an evil-minded introvert.

Chamillart only told me about her aversion after the King's death. He said it was so powerful he often had words with her about it, and that it had long kept me from regaining the King's good graces, before the period I am now describing. When Chamillart asked her for particulars, she could find none, but made vague charges that I was a proud and ambitious troublemaker. He was never able to change or attenuate her feeling, and she helped discredit me in the eyes of the King.

SAINT-SIMON AGAIN INCURS THE KING'S WRATH (1708)

One evening after supper at Chamillart's I was chatting with five or six members of his family and La Feuillade. We were all impatient with waiting for news from Mons-en-Peule, and I listened patiently to the bragging about the battle that would take place, the victory, and the rescue, even to the designation of the day and the moment. Firm in my own convictions, I finally lost my patience and interrupted Cany to bet him four pistoles that there would be no battle, and that Lille would be taken and not rescued.[1] This strange proposal drew great outcries from those

---

* A castle built by Colbert near Paris where the bastard son of Louis XIV held his own court and tried to attract distinguished and learned men.

[1] The British army and the German imperial army, led respectively by the Duke of Marlborough and Prince Eugène de Savoie, were marching on Lille, which was held by Monseigneur the duc de Bourgogne, the grandson of Louis XIV. Saint-Simon won his bet.

present, and they barraged me with questions as to my reasons. I was careful not to give away my real reason[2] and replied impassively that such was my opinion. Eager to make their point, Cany and his father protested that, besides the ardent wishes of Vendôme and the whole army, specific and repeated rescue orders had been given. They warned me that I was throwing my four pistoles out the window, and that Cany was betting on a sure thing. I told them with the same cool self-possession, which dissembled all that was seething within me, that I was ready to believe everything they said, but that it would not make me change my mind. In a word, I said, I would not go back on the bet. They kept at me, but I held fast, and with few words. At last, they consented mockingly, and Cany thanked me for the little present I had been kind enough to give him. We each drew four pistoles from our pockets and put them in Chamillart's care. Never was a man more surprised. Clutching the eight pistoles, he led me to the other side of the room and said: "In God's name, be good enough to give me your reasons, for on my word of honor I repeat that I have given the most emphatic orders, and there is no going back on them." I argued that the enemy would make good use of lost time, and that the army would be unable to carry out the orders. . . . There was nothing less sinister than this bet and the manner in which it was made, in a home where I spent a part of nearly every evening.

When Chamillart pressed me into the corner of the room and promised to keep what I told him secret, I would only give him vague, noncommittal, and public reasons. Despite his trusted friendship and discretion, I had not wanted to explain anything, except in a tête-à-tête. I learned thanks to a sudden and very unfortunate experience that nothing could have been more unwise. The very next day, my bet was the talk of the court. One cannot live at court without enemies, and although there was nothing in me to envy, I was considered unusual for my age because I had important friends. The Lorraines could not forgive certain things I had said and many other details not worth setting down. M. du Maine, whose prodigious advances I had sidestepped,

[2] Saint-Simon was convinced that the duc de Vendôme, who had promised to rescue Lille, would fail to do so because of his rivalry with the duc de Bourgogne.

and who could not ignore my feelings about his rank, did not like me, and consequently neither did Mme. de Maintenon. I had been too outspoken during the battle of Oudenaarde to be forgiven by Vendôme's cabal. They kept up the furore about my bet. Monsieur le Duc and Madame la Duchesse joined in, because I had stopped seeing them and because of the Lussan affair, which I have already described. D'Antin, still smarting at my choice for Rome (although I never went), which he had more than made up by his recent good fortune, worked against me more than anyone else. Perhaps my laconic attitude made the guilty guess to what and to whom I imputed the forthcoming loss of Lille. In a word, the matter created a dreadful uproar. The villains went to the point of saying that I disapproved of everything, reveled in discontent, and delighted in the nation's failures. These remarks were carefully brought to the King's attention, and he was skillfully made to believe that they were founded. The reputation for intelligence and wisdom which they had foistered on me after I had been picked for Rome was artfully renewed and refreshed, so that I found myself fallen completely from the King's grace. I did not realize it until two months later, and for a long time there was nothing in the King's behavior to make me suspect it. All I could do to keep matters from getting worse was forget about the whole thing and hold my tongue.

Saint-Simon Decides to Leave the Court (1709)

I had long realized that the bishop of Chartres' warning about the way I had been slandered to the King and the impression he had derived were only too true. His change of attitude could not have been more obvious, and although I was still invited to Marly, I knew the merit was not mine.[1] I realized that the roof had fallen in while I was standing under it. I could not put my finger on the real sore spot, and was thus unable to find a remedy. I had to cope with violent and powerful enemies whom I had done

[1] Saint-Simon thought he was invited because of his wife's popularity at court. There were times when she was invited without him.

nothing to deserve, such as Monsieur le Duc and Madame la Duchesse, the members of Vendôme's cabal, and the other enemies and envious persons that abound in courts. On the other hand my friends were powerless or weakened, like Chamillart and the Chancellor, the maréchal de Boufflers and the ducs de Beauvillier and de Chevreuse, who with all their good will could do nothing to help me. A victim of spite, I decided to leave the court and abandon all that touched it. Mme. de Saint-Simon, wiser than I, advanced many reasons for staying: She said that courts change continuously and unexpectedly, that the age itself evolves, and that we depended on the court for our fortune and even our heritage. Finally we agreed to spend two years in Guyenne under the pretext of inspecting a large family estate we had never seen. Thus we could prolong our absence without shocking the King, let time go by, and eventually see what course circumstances would advise. We discussed our decision with M. de Beauvillier, who brought along M. de Chevreuse, and later with the Chancellor. They agreed once they saw they were powerless to make me remain. They advised us to announce our departure far in advance so that it would not look like spite and to keep the rumor that I had been discreetly warned to leave from spreading. I needed the King's permission for such a long and distant journey. I did not wish to see him, since I was out of favor, but La Vrillière, a great friend who administered the Guyenne among other departments, spoke on my behalf, and the King agreed.

SAINT-SIMON'S IMPORTANT AUDIENCE WITH THE KING (1710)

I went to see Mareschal,[1] whose character and attachment for me have been described elsewhere. He was one of those who urged me most strongly not to give up the game, and he had written me at La Ferté to hasten my return. The conversation soon turned to my difficult situation. The grievances against me were

[1] Georges Mareschal was made the King's chief surgeon in 1703 and was knighted in 1709.

a collection of trifles both true and false, which had been ampli-
fied and poisoned so that they were more certain to sink me than
real and serious faults. After arguing along this line, I suddenly
told him that my greatest plight was an unapproachable master,
while if I were given the chance to talk to him at leisure I could
certainly dispel all the knaveries that had blackened my reputation. I followed this with a proposal, because I knew I could
count on his friendship and good will, and I specified that he
should answer freely, and not undertake something inconvenient
or beyond his reach. The proposal was that he should in his own
good time tell the King that he had seen me terribly afflicted
because I was on bad terms with him without deserving to be;
that this was the only reason I had spent four months in the
country, where I would be still had it not been for the death of
a man essential to my affairs, which had forced my return; that
I could not rest until I had had a long and forthright talk with
him and I begged him to kindly hear me out whenever he could.
I added that refusal would be a sign there was no hope left for
me, while if I were granted an audience, this success would reveal what hope remained. Mareschal thought a while and, looking at me, said passionately: "I will do it, and in fact that is the
only thing to do. You have already spoken to him several times,
and it always pleased him: Because of this previous experience he
will not fear what you have to tell him. I cannot guarantee that
he will see you if he is really set against you; but let me handle
it in my own good time." . . .

Alone with the King, Mareschal tested his mood by mentioning a trivial personal matter. The King having replied favorably,
he mentioned that there was another matter far dearer to his
heart.

The King asked him candidly what it was, and he said he had
seen me deeply distressed at being on bad terms with him; he
took the opportunity to praise me, my attachment to the King,
and my assiduousness at court. The King, although he did
not scowl, stiffened somewhat, and replied that he had nothing against me and could not imagine why I believed the contrary. But Mareschal insisted, said there was nothing in the
world I wanted more than an audience, and that he too would
be highly pleased if I obtained one. Pressed in this manner,

the King answered, without mentioning an audience: "But what does he have to tell me? There is nothing. Of course I have heard several trifles about him, but nothing serious. Tell him to relax, and that I have nothing against him." But Mareschal insisted again, saying that without the satisfaction of an audience there could be no others for me, and pointing out that one day was as good as another, as long as I could see him alone in his cabinet. The King finally replied rather indifferently: "All right! I don't mind; let him come when he likes." Mareschal assured me he felt the King had been distant but not angry, and said he hoped I could have a quiet audience alone with him. He said I should explain myself once and for all and take all the time I liked, since I had to list and clear up in detail all the exaggerated trifles. He advised me to speak freely and forthrightly, and to mingle respect with a kind of cordiality. Finally, he said I should present myself as soon as possible, to give the King the chance to pick a time to talk to me. . . .

It was, as I have said, Friday, the third of January, and it was the fourth time I was presenting myself to the King in the hope of the audience he had promised Mareschal. I was beginning to worry because it never came. I found lunch nearly over, and stood with my back to the bedstead.[2] When he was finishing his fruit, I approached a corner of his armchair and begged him to remember that I had been given to understand he would have the graciousness to hear me. The King turned toward me and replied with an honest air: "Whenever you like. I could see you right now, but I have some business that would not leave us enough time." A moment later, he turned to me again and said: "Tomorrow morning, if you like." I replied that I was born to attend upon his hours and graciousness, and that I would have the honor of presenting myself to him on the following morning. . . .

The next morning, Saturday, the fourth of January . . . Nyert, first valet of the King's chambers, emerged from the King's study, looked around him, and called me in. Entering the study, I found the King sitting alone on the low end of the council table, which was his way of showing that he wanted a casual talk. Coming up to him, I expressed my thanks for the honor he was doing me,

[2] The King sometimes ate alone in his bedroom.

and I prolonged my compliment the better to observe his air and attentiveness: The first seemed severe, the second complete. Without waiting for a reply, I went to the heart of the matter. I told him I could no longer live in his disgrace (a term I avoided by circumlocutions so as not to shock him, but which I will use here to epitomize) without seeking to learn how I had fallen. I said he might well ask how I could judge his change of sentiment toward me, to which I would reply that having been invited to every Marly trip for four years, I had been most sensitive to the deprivation, which had disgraced me, and which had kept me from the honor of paying him my court. The King, speaking for the first time, replied with a prideful and haughty air that this marked nothing, and meant nothing. Even had I not known the meaning of the Marly deprivation, the tone of his reply did not ring true. But I had to take it at face value, and so I told him that what I had just heard was a great relief. Since he was doing me the honor of hearing me, I begged him to allow me to unburden my heart in his presence (that was the term I used) and tell him various things that caused me infinite grief. I said I had been slandered ever since the start of persistent rumors that he had considered me for the embassy at Rome— rumors which my age and inadequacy had kept me from believing. (The rumors were well founded as we have already seen; but I had to present the matter in this way, since I had never actually been proposed the post because of the uncertainty of the cardinal de La Trémoille's promotion. As soon as the promotion was a fact, he no longer wished to send an ambassador.) Ever since then, I said, I had been the butt of jealousy and envy, as a man who could make something of himself and must be stopped in time, so that nothing I did was innocent; even my silences were guilty, and M. d'Antin had never ceased to attack me. "D'Antin!" interrupted the King more softly. "He never mentioned your name." I replied that the King's testimony pleased me greatly, but that d'Antin had pursued me so mercilessly at every opportunity that I could not but believe he had done me some disservice.

At this point the King, who was recovering his serenity, and whose open face showed a sort of kindness and satisfaction at hearing me, cut me off as I was launching into another discourse

with these words: "There is still another man . . ." and told me:
"Yes, but Sir, it is because you speak out and because you dis-
approve; that is why you are talked about unkindly." I answered
that I was careful not to speak ill of anyone; and regarding him
with fiery eyes, I told him that I would rather be dead than
speak ill of His Majesty. While for everyone else, even though
I took great pains to restrain myself, there were occasions when
it was difficult not to speak out. "But," said the King, "you discuss everything, all sorts of affairs, even the most unpleasant ones,
with bitterness . . ." It was my turn to interrupt the King, observing that his words showed increasing kindness toward me. I
told him I rarely discussed court affairs, and only in the most
measured terms, but that sometimes, outraged by some undeserved
success, there escaped from my overflowing heart reasoned disapproval. I mentioned an affair which, to my surprise, had created
an uproar and been most harmful to me. I asked him to be the
judge so that if the affair displeased him, I could beg his forgiveness, while if he judged it more favorably, he could absolve me.
I knew what prodigious and pernicious use had been made of
my bet on the capture of Lille, and I was determined to tell the
King about it. I took advantage of his acquiescence, which was
given casually, as it always was to those who were granted an
audience.

I told him that during the siege of Lille, in the heat of a discussion, I had bet four pistoles that the city would be taken instead of rescued. I said I had been moved by the need to keep
the city, that I had despaired at the enemy's diligence to increase
its strength and the sluggishness of our army after the order to
march had been dispatched three times, and that I had been impatient to hear of the relief of such a glorious and essential siege,
while I could see that the time lost by our army made this impossible and gave our enemies the advantage. "But," said the
King, "there is nothing wrong in betting on something because
it interests you and because you resent its lack of success. On the
contrary, there is nothing but good in that. But who is this other
man you just mentioned?" I told him it was Monsieur le Duc,
and he did not reply, as he had for d'Antin, that I was imagining
things.

I described the affair of Mme. de Lussan, as briefly as I could without omitting the essentials.[3] As I had carefully avoided naming Chamillart, Vendôme, and Msgr. le duc de Bourgogne when describing the Lille affair, this time I avoided naming his daughter Madame la Duchesse[4] so I could concentrate on Monsieur le Duc. I told the King I did not intend to bore him by recounting the whole affair, but that the Chancellor and the Council, the First President and the Parlement, who had heard her case, had been so indignant they had strongly reprimanded her. I said that since this woman had attacked me everywhere with all sorts of lies, I had been forced to defend myself with the truth, harsh as truth sometimes is, but just and necessary; and before publishing my defense, I had begged Monsieur le Prince[5] to hear it, which he had done, and then encouraged me to go ahead. I said I had been unable to reach Madame la Princesse or Monsieur le Duc, who seemed unusually interested in the affair, even more so than Monsieur le Prince himself, who had scolded Mme. de Lussan for her behavior. Finally, I pointed out that His Majesty had seen nothing wrong in the numerous suits that had been pressed against her, and that if she were allowed to lie and plead her case without being called to account, her position would be greater than the most powerful man in the kingdom. I added that Monsieur le Duc had never forgiven me and never lost a chance to show it. . . .

The King had let me run on, and I noticed that I was making quite an impression. He replied, in a didactic vein, that I had the reputation of being quick to take offense, that I had been mixed up in a great many affairs of rank, and that I took the lead and prompted others.

I said that, to tell the truth, I may have become involved in

[3] Saint-Simon had lost an inheritance suit against Mme. de Lussan and went to the assistance of others pressing similar suits. Mme. de Lussan denounced Saint-Simon's meddling, and he wrote and distributed a memoir defending himself by attacking her and giving "a lifelike portrait of this nasty creature." Mme. de Lussan was related to the Condés, and Monsieur le Duc (Louis III de Condé), who had publicly sided with her, never forgave Saint-Simon. "We felt we had nothing more in common," wrote Saint-Simon.

[4] Monsieur le Duc had married the bastard daughter of Louis XIV and the marquise de Montespan, who was legitimized under the name Mlle. de Nantes.

[5] Monsieur le Prince (Henri-Jules de Bourbon, duc d'Enghien) was the father of Monsieur le Duc.

affairs sometimes, but that I had never intended to displease him. I begged him to remember that since the offertory affair, which I had reported to him four years before, I had not been mixed up in anything. I briefly recounted the offertory affair, and that of the princesse d'Harcourt.[6] I said I believed he had been pleased with my behavior in these affairs, and he agreed, making remarks that showed he had not forgotten them. I rejoined that the house of Lorraine had not forgotten them either, and still held them against me. . . .

"That only shows," said the King, speaking with a truly fatherly tone, "on what footing you are at court, and you must admit that you somewhat deserve your reputation. If you had never concerned yourself with affairs of rank, or at least if you had been less outspoken, there would be no reason to criticize you. If you keep away from these matters, nothing more will be said about you. You can shed your reputation by keeping control of yourself and sticking to a cautious and consistent line of conduct." I replied that such had been my line of conduct for four years, as I had just had the honor of explaining, and such it would continue to be, and I begged him to realize how small my part had been in all these affairs, although I was still being held responsible for them. . . .

I also mentioned the long absence I had undertaken from grief at having fallen out of favor, and I took the opportunity to unburden myself more affectionately than respectfully on my attachment to his person and my longing to please him in all things. I went on in this familiar and expansive vein because I could tell how receptive he was from his tone, manner, attitude, and remarks. He listened to me with surprising open-mindedness, which

[6] According to Saint-Simon, the princesse d'Harcourt was part of a plot he tried to thwart to have the princesses better placed at ceremonies than the duchesses. He writes that in 1699, when the Earl of Jersey was being received by the duchesse de Bourgogne, "the princesses d'Harcourt slipped behind the duchesse de Rohan and told her to sit at her left. The duchesse de Rohan, highly surprised at the request, said she was comfortable where she was.

"At that, the princesse d'Harcourt, big and powerful as she was, grabbed her by the shoulders, spun her around, and took her place. Mme. de Rohan was so startled she thought she was dreaming, but seeing that she had actually been attacked, she curtsied to the duchesse de Bourgogne and changed places, still not really knowing what had happened or what she was doing. All the other ladies were scandalized and astonished."

convinced me that I was back in his good graces. I begged him to let me know if he ever heard anything displeasing about me, for my instruction, to forgive my lapses, or to see that I was not at fault.

Seeing there was nothing left to discuss, the King rose from the table. In parting, I begged him to think of me for an apartment at Versailles so that I could continue to pay my court assiduously. He replied that there were no vacancies, and started on his way to another study after a slight but graceful and amiable bow. I left with a deep bow by the way I had come, after a very favorable audience of more than half an hour, which was much more than I had hoped for.

Saint-Simon Comments on the Spectacle of the Court at the Death of Monseigneur [1] (1711)

The faces of those present were extremely expressive. No knowledge of court life was required; a pair of eyes was enough to distinguish the selfish interests of some, and the apathy of those who counted for nothing. The latter kept their composure, the others showed grief, gravity, and efforts to mask their joy and sense of freedom. I did not want to take the spectacle at face value and tried several times to inform myself, for I feared the alarm had been exaggerated. Finally, I withdrew into myself to consider mankind's common misery and the fact that I too would someday be at the doors of death. However, I could not keep my fleeting thoughts on religion and humanity from giving way to joy. My particular deliverance was so great and unexpected that it led me to the absolute conviction that this loss was a gain for the state. Among these considerations, I felt the nagging and shameful dread that he would survive his illness. Although preoccupied by my own thoughts, I had the presence of mind

[1] Monseigneur, the Dauphin, and the only legitimate son of Louis XIV to survive infancy, died in 1711 at the age of fifty, to Saint-Simon's relief, for Monseigneur's "cabal" had not been friendly to the little duke.

to have Mme. de Saint-Simon summoned. Then, with secret looks, I pierced each face, each attitude, each gesture, I satisfied my curiosity, I took away nourishment for the ideas I had formed about each person (and which have seldom misled me), and I meditated on the accuracy of first reactions, which give people away and which become for the initiated precise indications of feelings and friendships barely perceptible in more settled times. . . .

M. le duc d'Orléans called me from the door of the study and I followed him to a back room below the gallery. He was not feeling well, and my legs were shaking from all that was seething within me and happening around me. By chance, we sat across from each other, and imagine my surprise when I saw tears fall from his eyes.

I was so startled I rose and cried out, "But, Sir!" He understood immediately and answered in a halting and tearful voice: "You have reason to be surprised, I am surprised myself; but the spectacle is moving. He was a good man whom I knew all my life. As long as he was allowed to act on his own, he treated me in a kind and friendly way. I know my grief will not last long, but I will wait several days before finding reasons to be glad for his death because of the way we were set against one another. Right now, blood ties, the closeness of the event, humanity, everything moves me to the quick." I praised this sentiment but expressed my surprise because of his relations with Monseigneur. He got up, put his head in a corner, and sobbed bitterly, which I would never have believed had I not seen it. After a brief spell of silence, I urged him to calm down and pointed out that soon he would have to join the others with Mme. la duchesse de Bourgogne. If they saw him with red eyes, everyone would think it was a joke in bad taste, since the whole court knew on what terms he had been with Monseigneur. He did what he could to stop crying and to wipe and repair his eyes. He was still working at it when he was told that Mme. la duchesse de Bourgogne was coming and that Mme. la duchesse d'Orléans was going home. He went with her, and I followed. . . .

I must admit that for those who know the innermost workings of the court, there is extreme satisfaction in the spectacle that follows rare and interesting events. Every face reveals the

care, the intrigues, the efforts to advance one's fortune, the training, the cabals, the skill in holding one's position and keeping
others at a distance, the methods used, the alliances more or less
closely knit, the setbacks, the periods of coolness, the hates, the
bad turns, the maneuvers, the advances, the circumspection, the
pettiness, the general baseness, the loss of face of some who have
reached the halfway mark, who have nearly or completely
gratified their hopes, the stupefaction of those who have come
all the way, the importance their enemies or the opposite cabal
suddenly take on, the resilience that finally leads them to success,
the extreme and unhoped-for satisfaction they feel (and I was
among the most eager), the fury of the others, and their embarrassment and spite at trying to hide it. Favored by the first
shock of surprise and sudden disturbance, my eyes were quick
to fly everywhere and probe the very soul, and in the combination of all that I saw, there was the surprise of finding some unexpectedly lacking in heart or wit, and others showing more than
I would have imagined: This mixture of stimulating objects and
important matters provides for those who know how to interpret
it a pleasure which, although fleeting, is one of the greatest that
can be enjoyed at court.

Saint-Simon Hears
Some Distressing News (1714)

At first glance, I saw in Maisons[1] and the duc de Noailles two
bewildered men. After a heated but brief preamble, they told
me with crestfallen looks that the King had declared his two
bastards hereditary princes of the blood, assuming the complete
quality, rank and honors of their new title, and capable of succeeding to the crown after the other royal princes. I was dumfounded by this unexpected news, the secret of which had been
kept without the slightest leak. My head sank, and I remained
in a deep silence, absorbed by my own thoughts. Soon I was

[1] Claude de Longueil, marquis de Maisons, was a president of Parlement,
in a position to know about the change in the bastards' rank.

interrupted by cries. The two men were running around the room, stamping their feet, pushing and hitting at the furniture, cursing at everything, and making the house shake with their noise. I admit that their outburst seemed suspect, for the one had always been sober and measured, and did not care about matters of rank, while the other was calm, sly, and self-possessed. I could not imagine how such gloomy discouragement had given way to such sudden fury, and I suspected that their anger had been faked to excite mine. If that was their aim, they achieved just the opposite. I stayed in my chair and asked them coolly at whom their anger was directed. My detachment exacerbated their fury. I have never in my life seen anything so odd. I asked if they were mad, and said that instead of this tempest it would be better to reason and see what could be done. They screamed that they were outraged precisely because there was nothing to be done, the whole thing had been resolved, carried out, drawn up, and sent to Parlement; that M. le duc d'Orléans was on such bad terms with the King he would not dare protest; and that the princes of the blood would only tremble like the children they were, while the dukes were powerless and the Parlement was reduced to silence and slavery. From then on, it was a question of who could rant loudest and longest, for they spared neither language, topics, nor people. I was angry too, but their witches' revel made me laugh, and helped me keep my temper.

I agreed that I could see no remedy or measures but that in the meanwhile and until something could be done I would rather see them princes of the blood in line for the throne than the custodians of some intermediary rank. And I believed what I said. Gradually, the storm passed . . . and I left them to return to Marly, so my absence would not be noticed. It was almost time for the King's supper, and I went into the drawing room where I found him very gloomy. Courtiers stared at and hardly dared approach one another. At the most, there were stealthy signs or whispers when they brushed past each other. I watched the King sit down at table. He looked more surly than usual, and often glanced about him. It was only an hour since the news had broken, and everyone was still under the initial shock, and remained on guard. I decided to make the best of things, which I could do more easily and honestly because the promotion was not a direct threat, unlike the intermediary rank, upon which I never complimented the bastards. I made up my mind. As soon as the King was at table, I went to see M. du Maine (the King stared at me fixedly as I left). Although the hour was rather unusual for visits, the doors opened wide, and I saw a man pleasantly surprised by my arrival, who came to greet me as though on wings, lame as he was.*

I told him that for this once, I was coming to pay him a compliment, and a sincere one at that; that we had no demands to make on the princes of the blood, but wanted only that there be no one between the princes and ourselves; and that since he and his had become princes of the blood, we had only to rejoice that we would no longer have to suffer an intermediary rank, which I admitted I found unbearable. At this compliment, there was an explosion of joy from M. du Maine. It is impossible to convey everything he did, everything he said, his politeness, and his air of deference inspired by the rapture of triumph. I repeated my compliment the next day to the comte de Toulouse and Mme. la duchesse d'Orléans, who was a hundred times more ambitious than her brothers, whom she already saw with a crown on their heads.

Saint-Simon Refuses Two Government Posts, but Accepts a Third (1715)[1]

"But you propose others and do not mention yourself," said M. le duc d'Orléans. "What would you like to be?" I replied that it was not up to me to propose myself and to choose my

---

* The duc du Maine had a clubfoot.

[1] The King was on his deathbed and the duc d'Orléans was about to become Regent. He and Saint-Simon, with all the macabre concentration of grave-looters, were already picking the members of the Regency Council in anticipation of the King's death. For Saint-Simon, it was an unexpected opportunity to put his theories on government into practice, ousting the magistrates appointed by the King, and bringing back the dukes to important posts. It was also the reward for his loyal friendship to d'Orléans during the years he had been out of favor. Saint-Simon was slightly dismayed when he was offered only the ministry of finances.

place, but up to him to see if he wanted to use me, if he thought I was capable, and to determine the post I should occupy. I will never forget it—it was in his room at Marly. After some complimentary chitchat, he asked me to be president of the council of finances, that is to direct it with a fool like the maréchal de Villeroy, and said that would be the best thing for both of us. I thanked him for the honor and for his trust in me, and respectfully refused—that was the post I had picked for the duc de Noailles. M. le duc d'Orléans was most surprised and said what he could to convince me. I replied that I had no aptitude for finances and for its technical jargon, which I could never grasp; that I knew no more than the names of all matters essential to financial administration, such as commerce, money, rates of exchange, and bank issues; that I was ignorant of the most elementary rules of arithmetic; and that since I had never meddled in the administration of my own property and domestic expenses, how could I cope with the disorganized finances of an entire kingdom? He answered that I would be given instruction and assistance by the other members of the Council, and anyone else I cared to consult. He flattered me in every way and insisted on my honesty and impartiality, two essential qualities for the handling of finances. I replied that it would make no difference to the public whether it was robbed by me or by my incompetence. I said I could vouch for my integrity, but did not know enough to discern the most obvious tricks and numberless traps that come up in finances. At the end of an hour's discussion he lost his temper, and asked me to think it over until tomorrow. . . .

"And you then, what do you want to be?" M. le duc d'Orléans asked, and pressed me so that I finally explained that if he would have me in the council of internal affairs I felt I could do better there than elsewhere. "Then you shall preside it," he said eagerly. "No, not that," I answered, "I only want one of the council seats." Each of us stood his ground. I told him I was frightened by the thought of presiding, which included reporting internal affairs to the Regency Council, and said that if I accepted, there would be nothing left for Harcourt. "To give you only a seat on the council of internal affairs is an unpardonable mockery," he said. "Since you refuse to preside it, there is only one place that can suit both you and me, and that is to sit on the Council where I sit, the supreme council, the Regency Council." I accepted and thanked him.

SAINT-SIMON'S TRIUMPH
OVER THE ROYAL BASTARDS (1715)

*After Louis XIV died, Parlement met to read his will and codicil.
The stormy session, as related by Saint-Simon, pitted the duc
d'Orléans against the duc du Maine, a royal bastard, in a decisive
struggle for power. The King's will gave the duc du Maine
charge of the young King's education, guard, and household. It
also named the members of the Council of Regency, who had
been picked for their loyalty to the bastards. Saint-Simon was
sure that the duc du Maine had practically dictated the will and
codicil to the dying Louis XIV, and that the powers he was trying
to assume now would eventually lead to placing the legitimized
bastards in line for the throne. As he tells it, he guided the duc
d'Orléans' line of action in this critical session of Parlement, and
succeeded in getting parts of the will and the entire codicil revoked and in crippling the duc du Maine's bid for power. The
bastards never recovered from the defeat, and were to suffer an
even worse one three years later under Saint-Simon's relentless
prodding. This was one of Saint-Simon's most important vic-
tories, although historians say he greatly exaggerated the dangers
of the will. Saint-Simon could not keep from gloating, as the
following passage shows.*

A few minutes after we had been in session the royal bastards
arrived. M. du Maine was bursting with joy. The term may seem
excessive, but no other can describe his bearing. His happy and
satisfied air was even more apparent than his audacity and self-
confidence, which dominated his good manners. He greeted everyone right and left, and gave them piercing glances. Once on the
floor, he saluted the presidents with jubilation, which the First
President's acknowledgment seemed to reflect. His slow, respectful, deep and grave bows to the peers were more than eloquent.

Although he tried to raise his head, it remained lowered, such is the weight of misdeeds even on days when victory seems within grasp. I watched him carefully and noticed that the greetings he was given on all sides were stiff and brief. As for his brother, he was impassive as usual.[1] . . .

The deputation was not long in returning, and handed the will and codicil to the First President. He showed them to the duc d'Orléans, then had them passed by the high court judges to Dreux,[2] who was parliamentary counselor and father of the grand master of ceremonies, saying that Dreux had a loud and clear voice which from his seat on the high bench . . . would be heard by all. One can judge how attentively everyone listened, and how all eyes and ears seemed to lean toward him. Despite his joy, the duc du Maine could not mask the painful aftereffects of a serious and recent operation. M. le duc d'Orléans displayed only a quiet attentiveness. There is no point in going over the will and the codicil, which are hymns of glory to the royal bastards, Mme. de Maintenon, and Saint-Cyr, and which leave M. le duc d'Orléans completely at the mercy of the duc du Maine's unlimited powers, through the choices made for the King's education and the Regency Council.

As the reading continued, I noticed a sort of gloomy indignation on everyone's face, which turned to silently seething discontent when the codicil was read by Father Menguy.[3] . . . The duc du Maine, who scrutinized every face and realized the change, grew pale. As I listened, I looked from him to M. le duc d'Orléans.

When the reading was over, M. le duc d'Orléans took the floor, tipped his hat after a sweeping glance, and expressed a few words of praise and regret concerning the late King. Raising his voice, he said he could only approve the measures for the King's education and for such a beautiful and useful establishment as Saint-Cyr, according to the dispositions that had just been heard. As for the measures provided for governing the State, he would discuss the will and the codicil separately. He said he found it hard to recon-

[1] The rather colorless brother of the duc du Maine was the comte de Toulouse, whose main interests were gardening and hunting.

[2] Thomas II Dreux de La Galissonnière was, at the age of seventy-five, dean of Parlement.

[3] Abbé Guillaume Menguy, counselor at Parlement.

cile these measures with the King's last words to him, and with public assurances that nothing in the will would displease him, so that he had continued to ask the King for instructions, and told his ministers to do the same.

Looking in the direction of the duc du Maine, he said the King could not have realized the importance of what he had been forced to write, since giving authority to a pre-named regency council left none for him. He said the will was so prejudicial to his birth, his attachment to the King and his love and loyalty to the State, that he could not tolerate it without dishonor. He expressed his conviction that those present had enough confidence in him to declare the Regency as it should be, that is, whole and independent. This included the choice of the Regency Council, which he would have to approve, since to entrust it with power meant giving it his confidence as well as that of the people. This brief speech made a vivid impression, and the duc du Maine asked to reply. As he removed his hat, M. le duc d'Orléans leaned over M. le Duc and told the duc du Maine severely: "Sir, you will speak when your turn comes." From that moment on, things went according to M. le duc d'Orléans' wishes. The powers and composition of the Regency Council were revoked, and M. le duc d'Orléans was given the full authority of a regent, including the right to name the Council. Matters in the Council were to be decided by a simple majority, with the Regent's vote counting for two. Thus the duc d'Orléans kept a tight hold on all benefits and punishments. The acclamation was so great that the duc du Maine did not dare contest the decision. He reserved himself for the defense of the codicil, which, if upheld, would void everything M. le duc d'Orléans had just obtained.

After a few moments of silence, M. le duc d'Orléans continued. He expressed his surprise that those who had suggested the will to the King had not been satisfied with becoming the masters of the State and had sought other guarantees by controlling the King's person, the court, Paris, and himself. He added that Parlement had by rendering its decision on the will recognized the blow against his honor, but that the codicil was an even greater blow, which deprived him of his liberty and endangered his life, and made the young King entirely dependent on the very persons who had taken advantage of a dying King's weakness to obtain what he no longer knew he was giving. In conclusion, he said the Regency could not govern under such conditions, and that the parlement in its wisdom would doubtless revoke this invalid codicil which was sure to throw France into chaos.

His words were received with a deep and gloomy silence, and when the duc du Maine was allowed to take the floor, his face was flushed. He said that since the King's person and education had been entrusted to him, it was only natural that he should have full authority over the military and civilian household, for otherwise he could not guarantee the King's service or safety. He then praised his own sense of devotion, which the late King had believed in to the point of entrusting him with the young King's care. At the word "entrust," M. le duc d'Orléans made a brief interruption. Adopting a more temperate tone, M. du Maine praised his deputy, the maréchal de Villeroy, whom he said had been given the same duties with the same trust. M. le duc d'Orléans retorted that it would be strange indeed if he were not the first to enjoy the King's complete trust, and stranger still if he could only see the King with the permission of those who would have taken control of everything including Paris through the guards regiments.

The quarrel was turning into a shouting match, and the altercations were becoming almost indecent. When the duc de La Force, who was sitting between myself and the duc de La Rochefoucauld, made room for me, I signaled to M. le duc d'Orléans to finish the discussion in the fourth hearing room, which was empty and communicates with the main chamber. My decision was taken because M. du Maine was strengthening his position, M. le duc d'Orléans was weakening his by publicly pleading his case, and there were vague mutterings about compromise. M. le duc d'Orléans did not see my signal, because he was absorbed in the debate, and because he was nearsighted. I signaled again, without success, got up, moved forward, and called out from a distance: "Sir, you will be more at ease to speak in the fourth hearing room." Coming closer, I urged him with hand and eye signals that he could distinguish. He nodded, and as soon as I had gone back to my seat, I saw them both rise and go into the fourth hearing room. I could not see how many of those scattered through the chamber followed them, for everyone rose as they went out, and sat down again in motionless silence. Some time later, M. le comte de Toulouse got up and went into the room, and he was followed by M. le Duc and the duc de La Force. But not many followed. Coming back, the duc de La Force passed me and the duc de La Rochefoucauld, put his head between me and the duc de Sully (because he did not want La Rochefoucauld to hear), and said: "For God's sake, go join them right away, for it's going very badly. M. le duc d'Orléans is softening. Put an end to the dispute and make M. le duc d'Orléans come back to the chamber and suggest that it is too late to finish and that Parlement should go to lunch and return afterward. During this interval," added La Force, "we should put pressure on the King's household at Palais-Royal, on the peers we are not sure of, and on the ringleaders among the magistrates." This advice seemed to me both timely and pertinent. I went into the fourth hearing room and found a rather full circle of spectators. M. le comte de Toulouse stood near the entrance on the fringe of the circle, Monsieur le Duc was closer to the center, and all of them kept their distance from the fireplace, before which M. le duc d'Orléans and the duc du Maine stood alone, arguing in low voices with agitated expressions. After contemplating the scene for a moment I approached the fireplace, like a man who has something to say. "What is it, Sir?" asked M. le duc d'Orléans impatiently. "One urgent word," I replied. He continued to talk to the duc du Maine, almost in front of me, and when I tried again, he leaned toward me. "No, not here," I said, taking his hand. "Come with me," and I pulled him to the corner of the fireplace. The comte de Toulouse and all the others near the corner drew back, as did the duc du Maine. I whispered to M. le duc d'Orléans that he could not hope to win anything from M. du Maine, who was not about to sacrifice the codicil to his reasoning. I said that the length of the conference had become scandalous, useless, and dangerous, that he was making a spectacle of himself before all those who wished to see and examine him, and that the only thing to do was return to the chamber and call a halt to the session. "You're right," he said, "I will do it." "Yes," I replied, "but do it right away, this minute, and don't let yourself be distracted. You owe this advice to M. de La Force, who has sent me to deliver it." He left me without a word to tell

M. du Maine that it was too late and they could resume the session in the afternoon. . . .

We returned to Parlement shortly before four. I arrived alone in my carriage just before M. le duc d'Orléans, and found everything ready. It seemed to me I was stared at with great curiosity, and I wondered whether anyone knew where I had come from. I was careful not to betray anything in my attitude. I told the duc de La Force in passing that his advice had been salutary, that I had told M. le duc d'Orléans whose idea it was, and that I was hopeful of success.

M. le duc d'Orléans arrived, and after his bustling suite had settled, said he wanted to take things up where they had been left off in the morning. He told the members of Parlement that he was in total disagreement with M. du Maine, and asked them to look again at the monstrous clauses of a codicil torn from a dying prince, clauses which were stranger still than the revoked dispositions in the will. He said Parlement could not allow M. du Maine to control the King's person, the court, Paris, and consequently the State and the Regent's life and liberty, since he would be liable to arrest at any time as soon as M. du Maine became the absolute and independent ruler of the King's civil and military household. He said Parlement must realize that such a fantastic precedent would put everything in the hands of M. du Maine, and promised to abide by the decision of the company gathered, because of its wisdom, knowledge, prudence, equity, and love of the State.

M. du Maine appeared as contemptible in battle as he was dangerous in the secrecy of cabinets. He was usually very pink-cheeked, but now he looked as though he had been sentenced to death, and the paleness of death was on his face. He replied in a low and almost unintelligible voice, with a tone as humble and respectful as it had been arrogant that morning. The members were deliberating without listening to him, however, and the complete repeal of the codicil was decided in great uproar, as a single voice. It was premature, and provoked by rising indignation, as had been the repeal of the will in the morning. The members of the King's household were to have spoken before the deliberation, and the First President had not called for a vote. But the action had occurred spontaneously. Speeches were heard from Daguesseau, the Attorney General, and Fleury, the First Prosecutor. The first spoke briefly, the latter more at length, and made a fine speech. Since the speeches are available in bookshops, I will only mention their common conclusion, which was favorable to M. le duc d'Orléans. After they had spoken, the duc du Maine, seeing himself stripped of everything, made a final effort. He argued more forcefully than he had all afternoon, but with measure, saying that if he was stripped of the authority granted by the codicil, he wanted to be relieved of guarding the King and being responsible for his person, and wanted to keep only the supervision of the King's education.

M. le duc d'Orléans replied: "With pleasure, Sir, and that will be quite enough." Upon that, the First President, looking as defeated as the duc du Maine, took the vote. Everyone agreed with the opinions that had been given, and the decree was pronounced, so that all the duc du Maine's powers were handed over to the Regent.

THE PLOT TO REDUCE THE ROYAL BASTARDS (1718)

Saint-Simon was a major figure in the conspiracy to end forever the power of the royal bastards. After the death of Louis XIV in 1715, Parlement ratified the provision in the King's will that the bastards be given the same rank as princes of the blood and the right of succession to the throne if the other royal branches became extinct. To void the decision, a special session of Parlement or Bed of Justice had to be called, in which Parlement was summoned by the King (Louis XV was then eight years old and a passive instrument in the plan) and presented with royal decisions, which it had no power to refuse. The decisions of the Bed of Justice were: To have the royal bastards (the duc du Maine and his brother the comte de Toulouse) relegated to the peerages they had been granted at birth, whereby they would lose all claims to succession and to the rank of princes of the blood or any intermediate rank; and to have Monsieur le Duc (Louis Henri de Condé, the son of the Monsieur le Duc who was such a bitter enemy of Saint-Simon) take charge of the King's education in place of the duc du Maine. Only the Regent and four or five others were in on the secret. They feared Parlement would balk and the duc du Maine would start a counterplot. The Bed of Justice was set for August 26, 1718. Members of Parlement were roused from their beds at 6 A.M. and told to be at the Tuileries (the King's residence) at 10 A.M. The guards regiments were on duty at the Tuileries and had orders to arrest members of Parlement or others who demonstrated any serious opposition. Guards officers were to act on a secret signal of the Regent, such as handkerchief-waving or leg-crossing. The wax and the stamps to seal the decrees were ready in an adjoining room. Parlement went to the Tuileries on foot as a sign of protest, but finally accepted the royal decisions.

Since an exception was made for the comte de Toulouse, the measures finally affected only the duc du Maine. A Regency Council had been called to precede the Bed of Justice. This insured the presence of both royal bastards, as well as Saint-Simon and the others who had organized the day's events. Parlement was to arrive when the Council was over.

I heard someone call me. It was M. le duc d'Orléans, who was alone near the fireplace and wanted to talk to me. I joined him and found him troubled. "I have told him (the comte de Toulouse) everything," he said. "I could not help myself. He is the best fellow you could imagine and I am sorry for him." "And what, Sir, did you tell him?" I asked.

"He came to see me on behalf of his brother, who admitted being upset," he replied. "His brother said he could see something had been arranged, and that he knew he was not on good terms with me. He wanted to know honestly whether I wanted him to remain, or if it would not be better if he left. I admit I thought I was doing the right thing in saying he would do just as well to leave. Upon that, the comte de Toulouse tried to engage me in a discussion. I cut him off and told him he had nothing to fear, for his status would not be altered, but that unpleasant things might happen to M. du Maine, which it would be cruel for him to witness. The comte de Toulouse insisted that he could not stand by and see his brother attacked, for blood ties and honor made them one. I replied that I was very sorry, but could do no more than reward merit and virtue, and give him special consideration. I added several phrases of salutation, which he received rather coolly before returning to his brother. Did I do the wrong thing?"

"No," I said, "for there is no more need for discussion, and you should not have embarrassed a man who deserves reassurance. You did the right thing, you spoke clearly like a man who has made up his mind and fears nothing. Now that you have gone this far you must show even greater firmness." He seemed resolute, but also eager to have the bastards leave, which I believe was the real reason for what he had done. . . .

The duc du Maine, pale as death, seemed on the verge of illness. While the comte de Toulouse said a word to M. le duc d'Orléans, he tottered to the end of the table and began to walk away, hugging the wall. It was all done in a flash. The Regent, who was near the King's armchair, said in a loud voice: "All right, gentlemen, take your seats." Everyone went to his seat, and as I looked around from mine, I saw the two brothers near the door about to leave. I virtually jumped between the King's armchair and M. le duc d'Orléans, so I would not be overheard by the prince de Conti, and I whispered heatedly into the Regent's ear: "Sir, they are leaving." "I know it," he answered quietly. "Yes," I rejoined, "but do you know what they will do once they are out?" "Nothing at all," he replied. "The comte de Toulouse asked me for permission to leave with his brother and promised me they would behave themselves." "And what if they do not?" I asked.

"They will, and if they do not, there are orders to watch them closely," he said. "But what if they do something foolish and try to leave Paris," I said. "They will be arrested," he replied. "There are orders, you can take my word for it." His words relieved me, and I took my seat. As soon as I was settled he called me back and said that since they had gone, he would change his plans and tell the Council now about his intentions concerning the bastards. I said it would be a mistake not to tell the Council, since the only obstacle had been lifted by the departure of the bastards. He whispered across the table to Monsieur le Duc and called the

Lord Privy Seal. Both of them approved his decision, and at last everyone took his place.

These movements had increased everyone's uneasiness and curiosity. All eyes were on the Regent, so that most of the members with their backs to the door had not noticed the bastards' exit. When they sat down they looked about for them, and not finding them, waited. I sat down in the comte de Toulouse's seat. The duc de Guiche was next to me, and, turning up his nose, left a seat between us, for he was still waiting for the bastards. He told me to come closer to him because I had taken the wrong seat. I did not reply and considered those assembled, for it was a fascinating sight. At the second or third summons I asked him why he did not come closer. "What about M. le comte de Toulouse?" he asked. "Come over here," I said. He looked across the table to where the Lord Privy Seal [1] had taken the duc du Maine's place, and was so stunned that I had to pull him by his coat from my seat, saying: "Come here and sit down." I pulled him so hard that he dropped next to me, uncomprehendingly. "But what is all this," he said, "and where are they?" "I don't know," I replied with impatience, "but they are not here." The duc de Noailles, furious at having been left out of such great preparations, finally deduced through repeated investigations that I was involved. Unable to restrain his curiosity, he joined the duc de Guiche, leaned across him over the table toward me and said: "In God's name, sir, be good enough to tell me what is going on." I was not on good terms with him, as has already been seen, and this was a good chance to show it. I turned toward him with a cold and disdainful air, and after listening to him, I turned away. That was my sole reply. . . .

When everyone was finally seated and all eyes were riveted on M. le duc d'Orléans, he briefly considered those present and said he had called the Council so they could hear a reading of the resolutions made at the last meeting. He said the only way to ratify the Council's decrees was to hold a Bed of Justice. But because of the heat, he said he did not dare risk the King's health among the crowds of Paris and would follow the example

[1] Marc-René, marquis d'Argenson (1652-1721), became Lord Privy Seal in 1718 and lieutenant general of the police two years later.

of the late King, who sometimes made his Parlement come to the Tuileries. He said that since a bed of justice had to be held, he wanted to take advantage of it to have the Lord Privy Seal register his letters of appointment, and that the meeting could begin with a reading of the letters.

The only importance of the reading was to force Parlement to recognize the Lord Privy Seal, for it hated his person and his function. While it went on, I considered the expressions of those around me. I saw in M. le duc d'Orléans an air of authority and attentiveness so unexpected that I was startled. The brilliant Monsieur le Duc was cheerful and seemed to be thinking of nothing in particular. After his initial surprise the absent-minded prince de Conti seemed to be concentrating on his own thoughts, seeing nothing, and taking part in nothing. The Lord Privy Seal, grave and pensive, seemed to have many things on his mind; he also had a great many things to accomplish, and would not get a second chance. However, he got through the reading firmly, clearly, and decisively. The duc de La Force was scanning other faces with sidelong glances. The maréchaux de Villeroy and de Villars talked together briefly; they both had bloodshot eyes and defeated expressions. No one kept his composure better than the maréchal de Tallard, but even he could not completely stifle his unrest. The stupefied maréchal d'Estrées looked as though he could see about as clearly as into a mud puddle. The maréchal de Bezons, wrapped even more than usual in his enormous wig, seemed concerned and angry-eyed. Peletier,[2] very relaxed, looked at everything as a spectator. Torcy, three times stiffer than usual, seemed to be considering everyone furtively. Effiat, quick-tempered, irritated, outraged, ready to attack, frowning at everyone, was darting quick and intermittent glances on all sides out of haggard eyes. I could not examine the ones to my side very well. I could only see them for brief spells when they changed their positions, and it was only rarely that curiosity made me lean forward to cast them sidelong glances.

I have already mentioned the duc de Guiche's surprise and the duc de Noailles' spite and curiosity. D'Antin, who had always been so debonair, now seemed flustered and self-conscious.

[2] Michel Le Peletier de Souzy, director of fortifications.

The maréchal d'Huxelles was trying to keep a stiff upper lip, but could not hide his despair. Old Troyes was so dumfounded he could show nothing but surprise and confusion, and seemed hardly to know where he was. . . .

M. le duc d'Orléans, half rising from his chair, told the Council in a firm and masterful tone that there was a very important matter to discuss. At this preamble, everyone froze in surprise. The Regent said he had considered the quarrel that opposed the princes of the blood and the legitimized bastards (this was the term he used, without adding the word "prince"). He said there were reasons why he had let the matter rest until now, but that his obligation to do justice to the peers of France remained, and that the peers had presented a petition to the King, which His Majesty had received, and which the Regent had shown to the bastards. He said the judgment of the petition could no longer be deferred before such an illustrious body, made up of the kingdom's notables, the first lords of the State, and the most honored persons, most of whom had distinguished themselves by service to the State. He said that since he had decided not to answer the petition at the time it was made, he now felt urgently that justice, which is the peers' most cherished wish, could bear no further postponement. He expressed his grief at seeing persons (this was the word he used) so close to him attain positions which, instead of occupying honorably, they tried to improve illegally. He could no longer blind himself to the truth, he said, which was that the favors granted to a handful of recently elevated princes had transposed the rank of peers; but that the prejudice to their dignity could only last as long as the authority which had strained the laws. Thus, the ducs de Joyeuse and d'Epernon, as well as the two Vendômes, had been put back in their rank of seniority among the peers right after the deaths of Henri III and Henri IV.[3]

Thus M. de Beaufort never held any special rank under the

[3] The duc Anne de Joyeuse was the husband of Marguerite de Lorraine, sister of Louise de Lorraine, who became queen of France when she married Henri III; the duc d'Epernon was a favorite of Henri III named Louis de Nogaret who bought the barony of Epernon from Henri de Navarre, the future king Henri IV; César and Alexandre de Vendôme were two bastard sons of Henri IV by Gabrielle d'Estrées.

late King, and neither did M. de Verneuil,[4] who obtained his peerage and dukedom in 1663 with thirteen others, was received with them by Parlement when the King held his Bed of Justice, took the place he had been granted by seniority, and never aspired to any other. M. le duc d'Orléans repeated that justice must be done in keeping with equity, order, the dignity of the State and the cause of so many important persons. The legitimized bastards had been given time to reply, he said, but could present no valid defense against the force of law and precedent. He explained that it was only a matter of registering a petition in a pending suit which had already been examined, and that he had drawn up a declaration which the Lord Privy Seal was about to read for their consideration, so that it could be registered afterward during the Bed of Justice which the King would hold.

A deep silence followed this unexpected speech, which had added to the enigma of the bastards' exit. Many appeared to be in a brown study. Anger was flashing from Effiat's eyes, and in those of the maréchaux de Villars, de Bezons, and d'Estrées. Tallard was dumfounded for a moment, and the maréchal de Villeroy completely lost his composure. I regretted that I could only see the maréchal d'Huxelles and the duc de Noailles out of the corner of my eye. I had to compose my own expression, for all eyes were turning toward me. I added to my face an extra layer of gravity and modesty. I forced my eyes to move slowly, and never looked above the horizontal. As soon as the Regent had opened his mouth, Monsieur le Duc cast a triumphant glance at me, which almost made me lose my self-control, but which served as a warning to keep a tight rein on it, and I did not look his way again. Restrained as I was, careful to absorb the attitude of everyone, alive to everything and to myself, motionless, glued to my seat, my whole body stiff, I was penetrated by the keenest and most delicate joy, the most delicious excitement, and by a voluptuousness inordinately and steadfastly longed for. The outward suppression of my rapture made me perspire with anguish, but even anguish became a sensual pleasure unequaled before or

[4] The duc de Beaufort was the son of César de Vendôme and thus the grandson of Henri IV; the duc de Verneuil (who became Cardinal de Metz) was an illegitimate son of Henri IV by Henriette d'Entraigues, marquise de Verneuil.

since this happy day. How inferior are the pleasures of the senses to those of the spirit, and how true it is that the greater the difficulties, the greater the joy at overcoming them![5] . . .

Once the agreement of the Council had been requested and given, M. le duc d'Orléans said: "Well, gentlemen, that is over, justice is done, and the rights of the peers are secure. Now I have an act of mercy which I propose with confidence, for I have drawn it up so that it can injure no one, and I have consulted the interested parties, who are agreed. It concerns only M. le comte de Toulouse. Everyone knows that he disapproved of all the measures taken to favor the bastards, and since the Regency he has supported them only out of respect for the will of the late King. Everyone knows also of his virtue, merit, sense of purpose, integrity, and unselfishness. However, I had to include him in the declaration you have just heard.[6] But now that he is beyond criticism, I feel that we can reward his merit with what we took away because of his birth. We can make of M. le comte de Toulouse an exception that will confirm the rule, leaving him and him only in full possession of his honors, which will not be hereditary, if he marries and has children, and from which no one else can profit. I am pleased that the princes of the blood have consented and that those peers with whom I have discussed the matter have agreed and even encouraged me. I do not doubt that the esteem in which he is held here will make this proposal agreeable to you . . ."

When opinions had been taken . . . , M. le duc d'Orléans, rising with majesty from his seat, said: "Gentlemen, Monsieur le Duc has a proposal; I find it just and reasonable and do not doubt that you will agree." And turning toward Monsieur le Duc, he said: "Sir, will you explain yourself?" It is impossible to describe the disturbance these few words created among the members of the Council. It seemed as though, being pursued from all sides, they had been surprised by a new enemy just as they breathlessly reached a sanctuary. "Sir," M. le Duc said, addressing the Regent with familiarity, "since you have done justice to the dukes, I feel

[5] Readers may be struck by the sensuality of Saint-Simon's account, in which he appears to be describing the fulfillment of a physical act of pleasure.

[6] Calling for the return of the bastards to their rank as peers.

within my rights in asking it for myself. The late King turned over the education of His Majesty to M. le duc du Maine. I was then a minor, and to the late King, the duc du Maine was a prince of the blood in line for succession. Now I am an adult, and not only is M. du Maine no longer a prince of the blood, he has been reduced to his peerage. Today, M. le maréchal de Villeroy is his senior and outranks him everywhere: Thus, he can no longer remain the King's guardian under the supervision of M. du Maine. I am asking to be named in his place, and in view of my age, my rank, and my attachment to the King's person and to the state, I do not see how I can be refused. I hope," he said, turning to the left, "that I will profit from the maréchal de Villeroy's lessons and be worthy of the task, and that I will merit his friendship." When the maréchal de Villeroy heard the words "supervision of the King's education," he almost went under the table. He sat holding his head up with his cane and did not even seem to hear the end of the speech. . . .

Several moments of deep and mournful silence followed while the maréchal de Villeroy, pale and nervous, mumbled to himself. Finally, like a man who has made up his mind, he turned toward the Regent, his head sinking, his eyes vacant, and his voice feeble. "I have only this to say," he mumbled. "All the King's intentions have been subverted, and I cannot see it done without grief. M. du Maine has been very badly dealt with." "Sir," replied the Regent with a haughty and impatient air, "M. du Maine is my brother-in-law, but I would rather have my enemies in the open than under cover." [7] At these words, several persons lowered their heads, and Effiat shook his head from side to side. The maréchal de Villeroy seemed about to faint, and across from me I began to hear muted sighs. Everyone realized that this time the blade was out of the scabbard, and wondered if it would ever be resheathed. . . .

Now the Regency Council was over and the plotters waited anxiously for the arrival of Parlement and the start of the Bed of Justice.

[7] The duc d'Orléans had married the second Mlle. de Blois, sister of the duc du Maine and legitimized daughter of Louis XIV and the marquise de Montespan.

Finally Parlement arrived, and we all rushed to the windows like children. They came in two by two through the courtyard's main gate, wearing their red robes. . . . Although the two windows were piling up with onlookers, I was careful to keep the interior of the room in sight, so I could observe exits and conversations. . . . One after the other, several persons asked to go out to relieve themselves, either because they had to or to test what prohibitions were in force. The regent granted their request, on condition that they hold their tongues and return without delay. He even suggested that Vrillière go out with the maréchal d'Huxelles and several other doubtful elements, but the real reason was so he could keep track of them more easily, and it worked out very well.

I used the same tactic with the maréchaux de Villars and de Tallard, and having seen Effiat open the King's small door for the maréchal de Villeroy, I ran over and pretended to offer my help, but actually I wanted to prevent him from speaking at the door and sending a message to the bastards. . . .

When the members of Parlement were in place and the King was about to arrive, I entered by the same door they had used. There was almost no one in the passage, and the guards officers made way for me and for the duc de La Force and the maréchal de Villars, who followed in single file. I stopped for a moment at the chamber entrance, struck with joy at the sight, and anticipating the precious moments that were to come. I also needed a pause to pull myself together, to compose a new layer of gravity and modesty, and to be able to distinguish everything clearly. . . .

Seated as I was on a high bench . . . I was able to observe all those assembled. I began to look around as piercingly and as sweepingly as I could. Only one thing bothered me: I did not dare stare too long at certain people; I feared the fire and significant brilliance of my glances, for I was closely watched. The more I realized that almost everyone's eyes met mine, the more I restrained my curiosity. Nonetheless, I cast a withering glance at the First President[8] and the main bench, for I was sitting right across from them. Then my eyes swept over the entire Parle-

---

[8] Jean-Antoine III de Mesmes had been First President of Parlement since 1712.

ment and saw surprise, immobility, and unexpected consterna-
tion, which to me seemed good signs. The most pleasant sights
were the First President, who looked shamefully defeated, and
the other presidents, who were abashed but expectant. Simple
observers, among whom I list all those without power of deliberation, did not seem less surprised, but looked calm and un-
bewildered. In a word, everyone felt a great sense of expectancy,
and tried to guess what would happen by observing those who
came out of the Council. But I could not prolong my investiga-
tion, for at this point the King arrived. . . . He looked serious,
majestic, and as pretty as could be, with a gracious gravity in his
bearing. His manner was attentive and not at all bored, and he
seemed to understand everything without difficulty. . . .

After the Lord Privy Seal had spoken, there was some commotion on the main bench. The First President wanted to speak.
His admonition was full of refined malice, impudence to the
Regent, and insolence to the King. And even so the scoundrel
trembled as he pronounced it. The broken voice, the fearful eyes,
the spasms and visible discomfiture of his whole person, belied
the residue of venom which he could not keep from spitting out
for himself and for the company. . . .

When the remonstrance was over the Lord Privy Seal went up
to the King, returned to his place without seeking other advice,
stared hard at the First President, and said: "The King wishes
to be obeyed, and obeyed immediately." These strong words
were like a bolt of lightning, and struck down the presidents and
counselors in the most unmistakable way. Their heads sagged, and
most of them did not rise again for a long time. The others, apart
from the marshals of France, did not seem very touched by their
desolation. . . .

Finally the Lord Privy Seal spoke, and with his very first words
announced the downfall of one brother and the preservation of
the other. It is impossible to express the effect of his words.
Preoccupied as I was with composing my own expression, I lost
nothing of the spectacle. Surprise seemed to be the most widespread reaction. A few were consternated, and many seemed relieved, either from a sense of justice, hatred of the duc du Maine,
or affection for the comte de Toulouse. The First President completely lost his composure; his smug and arrogant face was con-

vulsed; only the force of his rage kept him from fainting. It was even worse when the declaration was read. Every word had force of law and magnified his defeat. Everyone was motionless, so as not to miss a single word, and all eyes were on the clerk of the court, who was reading. When the reading was about one third over, the First President, gnashing his few remaining teeth, let his head fall on his cane, which he held with both hands. In that singular position, he finished listening to the reading, which was so crushing for him, and brought new life to us. Meanwhile, I was almost dying of joy. I feared I would faint, for my heart was bursting. Self-control and careful observation were infinitely painful, and yet my torment was delicious. I compared the years of bondage, the baleful days when I was dragged before Parlement several times as a victim served up to the triumph of the bastards, the diverse methods they used to climb to the heights at our expense, with this day of rule and justice, this terrible fall, which acted as a spring to restore us. I recalled with delight what I had dared tell the duc du Maine on the day when, under the despotism of his father, the scandal of the bonnet broke out.[9]

Now my eyes could behold the accomplishment and outcome of my threat. I congratulated myself repeatedly for having carried it out. I had triumphed, I was avenged, I wallowed in my vengeance, I enjoyed the fulfillment of the strongest and most sustained desires of my life. I was tempted to forget the rest, and yet could not help listening to this revivifying reading. Every word touched my heart like the bow of a violin. . . .

I had watched the King most carefully while his education was being discussed, and remarked in him no alteration, change, or even restraint. It was the last act of the drama, and he still looked alert when the decrees were drawn up. However, since there were no more speeches to occupy him, he began to joke with those about him, to laugh at everything, and even to mock how

---

[9] On that day in 1714, Saint-Simon learned that the duc du Maine had defected in the vital affair over whether the presidents of Parlement should take off their bonnets when addressing the dukes. Saint-Simon was beside himself, and told the duc du Maine: "Sir, you have broken your word, and have made us the toy of Parlement and the laughingstock of the world . . . there may come a time when it will be too late to repent your abuses of power and your cold-blooded betrayal of all the principal lords of the kingdom, who will never forget it."

warm the duc de Louvigny must be, because he was wearing a velvet coat; and he did all this with grace. His indifference to the duc du Maine struck everyone and served as a public denial to rumors being spread by his supporters that the King's eyes had reddened, but that he had not wanted to betray emotion at the Bed of Justice. The truth was that his eyes remained dry and serene and that he only uttered the duc du Maine's name once, that same afternoon, when he inquired very indifferently where he was going, and asked nothing else about him. . . .

While the decrees were being drawn up . . . I could not resist the temptation of getting even with the First President. A hundred times during the session, I crushed him with the weight of my withering and lingering glances. My eyes darted scorn, contempt, disdain, and triumph into his very marrow; when his eyes met my gaze he often lowered them. Once or twice he stared back at me, and I took pleasure in insulting him with stealthy, evil smiles, which finished him off. I bathed in his rage and delighted in letting him know it. Sometimes I used my two neighbors to mock him, by pointing him out to them with a wink when I was sure he would notice it. In a word, I tormented him mercilessly and relentlessly.

The Making of a Regent (1715)

I told the Regent that I had long abstained from mentioning his private life, having recognized it would be useless, but that now I was forced to speak because his new position made radical changes necessary. I begged him to consider with sober good will what he himself, if he was fastidious, would think of a regent more than forty years old who was still behaving like an eighteen-year-old musketeer, with obscure companions respectable people would fear to meet. I described the consequences of such behavior on his authority, his reputation abroad, and his prestige once the King was old enough to judge him. I mentioned the inconvenience to his affairs, the spread of indecency, the influence his fellow carousers would have, the shame and embarrassment he would suffer from French and foreign dignitaries, the open door to criticism, and the constant peril of contempt and disobedience. I added that nothing could be worse than open impiety, which would make enemies of all the nation's devout elements, the clergy, the monks (both of whom could be extremely dangerous), and which would estrange him from honest people, those with morals, gravity, sober habits, and piousness. I said the argument of the libertines, which he loved to praise and repeat, could here be used against him: That religion is an illusion invented by clever men to contain mankind, to make men submit to the laws that govern society, to make them fear, respect, and obey these laws, and that it is so vital to kingdoms that governments have always carefully maintained religion; even savages were governed this way by their elders and their council. Thus he should understand that even according to his own principles, the need to respect religion was great, while a display of impiety would make him despised.

I kept insisting on this essential point, and said there would be no danger of hypocrisy (which is also extremely contemptible) if he simply kept from speaking out about religion, treated it seriously, and observed the simplest forms of practice, never trying to pierce the surface. I said he should never tolerate jokes or offensive remarks about religion made in his presence, and simply live like an honest man of the world who respects the religion of the country he inhabits without displaying his indifference to it.

I made him feel the danger of having a permanent mistress in his new position and entreated him to change them often if he weakened, so that he would not fall victim to a love that was the creature of habit. I asked him to conduct his miserable affairs with all the precautions used by certain prelates who hide the profound disorder of their lives to maintain their reputations. I pointed out that he would henceforth have so many absorbing occupations, and such an urgent need to make himself loved, respected, considered, and obeyed, that his mind would be completely occupied, unless it was already corrupted, and that he would no longer feel the need to indulge his flesh. I said that in all things the mechanics are far more important than they seem, so that the regulation of his days should be entirely devoted to his affairs and his reputation, avoiding a clash of one with the other and never recalling or regretting his debaucheries. The first thing was to organize a daily schedule filled with business, court affairs, and some harmless relaxation, which he would keep as faithfully as the King's ministers, who could truthfully say they did not have time to stay away from their work a quarter of an hour. I told him that the novelty and apparent urgency of matters should not lead him to do too much at first, for he would soon weary of it, and end up doing too little at the expense of his prince and his country. I warned him not to lose too much time with audiences, especially when receiving women, who usually come for trifles (although they might have a secret purpose he would not realize), fall into banter and conversation, and find a source of vanity in the length and frequency of their audiences. They should, I said, become accustomed to waiting with Madame or Mme. la duchesse d'Orléans for his regular visits, and could talk to him alone in the antechambers when he left. I said he should listen well to the essentials, and carefully follow the practice of the late King,[1] who almost always answered "I will see." Otherwise, he should politely cut off the conversation, never receive women at other times and places (except in rare cases), and establish that once he had come into the room to visit Madame or Mme. la duchesse d'Orléans, no woman should draw him aside or talk to him. One polite but stern refusal to the first who attempted any unseemly familiarity would surely prevent the others.

As for men, they would speak to him in passing as they did with the King, so that he would hear a great many. The members of councils could easily address him during work sessions, while other distinguished persons could wait for him in the council antechambers, where he could talk to them as he did to ladies. This type of audience should also be limited to few people, and only to those who have already explained the purpose of the audience. It would be up to him to decide if the matter warrants an audience or can be explained in a few words. Generally, he should show discernment in granting audiences, which can be a

---

[1] Louis XIV was still alive when Saint-Simon was giving this advice, but had died (September, 1715) by the time he was setting it down in his *Memoirs*.

great waste of time. If he is careful to avoid superfluous detail, to discuss council matters only in the Council, and to maintain jealously each council within the confines of its duties, he should find little need for audiences. He should not forget to visit the King every day, staggering the hours to make the visits seem natural and to make his presence familiar at all times. He should show respect, because none are more vainglorious than children[2] and because those who surround the King will be watching, but also the familiarity suitable to his birth and his rank, which accustoms and tames children when it is blended with wit. He should sometimes help with the King's dressing, treat the servants with an open grace, be accessible to them, and listen patiently if one should address him as he arrives or leaves. He should be attentive to please them, and yet limit his answers to those he had for others. Princes and princesses of the blood whom he could not keep from barging into his study he should receive standing and allege urgent business to cut things short, and propose that they save themselves the trouble by sending someone they trust to clear up the affair, which would also save time. He should hold his tongue with foreign envoys, ply them with civilities, and firmly send them to his advisers on foreign affairs, for the envoys will all try to make him reveal more than is wise. Thus he will always keep himself uncommitted and have the leisure to examine and deliberate. The King never dealt with any of them. He knew the purpose of the audience in advance, and replied briefly without getting involved or committing himself. If the envoy insisted, which he rarely dared, the King told him candidly that he had nothing more to say, and pointed to the ever-present Torcy as someone who knew his intentions and with whom the minister could deal.

That was his way of getting rid of them, and if the envoy pretended not to notice, the King left for another study after giving a slight nod. Then the foreign minister had to leave, and Torcy very civilly showed him the way. I was proposing absolute imitation of the King to M. le duc d'Orléans, with a supplement of politeness required by the difference between a regent and a king, especially a king like Louis XIV.

[2] The Dauphin was five years old when Louis XIV died.

SAINT-SIMON AND THE DUC D'ORLÉANS (1717)

I had more than once strongly opposed the duc d'Orléans' decisions in state and other matters. One afternoon I went to see him after successfully disputing some decree he wanted to have passed in the Regency Council. He was alone, and as soon as he saw me come in, he said: "You must have the devil in you, to make an important matter like that slip through my fingers." "Sir," I replied, "I am sorry indeed, but all your arguments were worthless." "Don't you think I know it?" he said. "But before all those people I could not give my real reasons," and he went on to explain them. "Again I am sorry," I said, "if I had known your reasons I would have accepted your pretexts. Next time be good enough to explain them beforehand, for as devoted as I am to you, when I sit in the Council, I owe my vote to God and the State, to my honor and conscience; I decide what I feel to be wisest, most useful, and most necessary in matters of State and government, or what is most just in other matters, and no amount of respect, attachment, or any other outside consideration can sway me. Thus, despite my indebtedness and gratitude toward you, never count on me for any other opinion than that which I deem to be the best. If you have some doubtful or troublesome matter to put before the Council, or if you intend to leave some matter unexplained, be good enough to warn me and give me your real reasons beforehand, or have someone else explain them if it takes too long. Then, when I know what is at stake, I will either agree with you, or if I cannot, I will tell you frankly. The Regency Council decree gives you the right to name or ban whomever you wish, so that you can easily ban a member for a single or for several sessions. Thus, if we disagree, tell me not to come to the Council when the affair is discussed. I will not feel hurt, I will even find some pretext for my absence, so that you will not be suspected of provoking it. I will never breathe a word about the matter to anyone in the Council, feigning ignorance, and will faithfully keep your secret." M. le duc d'Orléans thanked me for the proposal, said I had spoken like a friend and an honest man, and promised to take advantage of my good will. It will be seen that he did in fact take advantage of it several times. . . .

One day when I was walking alone with M. le duc d'Orléans in the little garden of the Palais-Royal, he stopped abruptly, turned toward me, and said: "I am going to tell you something that will give you great pleasure." He told me he was weary of the life he was leading, which his age and needs no longer demanded, and other things along those lines. He said he was determined to give up his nights of debauchery and to spend his evenings soberly and properly, sometimes alone, and often with Mme. la duchesse d'Orléans. He said his health would improve and he would have more time for work, but that he would only make the change after the imminent departure of M. and Mme. de Lorraine, for he would die of boredom having to eat every night with them, Mme. la duchesse d'Orléans, and a troop of women. As soon as they were gone, he said, I could be sure there would be no more suppers with rakes and whores (those were the terms he used), and that he would lead a sober and reasonable life appropriate to his age and rank.

I admit I took such an interest in him that I expressed a delighted surprise. I thanked him warmly for confiding in me and reminded him how long it had been since I had mentioned the scabrousness of his life and the time he wasted, for I realized that I would only be wasting mine. I said I had painfully abandoned all hope that he would ever change, but that he must have known from our repeated discussions how fervently I had wished it, and how surprised and pleased I was now. He assured me that his resolution was firm, and I left him because it was getting dark.

The next day I learned from persons who had heard it from the rakes themselves that no sooner had M. le duc d'Orléans sat down to table with them than he started to laugh and clap and tell them that he had just put over a good one on me, and that I had been completely taken in. He repeated our conversation, which made for marvelous mirth and applause. It was the only time he ever diverted himself at my expense. But it was also at his expense, for it was more to my credit than his to have been foolishly taken in by a story because my joyful surprise overcame my reason. I did not wish to give him the pleasure of telling him I had found out his joke, or of reminding him of his resolution, and he never dared mention it.

I never could divine what fantasy had made him tell me such a story, since for years I had not even opened my mouth about the kind of life he led, and he in turn never mentioned it in my presence. . . . I used to tell him that if he wanted to joke, I would joke as much as he liked, but that I could not bear to have serious matters mixed with sessions of buffoonery. Although these occasions were not infrequent, I was always taken by surprise and lost my temper, at which he laughed heartily before resuming the topic of discussion. I suppose there are times when princes must relax and make sport with those they treat as friends. . . .

I learned one day by accident what he really thought of me. I will repeat it here, so as to leave all these trifles behind. M. le duc d'Orléans was returning from an afternoon session of the Regency Council in the Tuileries to the Palais-Royal, alone in his carriage with the duc de Chartres and the bailiff of Conflans, who was then first gentleman of his chambers. He began to talk about me when they had reached the courtyard of the Tuileries, and praised me to such an extent to Monsieur his son that I hesitate to report it here. I cannot recall what had occurred in the Council to prompt his praise. I can only say that he insisted on his good fortune at having in me a friend so loyal, constant, competent in everything, sure, true, disinterested, firm, unequaled, trustworthy, obliging, and who always discussed matters truly, uprightly, forthrightly, and disinterestedly. This eulogy lasted until they set foot in the Palais-Royal, when he said his son should meet me, and know what happiness and support he had always found in my friendship and advice (for those were his exact terms). The bailiff of Conflans, astonished by such an abundance of praise, reported it to me secretly two days later, and I admit I have never forgotten it. . . .

He was never content with a single mistress, but needed variety to stimulate his taste. I had no more to do with them than I did with his rakes. He never mentioned them to me, nor I to him, and I ignored almost all their adventures. These rakes and valets pressed women on him, and there was always one in the bunch he would take a fancy to. . . .

His suppers were always spent in strange company, with his mistresses, or a girl from the Opéra, or often Mme. la duchesse de Berry,[1] and a dozen men, who were not always the same but whom he always called his rakes in an offhand way. There was Broglio, the eldest son of the one who died a duke and a marshal of France; Nocé; four or five of his officers, but not among the highest-ranking; the dukes of Biron, Brancas, and Canillac, several young men he had met by chance, and an occasional lady of the court, but of moderate virtue; there were several persons whose names were obscure, but who shone by their wit or their debauchery. The food was exquisite, and was prepared in specially equipped kitchens; they often helped prepare it, and all the tableware was silver. It was during these sessions that everyone at court, including the ministers and the Regent's intimate friends, was lampooned with unbridled effrontery. Affairs of the heart, past and present, at court or in the city, were discussed mercilessly. They recounted old tales, quarrels, practical jokes and ridiculous stories, and no one and nothing was spared. M. le duc d'Orléans joined in with the others, but it is true that these remarks rarely left any impression on him. Everyone drank a great deal, became overexcited, and rivaled at shouting full-throated obscenities and impieties. When they were good and drunk and had made enough noise, they went to bed and started up again the next day.

Whenever the time for these suppers came, they barricaded themselves in so that whatever happened, it was impossible to reach the Regent. I do not mean only for the unexpected affairs of individuals, but for affairs that could have been essential to the State or his personal safety. They remained sequestered until the next morning. Thus, the Regent lost an infinite amount of time in amusements, debaucheries, and time spent on his family. He also lost time in audiences that were too easily given, too long, too windy, during which he buried himself in the kind of detail for which he and I used to criticize the late King. When I called it to his attention he agreed, but still could never help

[1] His daughter, with whom he was said to have incestuous relations.

himself. There were a thousand particular matters, and many others dealing with public administration, that he could have investigated in half an hour and sped on their way. Instead he let them drag on, sometimes from weakness, and sometimes from his miserable desire to confuse the issue and implement this favorite but poisoned axiom which sometimes escaped from his lips: *Divide et impera*. Most of the time he was moved by a general suspicion of all things and all men.

It is very extraordinary that neither his mistresses nor Mme. la duchesse de Berry, nor his rakes, could ever find out from him anything of importance about the government or his affairs, even when he was drunk. He lived publicly with Mme. de Parabère, and at the same time lived with other women. The jealousy and spite of these women amused him, which did not prevent him from being on good terms with them all. The extreme scandal of his public harem and the daily obscenities and impieties of his suppers had spread everywhere.

Saint-Simon Helps the Duc d'Orléans Pick the Members of the Regency Council (1718)

"He (the duc de La Force) wants very badly to be a member of the Regency Council," said M. le duc d'Orléans with a smile, as if seeking my approval. "I know it," I replied, "but we are already many." "That is true," he said, "too many." I held my tongue to remain uncommitted, and was pleased to have put my finger on the sore spot, so that I could explain it to the duc de La Force. But a moment later M. le duc d'Orléans added, as though to himself: "He would make only one more." "Yes," I said, "but the duc de Guiche is vice-president for war, as the duc de La Force is vice-president for finances, and Guiche is colonel of the guards besides, how then could you leave him out?" "By heaven, you are right," said the Regent, "and I will not have M. de La Force."

I had said it on purpose, and my conscience bothered me for

having cast aside a man who confided in me. After thinking it over for a while, I gave the Regent the fruit of my silence. "But you promised him," I said. "There is something in that," he replied. "Let us consider again," I said. "As for me, my role is simply to remind you of a man whom you would wrong by discarding." "You please me by saying that," he said, "for in fact one cannot go without the other." And after a brief silence, he said: "And finally, the way things are now, two more or less will not matter much." "Well," I said, "do you want to have them?" "By heaven," he said, "I believe I do." "If that is the case," I replied, "you can do it more gracefully by asking them both right now. The duc de Guiche is next door—shall I call him in?" "Go ahead," he said promptly. I opened the door and summoned the duc de Guiche in a loud voice.

Saint-Simon's Vindictiveness [1] (1715)

I paid an unaccustomed visit to Pontchartrain, and fell upon him like a bomb, which is usually more unfortunate for the bomb than for those on whom it falls. But this time the only victims were those present, which doubled my pleasure. The ministers were groaning about their fate. Fear of the King still kept them from turning to M. le duc d'Orléans. They were held back by the vigilance of the duc du Maine and the wrath of Mme. de Maintenon, for there was still enough life left in the King to have them banished, in which case M. le duc d'Orléans would consider less their martyrdom than their poor political timing. I wanted to enjoy Pontchartrain's embarrassment and goad the

---

[1] Saint-Simon hated Pontchartrain's son as much as he had loved the Chancellor, his father. The son, who "had lost one eye to smallpox and been blinded by his good fortune," had the audacity to remove some minor responsibilities from Saint-Simon's governorship, and the little duke never forgave him. With Louis XIV on his deathbed and the duc d'Orléans about to become Regent, Saint-Simon's star rose. He knew he could have Pontchartrain sacked (he was secretary of the King's household, of the clergy, of the navy, and of commerce), and went to see him to gloat in anticipation of the happy event.

detestable cyclops. He was shut in with Bezons and d'Effiat,[2] but his servants, after a moment's embarrassment, did not dare bar my way. I went into his study where I saw at first glance three men sitting with their heads together who, as I came in, jumped up with an air of distrust that soon changed to contrived compliments. The more I realized that my unannounced visit had embarrassed and interrupted them, the more I was amused, and the less I wanted to leave, as I would have done at any other time. They were hoping I would leave, but when I began making innocent conversation like a man who does not realize he is unwanted, d'Effiat left with a stiff bow, and Bezons soon after. . . .

As soon as they were gone, I said maliciously that I was afraid I had interrupted them, and should have left them alone. Between compliments, Pontchartrain agreed so I would get the idea the two men had promised to help him. The fear of losing his position blinded him to the point that he could not see I was drawing him out to mock him. He forgot his misdeeds and everything that had passed between us, flattered himself on receiving my visit, and confided in me with an ornate respectfulness I had never seen before. I did not even have to lure him with vague compliments and court banter.

He got in deeper and deeper, described his troubles, his anxiety, his difficulties, and apologized for his past conduct toward M. le duc d'Orléans. This man who had lorded it over others had by now completely swallowed his pride, admitted his appeals to Bezons, and through him to d'Effiat, and praised their friendship and kindness. He returned to his anxieties, larding his phrases with hints to show how strongly he desired my protection and how embarrassed he was to ask for it. After rejoicing for a while to see him crawl, I expressed my surprise that a man of his intelligence, who knew the court and the world as well as he did, could worry about what he would become after the King, who it was true (and here I looked him straight in the eye) did not seem to have much time left. I said that with his experience and capacity in naval affairs, where there was no one who could touch him, M. le duc d'Orléans would be only too pleased to

[2] Bezons was a marshal of France, friend of the duc d'Orléans and member of the Council of Regency; the marquis d'Effiat was governor of Montargis and also became a member of the Council of Regency.

keep him in office, since there was no one capable enough to replace him. It seemed to me these words brought him back to life. But since he was very long-winded, he kept referring to his fears, which I sometimes half acknowledged to see him pale. Then I reassured him with the arguments that he was the right man in the right place, that he was indispensable, and that he was his own man and could rest easy. This delectable farce lasted a good three quarters of an hour. I was careful not to say a single word that smacked of advice, past friendships, or offers of help. I only had to intersperse his flow of words with a few of my own from time to time to learn that Bezons and d'Effiat had become his protectors. I was assured daily by M. le duc d'Orléans that he would not be on the next naval council, and I took delight in my secret scorn, and in seeing myself on the verge of keeping the vow I had made long ago.*

Saint-Simon's Malice [1] (1716)

Another time . . . the duc de Noailles began holding forth on the danger to royal manufactures in granting licenses to sell and wear prohibited fabrics.[2] He dwelt with marvelous grandiloquence on the evils of wearing painted cloth, a fashion which defied all rules and reason, for it was worn publicly and with impunity by great ladies everywhere, and by other ladies who felt protected by their example and imitated them, with the most scandalous public contempt for laws and fines, which had been repeatedly enforced. He finally concluded with the same fiery eloquence that such a great and insidious evil must be

---

* The vow to avenge himself.

[1] Saint-Simon had suggested to the duc d'Orléans that the finance portfolio be given to the duc de Noailles, and delighted in mocking poor Noailles at every Regency Council.

[2] Cloth not woven by the royal manufactures could not legally be worn by anyone, and violators were liable to heavy fines. This puerile form of protectionism extended to cloth-covered buttons, which for a time were in fashion. Another curious restriction was that the bourgeoisie was not allowed to wear cloth of gold and silver, embroidery, lace or other ornamentation by which they might have been confused with the nobility.

fought with efficient methods, but did not propose a single one, apparently to avoid falling out with the fair sex. There was then some long-winded discussion of the matter, which was nothing but words. When my turn came, I gave high praise to the duc de Noailles' zeal in upholding the interests of France's textile mills and castigating the abuses of wearing prohibited fabrics. I particularly insisted on the dangers of painted cloth, and even added several points to what the duc de Noailles had already said. I remarked gravely how important it was to put a stop to such a widespread fashion and contempt for the law which had spread to women of every station. I proposed a severe punishment, in view of the gravity of the situation, which would serve as an example for all. And my advice was that after renewing the bans, madame la duchesse d'Orléans and Madame la Duchesse should be put in iron collars if they were ever caught wearing painted cloth. The grave tone of my preamble joined with my sarcastic conclusion prompted a great roar of laughter, and the duc de Noailles was so put out he could not conceal it from the Council, and left in a huff. . . .

I never missed a chance to amuse myself and the others at his expense, and he never got used to it. M. le comte de Toulouse and I noticed that he never brought his files when discussing financial matters, although many cases he discussed were in dispute. In this way, he could say whatever he wanted without fear of contradiction, and we decided to tolerate this abuse no longer. At the next financial council, I interrupted the duc de Noailles as he was discussing a case and asked him where his files were. He mumbled something, looked angry, and did not know what to answer. Looking at those assembled and addressing myself to the Regent, I said that however trusting one might be, it was a mistake to judge without proof, and that I had my own reasons for doubt. The duc de Noailles' face flushed, and he tried to speak. I interrupted him again to say that my proposal was current practice in all tribunals, and would moreover bring him relief and merit. He grumbled some more, and I looked at the Regent and shrugged my shoulders. The comte de Toulouse said he did not see what objections there could be to bringing the files. This silenced Noailles, who buried his head between his shoulders and continued his report, which he made as brief as he could. At the next financial council, he brought in a great bag filled with papers.

For his sins, he was always seated next to me, since the only ranking peer between us was the maréchal de Villeroy, who could not sit next to me at financial councils or any others.[3] When Noailles began to speak, I asked: "What about the files?" "There they are, in my bag," he replied. "I can see the bag," I said, "but I don't see the files. Put the ones pertaining to the case you are discussing on the table." He opened the bag angrily, removed the files, and put them in front of him. As he read his report, I began to look through the files like a self-appointed auditor. Never was there a man so put out, and who tried so hard not to show it, for you could see it all seething inside him. When he got home he unleashed it, snorting with anger, heaping abuse, and saying that I infuriated him and that he could put up with me no longer. I got a good laugh out of it, and kept him on the alert. I often made him find the documents to prove what he was saying, and read them to myself alongside him as he read them out loud, as though I mistrusted him and wanted to show it to spite him. M. le duc d'Orléans never reprimanded me for it, either in the Council or in private.

Sometimes, in full council, I made him draw up under my dictation a decree that had just been pronounced, and here and there take out what he had put in, or add what he had left out, or make him change the terms he had substituted for those pronounced. On these occasions, rage oozed from his every pore. His every attitude and gesture, and his furiously inflamed face, betrayed him. And yet, afraid of attracting more trouble, he kept his temper and avoided superfluity.

I would swoop on him like a bird of prey, and when the council was over, everyone would have a good laugh, and spread the story around court. Noailles, who was neither liked nor respected because he was surly and difficult, became a general laughingstock. He knew it, for he was very nosy, which increased his despair at these oft-repeated scenes. That is enough for a sample of his behavior, which is not worth expanding upon.

[3] The maréchal de Villeroy had been entrusted with the King's education, and had a special seat at the Council when he was able to attend.

SAINT-SIMON'S SCRUPULOUSNESS (1719)

Law[1] was still accomplishing miracles with his Mississippi project. You had to know a special jargon to understand his maneuvers. I will not attempt to explain it, or any other financial operations. There was a tremendous run on Mississippi stocks, and huge fortunes were made overnight. Law was besieged by supplicants. They forced his door, climbed through his windows from the garden, and fell down the chimney into his study. The talk was always in the millions. Law, who as I have already explained, came to see me every Tuesday between eleven o'clock and noon, had often urged me to accept some stock as a gift, which under his management would reap a multimillion profit. So many people of all kinds had already profited, some of them only by acumen, that I had no doubt Law could obtain better and quicker profits for me, but I would have nothing to do with it. Law went to Mme. de Saint-Simon, whom he found just as inflexible. As far as making anyone rich, he would rather it were me than a good many others, for he could thus involve me in his interests, knowing of my influence over the Regent. He even asked the Regent to persuade me to accept. The Regent mentioned it to me more than once, but I always avoided the issue. Finally, one day he asked me to meet him at Saint-Cloud, where he had gone to work and take a stroll. We were both sitting on the Orangerie railing which leads to the bois des Goulottes, when he mentioned the Mississippi stock again, and urged me to accept some from Law. The more I resisted, the more he urged and reasoned; finally he lost his temper and told me I was vainglorious and stubborn to refuse something offered in the King's name, which many others of my quality and rank would be only too glad to have. I replied that if these were my reasons I would be

[1] John Law, the Scotch financier who founded the French Compagnie des Indes and whose novel system of banking under the Regency ended in bankruptcy, had been befriended by Saint-Simon, who did not however share his views on finance.

more of an impudent fool than vainglorious, and that since he pressed me so, I would give him my reasons. I said that since King Midas, who would have to be seen to be believed, I had not heard of anyone able to turn everything he touched to gold; that I did not believe Law had the secret, and that I thought all his wisdom was an intricate game, a new and clever trick, which robbed Peter to pay Paul, and enriched some at the expense of others. Sooner or later, I said, things would spoil, the game would be exposed, and an infinite number of people would be ruined. I mentioned how difficult, and even impossible, it would be to make restitution, for to whom should this kind of profit be restituted? I said I abhorred other people's goods, and would not assume even an indirect responsibility of this kind for anything in the world. M. le duc d'Orléans did not know what to answer, but he kept belaboring his points discontentedly, and repeating his idea about refusing the King's bounty.

SAINT-SIMON AS A SOCIAL REFORMER (1718)

Although I never took part in finances, I had my own experience with financiers, controllers, and other financial magistrates. I had never forgotten President de Maisons' explanation of the salt tax, the enormity of employing 80,000 persons to collect it and the abuses practiced at the expense of the people. I had also been struck by the differences in provinces which were all equally subject to the King. In some provinces the salt tax is severely enforced, while in others salt is tax-free, although the King gets the same revenue.[1] The latter enjoy a freedom which make the others appear to be under the arbitrary yoke of roguish tax collectors who grow rich from graft and looting. I therefore conceived a plan for lifting the salt tax and putting salt freely on the market. The King would only have to buy the few privately owned brine pits at one third more than their real value.

---

[1] It would be more accurate to say that in some provinces the sale of salt was a state monopoly, while in others private concerns were enfranchised to sell it and get what price they could, as long as the King got his share.

When the King owned them all, he could sell salt to his subjects at a given price, and no one would have to buy more than he needed. The brine pit of Brouage was practically the only one he would have to acquire. The King would save the odious expense of farming out taxes; the nation's cattle would profit visibly, for there was a great difference between the cattle fed a little salt in the tax-free provinces and the cattle deprived of salt because it was too dear; the people would gain more freedom, and rid themselves of the monstrous number of employees who were paid starvation wages and had to subsist by looting. I proposed my plan to the Regent, who agreed enthusiastically. The matter was discussed and was about to be settled when Fagon and others in the finance ministry, who had not been able to oppose it before, took measures that made it founder. Some time later I tried again and I was given every reason to believe I had succeeded and that the project would be enacted within a week; but the same group, getting wind of it, made it fail again.

Aside from the advantages I have just described, it would have been an excellent thing to convert the army of bloodsucking tax collectors into soldiers, artisans, or laborers.

This incident brings to mind a truth which I learned from sad experience while serving on the Council: It is impossible to work for the common good. Every worthy project is taken up by a few men of good will and opposed by a great many more who have special interests. Those who wish to do good ignore the byways of success and are powerless to ward off the cunning and influence of their opponents. Their cunning, added to the influence of men of power and authority, is so great and sinister that good works are bound to fail. This distressing truth will always hold true in governments such as we have had since Cardinal Mazarin, but it can be a source of infinite consolation to men of feeling and intellect who are no longer involved in affairs of state.

SAINT-SIMON AS A POLITICAL THINKER (1746)

Let us now compare our government with that of our enemies, and see if we can find the deplorable origin of our misfortunes. France and Spain have been governed by magistrates of little worth, and then by prime ministers of even lesser ability. Both were continuously on guard against high birth, intelligence, merit, and experience, and were mainly preoccupied with keeping deserving persons at a distance, watching from their cabinets over the few they employed, and commanding the army. I will say no more about it, and refer the reader on this vital matter to what has already been said about the reign of the late King and what has been briefly said about the prime ministers who since his death have governed France and Spain. The courts of Turin, London, and Vienna have been fortunate in their continuous abhorrence of this form of government. In these courts there has not been a prime minister for centuries, and magistrates are given, in all due honor, the duties they deserve. The neckband as a condition for all the civilian, political, and military offices of government, excluding all other professions and conditions, is a gangrene to which these courts have never fallen victim, and from which our fatal example should preserve them.

These powers only employ the most distinguished persons of quality in their councils, convinced as they are that their high purpose and attachment to the State stemming from their birth, their land, and their marriages will be certain to govern their conduct. Thus they will be preserved from indifference to the general good, eagerness to amass a quick private fortune, and underhanded stabs at quick honors, since they already possess the honors due to their quality. Appointments must be made with care, so that incompetents are not named to the most important portfolios. These courts have never been sullied by the pernicious belief that power and prosperity lie in making everything accessible to the base and ignorant people. On the contrary, they have selected candidates among their subjects for various ministries in all parts of the administration, promoted them by degrees in the civilian and political as in the military offices, so that the incompetents fall by the wayside, the others rise according to their talents, and no one with talent is allowed to languish. . . .

I will not go further in a matter as futile as it is important. Theories, comparisons, experience, everything points to its importance, and the fatal path taken in France shows the futility of hoping for any salutary changes. I have quite naturally let myself be carried away by this digression because of the chain of events, and France's present situation pains me so that I cannot keep from stating its causes. At my age and with my family in its present condition,[1] it can readily be judged that these truths are not prompted by any selfish interests. I would be pitiful if I regretted my idleness since the death of M. le duc d'Orléans. I have learned that mixing in politics is only fine or pleasant when seen from the outside, and even if I had stayed, what would the conditions have been? Now the time has come to draw back and consider the account I will have to settle with the One who dominates time and eternity. He is sure to be far more severe with the powerful of this world than with those who had a part in little or nothing.

SAINT-SIMON ON FOREIGN AFFAIRS (1718)

The experience of several centuries should have taught us what England is to France: A rival with claims on our harbors and provinces, a rival for control of the seas, a rival as a neighbor, a rival in commerce, a rival in the colonies, and a rival in her form of government. And the crowning rivalry is religion, and the attempts to restore the Stuarts despite the will of the nation. What England has in common with the rest of Europe, what has united her with the other powers against ours, and maintained the alliance, is the extreme jealousy of seeing Spain ruled by the house of France, and Europe's terror at what these two royal

[1] Saint-Simon was seventy-one when he wrote this passage, which is not in the *Memoirs*. His eldest son had just died, and his other son was childless.

branches could achieve for their common greatness, if only they were guided by wisdom. . . .

The same experience also shows that France has always had everything to fear from England when she was at peace with herself. France, although she did not meddle in them, has always reaped the greatest advantages from the long and cruel divisions of the White Rose and the Red Rose, the intermittent jolts caused by the authority and passions of Henry VIII, and the lengthy turbulence that brought Cromwell to supreme power. Mary's rule was brief, and marred by her efforts to bring back Catholicism after the brief rule of her younger brother.[1] The famous Elizabeth was a personal friend of Henri IV, and her reign was troubled by Scotland, Ireland, and her very sex, for her subjects were always pressing her to marry, and she did not dare refuse them although she did not want to share her throne. The weakness of James I, his unfortunate bent for writing and erudition,[2] his passion for the hunt, and his distaste for work kept England from becoming dangerous during his reign. His grandson[3] was restored after some strange revolutions and had to cope with a good deal of domestic trouble. He was a personal friend of the late King, and yet was forced by Parliament to declare war on him.

The brief reign of James II is not even worth mentioning. France cruelly felt all of William's reign, and although the end of Queen Anne's reign was some compensation, it was dearly paid for, thanks to Dunkirk and the exposure of our best-protected coastline. One can also observe the attitude of the English toward Dunkirk after the peace, which they hated.[4] One has only to read Torcy's reports. . . . It is thus clear that France's perceptible interest is, if she can do it with circumspection, to excite and maintain domestic strife in a country which has its own inclinations for it.

[1] Mary Tudor succeeded her brother Edward VI (son of Henry VIII and Jane Seymour) in 1553, and died in 1558.

[2] He published works in English, French, and Latin.

[3] Charles II.

[4] According to the Peace of Utrecht, which in 1713 put an end to the War of the Spanish Succession, the French fortifications of Dunkirk were to be razed and the harbor to be filled up. The treaty signed between England and France put a stop to French expansion in Europe and forced Louis XIV to recognize the house of Hanover for English succession.

SAINT-SIMON'S ANONYMOUS LETTER
TO THE KING [1] (1712)

The nobility is not happy. It is exhausted by almost continuous warfare. Since it cannot hope for other then military distinction, it has cast aside all other studies and occupations. It is deeply dejected by the yoke of ministers, governors, and taxes. To survive, it is debased—forced to mingle with the lowest sort of people through shameful misalliances. All the oldest houses have been completely ruined. There is no more credit or consideration for officeholders or for governorships whose titulars refuse to connive. The same despondency exists on estates where the owners are absent, and the few who have remained on their land can only be distinguished from their vassals and peasants by the favor or disfavor of their overseers and subordinates. The court is deprived of all positions by the Crown, and debased in its essential dignities by the countless changes Your Majesty has made or tolerated, and by the forty-six new peerages: Of these, there now remain twenty-eight peers and eleven hereditary dukes, while all your predecessors together named only fifteen. You have also raised three particular houses to ranks that stifle and corrupt all the rest, and have created a dozen other special warrants without royal titles.

Other, lesser honors are rarely given to the old nobility, and particularly the important duties of your household, which are left to the families of your ministers. The nobility devoted itself to war, and was wasted in subordinate commands because it could not buy or keep up regiments. It was constantly submitted to the whims of the minister, his clerks, and his underlings, who tarnished every rank up to and including that of marshal of

---

[1] There is no autograph copy of this letter, but scholars agree that its author is Saint-Simon and that he wrote it in 1712, discouraged by the death of the duc de Bourgogne. The letter deals largely with Saint-Simon's obsessions, the hatred of the bastards, the deterioration of the nobility, and the ruin of the country thanks to useless wars. The complete letter is roughly 20,000 words long.

France. The great choice and number of ranks led to a falling off of discipline and produced mishaps hitherto unknown to French arms. The provincial nobility is more miserable than the vilest peasants, and only those are happy who own a plow they can draw themselves in the fields.

Under these conditions, French nobility, the flower of Europe, the terror of the kingdom's enemies, the mainstay and honor of the nation, this forever faithful and forever willing nobility, whose powerful assurance is equal to all times of hardship, this nobility which despite terrible obstacles restored to the throne of his fathers the great King Henri* your ancestor and assured your own reign, is no more than a severed head, an impotent husband, a lost crowd, dissipated, idiotic, sterile, incapable of anything except resignation.

Saint-Simon's Disgust with Court [1] (1723)

This year, the last in the memoirs, will not have the fullness and abundance of the others in these writings. I was embittered by the precedents set at the sacring of Louis XV, which I felt would lead to the complete re-establishment of all the bastards' privi-

---

* Henri IV.

[1] This passage, one of the last in the *Memoirs*, shows a new note of resignation mixed with Saint-Simon's bitterness and announces his retirement from court. The memoirs end in 1723, with the death of the Regent, a great personal blow to Saint-Simon and the end of his influence at court. Although he lived until 1755, he practically stopped going to court after the Regent's death. Monsieur le Duc became prime minister, and was later replaced by Cardinal de Fleury. Almost indifferently Saint-Simon watched them govern and his violent passions of earlier days gave way to a conviction that worldly life is futile. There were a few exceptions. In 1724, Saint-Simon was on the list to receive the Order of the Holy Ghost. There was some intriguing behind the scenes, and when Monsieur le Duc presented the list to Louis XV, the little duke's name had been mysteriously removed. That was the end of his friendship with Monsieur le Duc, whom he prohibited even his children from seeing. In this state of affairs, "dead to the world," he spent the rest of his life between his property of La Ferté and his house in Paris, with his friends and his books, attending court only once or twice a year.

leges.[2] My heart was heavy at seeing the Regent chained to his unworthy minister[3] and unable to make a move without him. The state was prey to the personal interests, avarice, and folly of this scoundrel, and there was no remedy. Whatever had been my experiences with M. le duc d'Orleans' astounding weakness, they reached new heights right before my eyes when he picked this prime minister despite my warnings and his own misgivings. I have told elsewhere the complete truth on the incredible manner in which this was done. Now it was only with repugnance that I approached this unfortunate prince, who had so many notable but hidden talents. I could not help feeling strongly what bad Jews said about manna in the desert: We are disgusted with this food. I no longer dared speak to him. He felt it and it distressed him. He sought to bring me around, and although he tried to keep from discussing current affairs, he could not. I barely answered, and cut off the conversation as soon as I could. I made my audiences less frequent and accepted his reproaches coolly. I had nothing to say to a regent who was no longer serving the kingdom, no longer his own man, and who had let everything fall into disorder.

[2] At the King's sacring (religious ceremony by which a king is consecrated) at Reims in 1722, Saint-Simon was shocked by three things: After the religious ceremony and before the royal banquet, the King's shirt was burned because it had been spotted by holy oils. This was contrary to custom, which dictated that only the gloves could be burned, and that otherwise the King had to wear the same clothes to the banquet he had worn to the ceremony.

Certain bishops were allowed to eat at the same table as the ecclesiastical peers, which Saint-Simon considered an offense to the dignity of peers and a lack of respect to the King.

Ambassadors were seated farther down than the bishops who were at the peers' table, which was an insult to them. Another "enormity" was that the court's two ambassadorial ushers were seated at the same table as the ambassadors.

[3] Cardinal Guillaume Dubois, whom the Regent had chosen despite Saint-Simon's opposition.

SAINT-SIMON AND RELIGION

INTRODUCTION

*S*AINT-SIMON'S *attitude toward the Church was a blend of suspicion and piety, irreverence and fervor, hatred for the secular powers the Church had gained under the Bourbons and love for all signs of spiritual vitality. He despised the church hierarchy, and considered the Pope more as a sovereign ruler of the papal states than as the spiritual head of the Church. One can imagine Saint-Simon's outrage had he lived until the first Vatican Council when the doctrine of papal infallibility was proclaimed. To him a cardinal was not a prince of the Church, but a base intriguer who used the purple to attain high political office. He could never forgive Richelieu, Mazarin, and Dubois for having confused the issue of Church and State by wearing birettas while running the country. He could not tolerate the venality and venomous rivalry of the religious orders. His suspicions were so ingrained that he could write without afterthought that a certain priest was "a Jesuit, but not a bad fellow withal." He was just as critical of other orders and refers to "the dirty beards of Saint-Sulpice" and the "ignorant and stubborn Ultramontanists." His visit to Spain increased his anticlericalism, for he saw in the Spanish Church a coarser and more retrograde model of the French. "I never saw such fat, vulgar, roguish monks," he wrote. "Pride and vanity showed in their eyes and countenance."*

It is probably on religious issues that Saint-Simon was at his most liberal and disinterested. He had no court privileges to protect, his ducal rank was not at stake, and he realized that the fanatic persecution of heretics would ultimately weaken the Church. Of his many quixotic crusades, his positions on the two principal religious issues of his time are the only ones untinged by querulousness or malice.

He considered that the revocation of the Edict of Nantes by Louis XIV in 1685 and the persecution of the Protestants throughout France was the monarch's worst single mistake. In eloquent pages, he describes a smug King surrounded by sycophants who assure him that the whole country has been converted to Catholicism. The reader cannot escape the conviction that for Louis XIV, religious persecution was a way of receiving indulgences to ease his passage into heaven, much like telling his beads or kissing the foot of a holy statue. Saint-Simon's contrast between the human tragedy of the persecuted and the shallow motives of the King is an effective indictment of the court's hothouse climate.

The second pressing religious issue of the time, Jansenism, was more perplexing. Saint-Simon deplored the hounding and banishment of Jansenists, but would not condone the heresy, and put himself in the position of a man "who doth protest too much." He was forever explaining why he was not and never would be a Jansenist. And yet he had a passion for the Abbey of Port-Royal, the intellectual center of Jansenism, and considered the razing of its Paris buildings in 1710 to comply with the Bull Unigenitus of Pope Clement XI an act of barbarism. Saint-Simon knew the virtue and genuine piety of the nuns at Port-Royal. He was sensitive to the absurdity by which a spiritual renewal can be branded heresy while the slothful, corrupt, and greedy elements of the Church remain immaculately orthodox. One of his grudges against the Jesuits was their denunciation of the cardinal de Noailles, which sparked the persecution of Jansenism. However, although the emphasis of Jansenists on personal holiness and St. Augustine's teaching on grace certainly appealed to Saint-Simon, he never swallowed the doctrine whole.

One aspect of Jansenist persecution he held in particular contempt was the Formulary, a certificate Catholics had to sign and show their confessor to prove they were free from heresy. In his attack on this "pernicious document" Saint-Simon emerges as an early critic of loyalty oaths.

The Jesuits' Strange Cargo (1702)

When the vessels were unloaded in Spain, there were eight huge cases of chocolate, each one marked: CHOCOLATE FOR THE VERY REVEREND FATHER GENERAL OF THE COMPANY OF JESUS. Twice the usual number of dock hands were needed to unload the cases, which nearly broke their backs. The great trouble they had, despite reinforcements, aroused curiosity. When the cases arrived in the storehouses of Cadiz, those in charge opened one and found only great fat balls of chocolate in neat piles. They took one out, and were startled by its weight, then a second and a third, each one just as heavy. They tried to break one open and could not; but the chocolate coating broke off and they found that the balls were solid gold covered with a layer of chocolate as thick as a finger; they examined the rest of the case and all the other cases. They sent notice of their findings to Madrid, where despite the esteem in which the Society is held, a trap was set. The Jesuits were told their cargo had arrived, but in vain: They were too clever to claim the precious chocolate, and preferred to lose it rather than admit ownership. They protested that it was an insult to think the gold was theirs, and that they did not know whose it was. They persevered with such firmness and unanimity that the gold went to the King, and it was no mean amount, as one can judge from those eight large cases full of great, fat, solid balls of gold; as for the chocolate layer, it was left to those who had performed the service of discovering the gold.

A Papal Bull (1702)

Cardinal Borgia, who was patriarch of the Indies, was on board one of the ships.[1] He was a very ignorant man and the most

[1] During a trip of Philip V of Spain to Naples.

extraordinarily base type of courtier. Louville, who was on the same ship, was invited by the cardinal for lunch on Good Friday. No man was ever more surprised than he when, sitting down at table, he saw there was only meat. The cardinal told him he had a bull from Pope Alexander VI* that gave him and his guests the right to eat meat any day they liked, and particularly on Good Friday. The authority of such a strange pope so strangely used did not impress his guest. The cardinal grew angry: He claimed that doubting the bull's powers was a crime that could lead to excommunication. Respect for the day won out over respect for the bull and the cardinal's example. Nevertheless the cardinal ate meat and forced all those whom he could persecute, intimidate, and threaten with penalities to do likewise. Such abuses defy comment.

Aversion of the King for Jansenism (1707)

The King asked M. le duc d'Orléans who he was taking to Spain, and Fontpertuis was one of those named. "What, my nephew?" replied the King heatedly. "The son of that madwoman who followed M. Arnauld[1] everywhere—a Jansenist? I want none of that sort to go with you." "By my faith! Sire," replied M. le duc d'Orléans, "I don't know what the mother did, but as far as the son being a Jansenist, why he doesn't even believe in God!" "Can that be true?" replied the King. "And can you vouch for it? If so, then there is no harm; you can take him." That afternoon M. le duc d'Orléans told me the story and almost fainted from laughter. The King's prejudices had taken him to the point where he preferred an atheist to a suspected Jansenist! M. le duc Orléans found this so amusing he could not keep it to himself;

---

* Alexander Borgia (1431-1503), the father of Cesare and Lucrezia Borgia. The papal bull in question had probably been handed down to deserving members of the Borgia family.

[1] Antoine Arnauld was the foremost French Jansenist and was expelled from the Sorbonne in 1656.

it became a joke at court and in town, and libertines admired the extremes to which the blindness of the Jesuits and Saint-Sulpice[2] could lead.

THE KING'S CONFESSOR (1709)

Father Tellier, whose talent had been recognized by the Society of Jesus, was privy to all its secrets. Since becoming a Jesuit, he had dedicated his life to the Society's advancement and to the belief that all means were proper to attain its ends. He was hard-headed, hard-working, stubborn, bereft of all other desires, opposed to all dissipation, all social occasions, and all amusement. He was incapable of easy mingling with his fellow Jesuits, and only noticed them if their passion conformed with the one that consumed him. He had made this cause a personal matter, the only matter to which he applied himself, and he was tireless in his efforts. He could not bear temporizing or circumspection and only suffered them when he was forced to, or when he saw a way to reach his goals more surely; all other equivocation was to him a crime and a shameful weakness. His life was austere by habit and inclination: All he knew was assiduous and uninterrupted work and he demanded it of others, without ever showing them any consideration. His head, his backbone, and his health were made of iron, and he had a cruel and fierce nature. He was as steeped in the maxims and policies of the Society as his unbending nature would allow. He was profoundly false, deceiving, and hid his true meaning under a thousand folds and creases. As soon as he was able to make himself feared, he demanded everything, gave nothing, broke solemn promises when he no longer had anything to gain by keeping them, and relentlessly pursued those to whom he had made them. He was a terrible man, whose secret aim was nothing less than to crush everything in his way. When he became powerful, he came out into the

[2] The church of Saint-Sulpice at that time housed the order of Oratorians, who backed the Jesuits in their witch-hunts.

open. Then, he became inaccessible even to the Jesuits, except for four or five of his stamp; he was the terror of all the others. Even the four or five approached him with great trepidation and only dared to contradict him if they could show that his proposal would not further his aim, which was the despotic rule of the Society, with its dogma and its maxims, and the complete destruction of everything opposed to it, and of everything which did not blindly submit to it. The most remarkable aspect of his obsession, which nothing interrupted even for a single moment, was that he never sought anything for himself and had neither friends nor family.

He was born evil, had never been touched by the desire to please, and made no effort to conceal his low birth. He was so violent that even the wisest and most ardent Jesuits were afraid he might have them expelled. His physical appearance matched his character. You would not have wanted to come upon him in a dark wood. His appearance was sinister, shifty and terrible; his eyes were crooked, shining, and evil-looking: The sight of him was very striking. He had consecrated himself body and soul to the Society, his only nourishment was its most obscure mysteries, and his whole life had been devoted to its study. It was his only God. From this faithful and accurate portrait of the man, and because of his low extraction, it is not surprising that in everything else he was coarse, ignorant, insolent, impudent, impetuous, antisocial, excessive, uncompromising, all of a piece, and that any means were proper to reach his ends. It was in Rome that he perfected himself in the maxims and policies of the Society. He had been noticed because of his fervor and inflexibility, but was sent back to France when his book was put on the Index and he became notorious. The first time he saw the King in his study, after having been formally presented, they were alone save for Blouin and Fagon. Fagon, all bent and leaning on his cane, paid close attention to the interview and noted the new confessor's bows and remarks. The King asked him whether he was related to M. Le Tellier. The priest acted dumfounded: "Me, Sire," he replied, "related to M. Le Tellier! far from it; I am only a poor peasant from lower Normandy, where my father was a farmer." Fagon who had not missed a word, turned and whispered to Blouin, while pointing at the Jesuit:

"Sir, what a sacre!" * And, shrugging his shoulders, he leaned on his cane. It turned out that he was right in his strange judgment of the confessor. With hypocritical grimaces, Tellier had given the impression that he dreaded his position as the King's confessor and had accepted it only out of obedience to the Society. The reason I have gone on about the new confessor is that he was the source of the incredible storms which are still shaking the Church, the State, knowledge, doctrine, and all sorts of distinguished people; also because I knew this terrible man more deeply and more fully than anyone at court.

SAINT-SIMON'S POSITION ON JANSENISM (1711)

The celebrated abbé de la Trappe was my guiding light in this matter (Jansenism) and in many other things I knew in theory but not in practice. I hold all parties in the Church and in the State to be particularly loathsome. The only party is that of Jesus Christ. I also hold the five direct and indirect propositions[1] to be heresy, and consequently any book that contains them, without exception. I also believe there are people united among themselves who hold them to be good and true, and who form a party. Thus, whatever way you look at it, I am no Jansenist. In addition, I am, more by conscience than because of sound political views, intimately attached to what has been wrongly called the liberties of the Gallican Church. These liberties are neither privileges, nor concessions, nor usurpations, nor even matters of usage and tolerance; they are the constant practice of the universal Church. The French Church has jealously kept and defended them against the ventures and usurpations of the court

* A *sacre* (*saker*) is a bird of prey. Fagon was probably punning sourly on *sacre*, in its religious sense, the anointing or consecration of bishop or king, with further suggestions of sycophancy.

[1] The five propositions were Jansenist doctrines condemned in 1653 by Pope Innocent X. Cornelis Jansen was a Dutch theologian who gave birth to a Roman Catholic splinter movement based on a return to personal holiness and salvation for a chosen holy few. Saint-Simon is hedging here, for the main issue was whether Jansen's "Augustinus" contained the heretical propositions.

of Rome,[2] which overcame and enslaved all the other churches and did infinite harm to religion. I say "the court of Rome" out of respect for the Bishop of Rome, who is Pope in name only. It is a matter of faith that he is the head of the Church, the successor of Saint Peter, with God-given superiority and jurisdiction over all the other bishops. The care and supervision of all the churches in the world is his concern only, for he is pre-eminently the vicar of Jesus Christ, that is to say first among all the vicars, who are the bishops. To this I add that I hold the Church of Rome to be the mother and the mistress of all the others, who must remain in communion with it; by mistress, I mean MAGISTRA, and not DOMINA;[3] nor do I hold the Pope to be the only bishop, nor the universal, natural, and diocesan bishop of all the dioceses, nor that he is the only holder of episcopal power and that it emanates from him to all the other bishops; these are the teachings of the Inquisition, which I hold abominable to God, and execrable to man. I believe the signature of the well-known Formulary[4] was a pernicious invention, which can only be tolerated if followed to the letter according to the Peace of Clement IX.

As a result I am far from believing that the Pope is infallible in any sense, or superior, or even equal to the ecumenical councils which alone have the power to define articles of faith without erring. As for Port-Royal, I agree with the late King's grieved explanation to Mareschal:[5] That over the last few centuries, Port-Royal has produced what is saintliest, purest, wisest, clearest, most instructive, most practical, most elevated, and most luminous; that the name of Jansenist and Jansenism is a convenient pitch pot to blacken the name of anyone, and that out of a

[2] There was no central government in Italy, and the Pope was the sovereign of the Papal States and of what Saint-Simon refers to as the court of Rome.

[3] Saint-Simon accepted the magisterium, or teaching authority of the Pope and the Church of Rome, but not their jurisdictional domination.

[4] The Formulary was a document that Catholics had to sign and show their confessor to prove they did not adhere to Jansenism.

[5] Port-Royal was a women's abbey in Paris that was accused of Jansenism. Mareschal, who was Louis XIV's surgeon, went there to perform an operation and reported to the King that they seemed to be saintly women. The King was impressed, and said publicly that they had been persecuted wrongly. But under the influence of his Jesuit confessor, Father Tellier, Port-Royal was suppressed and the buildings were razed in 1710.

thousand persons accused of it, there are probably not even two who deserve it; to be stained with Jansenism it is enough to lead a simple, retiring, laborious, and disciplined life, to associate with others accused of the same, or to shrug at the claims of the court of Rome in spiritual and temporal matters; such unfounded rumors are so widespread, and so convenient and profitable for those who inspire them and profit by them, that they have become a cruel affliction for religion, society, and the State. I am convinced the Jesuits are useful when they hold themselves to the principles established by Saint Ignatius. The Company is too numerous not to include many saints, and I have known some, but it also includes many who are not. Their politics and jealousies were and are still the cause of many evils; their piety, their diligence in the instruction of youth, and the scope of their learning and knowledge does great good.

THE REVOCATION OF THE EDICT OF NANTES (1715)

The needless and inexcusable repeal of the Edict of Nantes[1] and the various proscriptions that followed were the fruit of a horrible plot that depopulated the kingdom by a fourth, wrecked its trade, and weakened it in every way; the populace was long subjected to the open and admitted looting of the dragoons, whose tortures and torments killed thousands of innocent men and women.[2] The repeal ruined a great people, split a vast number of families, caused sons to run off with their parents' possessions and leave them to starve, and allowed much of our industry to fall into the hands of foreigners. Foreign states were enriched at our expense, able to build new cities, and granted the spectacle of a prodigious people turned into fugitives, proscribed and poor. They fled though they had committed no crime, and sought asylum far from their native country. The noble, the rich, the

[1] The Edict of Nantes, signed in 1598 by Henri IV, granted religious freedom to Protestants. Louis XIV had it revoked in 1685.

[2] The dragonnades consisted in billeting rowdy dragoons in the homes of Huguenots and disregarding their violence and looting. The outrages of the dragoons led to the mass emigration of the Huguenots.

elderly, the pious, the learned, the virtuous, the well-to-do, the sickly, the delicate, all were condemned to the galleys and fell prey to the whips of convict gangs; and only because of their religion. Finally, crowning all the other horrors, the provinces of the kingdom became the scene of perjury and sacrilege, and the howls of unfortunate victims mistakenly accused echoed everywhere. Meanwhile many others sacrificed their conscience for the sake of their possessions and tranquillity. The price they paid was simulated apostasy, after which they were immediately dragged off to adore what they did not believe and to receive the divine body of the Saint of Saints, which they remained convinced was only bread and must be abhorred. Such was the widespread abomination fathered by flattery and cruelty.

From torture to perjury to communion there was often less than twenty-four hours, and the torturers became guides and witnesses. Those who had pretended to renounce peacefully soon showed, by their flight or behavior, what their true feelings were. . . .

The King received from all sides detailed news of these persecutions and conversions. Those who had renounced and received communion could be counted by the thousands: Two thousand in one place, six thousand in another, they had all renounced together and at once. The King congratulated himself on his power and piety. He thought he was back in the time of the Apostles, and took all the credit. The bishops wrote him panegyrics; the Jesuits made their pulpits and monasteries reverberate with praise. All France was full of horror and confusion, but never had there been such triumph and joy, never such a profusion of praise. The monarch did not doubt the sincerity of these collective conversions. Those responsible took great care to persuade and beatify him in advance. He swallowed their poison in long draughts. Never before had he considered himself so great a man, or so successful in having repaired before God his sins and the scandal of his life. All he heard was praise, while good and true Catholics and holy bishops bemoaned with all their heart that the orthodoxy was acting against the heretics as pagan and heretic tyrants had acted against truth, confessors, and martyrs. Above all, they could not get over the numberless sacrileges and perjuries. They wept bitterly over the irremediable and odious results these hateful methods would have on true religion. Meanwhile, our neighbors exulted to see us weaken and destroy ourselves. They took advantage of our folly and the hate we had incurred from all the Protestant powers to hatch plots against us.

Separation of Church and State (1719)

I cannot keep myself from mentioning here one last time what blindness it is to suffer the clergy in affairs of state. This is particularly true of cardinals, who have special license to commit with impunity all sorts of crimes and infamies. They can display independence and unfaithfulness, be guilty of felonies and revolts, and go unpunished. However the conduct of everyone toward these eminent criminals remains unruffled, and popular opinion has accustomed itself to them thanks to numberless examples. . . .

Every clergyman who through purposeful baseness manages to have a hand in state affairs, intends to become a cardinal and will sacrifice everything, without exception, to that end. This truth is so apparent, and so strengthened by examples from all eras including our own, that it can only be considered the most evident and certain of axioms.

Hypocrisy of the Jesuits (1722)

One day when I had seen the Queen sniff tobacco several times, I remarked that it was rather extraordinary to see a king of Spain[1] who took neither tobacco nor chocolate. The King replied that it was true he took no tobacco; the Queen excused herself and said that to please the King she had done everything she could to rid herself of the habit, and was sorry to admit she

[1] This was during Saint-Simon's embassy to the court of Spain.

had not been able to. As for chocolate, the King added that he only took it for breakfast with the Queen on days of fast. "How so, Sire," I asked with passion, "you take chocolate on fast days?" "Why certainly," answered the King gravely, "chocolate does not break the fast." "But Sire," I said, "it is food, and very good and nourishing too." "And I can assure you," replied the King heatedly, his face reddening, "that it does not break the fast; for the Jesuits, who told me so, take some every fast day, without the bread which they use on other days for dunking." I held my tongue, for I was not there to give the King lessons on fasting; but I secretly admired the morals of the good Fathers and the instruction they give, the blindness with which they are obeyed and believed by everyone, the little credit given to the maxims of the Gospels and the teachings of religion, and the deep and untroubled darkness in which kings guided by the Jesuits live.

A Visit to Toledo (1722)

Although there were nearly twenty leagues between Madrid and Toledo, thanks to well-ordered carriage relays I made the trip in one day, and arrived before dark. The road is beautiful, open and smooth; but Toledo begins at the foot of a mountain. When I had reached the outskirts of the village at the foot of a high cliff on which the remains of the old castle are perched, I was asked to turn my back on the city and visit the Franciscan monastery where the famous councils of Toledo[1] were held. As soon as I had stepped down from my carriage, the monastery's notables gathered around and asked me to look at an old grilled window in the castle. They said it was from there that King Rodrigo had first seen the daughter of Count Julien, who had lived on the site of their monastery, and that this had inspired the king's love, which proved so disastrous for him and for Spain. The story did not impress me much, particularly since the

[1] Toledo was the seat of church councils in Spain from the fourth to the sixteenth century.

window and its emplacement seemed far short of a thousand year's antiquity. The monks showed me their church, which seemed very ordinary, and its portal was of recent origin. As soon as I had entered they stopped and asked me whether I did not notice something very extraordinary. Above the main altar I saw a life-size sculpted crucifix in loincloth and wig, which did not surprise me since almost all Spanish crucifixes are like that and I had seen many of them. When I did not reply, trying to divine what it was they wanted me to notice, they said: "The arms, the arms!" I saw that one was nailed to the cross while the other hung alongside the body. It was my turn to ask what it meant. They assured me in pious and solemn tones that it was a miracle which was still operating and without mentioning the date or who was then responsible for the church, they immediately told me that a commoner had made a village girl pregnant after promising to marry her. He went back on his promise and made a fool of her, at which her parents, lacking proof, asked her to go before the crucifix. They all came to the church, followed by a large crowd, and the girl and the boy had no sooner come before the crucifix than its left arm detached itself from the cross and fell loosely at its side, where it remains as we see it now. Everyone cried that it was a miracle and the boy married the girl. Although I was protected from the Inquisition by my rank of ambassador, I did not want to provoke a scandal in a country so dominated by superstition: I swallowed the monks' pious fairy tale as gracefully as I could, while they continued exalting it and calling on me to admire it. They asked me to kneel at the foot of the main altar, then took me to visit all the chapels of the church; each one had its particular miracle, and I was told about them all. As we progressed from chapel to chapel, I begged them to lead me to the council chamber, or what was left of it, for that was the sole purpose of my visit. They replied, "In a little while; but first there is this chapel, which is very remarkable"; and I had to submit, and hear about the miracles, which dampened my enthusiasm. Finally, when the chapels had been exhausted and I was ready to visit the council chamber, they told me there was nothing left of it as they had destroyed the remains five or six months before to build their kitchen. I was seized with such violent resentment that it was all I could do not to strike them with all my might. I turned my back, upbraiding them with very harsh words for what amounted to a sacrilege, returned to my carriage without having set foot in their monastery and climbed into it without giving them the slightest mark of courtesy. This is what happens to the most precious monuments of antiquity through avarice, ignorance, or expediency, when no one, not even the police, bothers to claim and preserve them. I felt extreme sorrow at the loss.

VI

SAINT-SIMON AS A WRITER

INTRODUCTION

*T*O praise Saint-Simon for his literary gifts is to disregard his real motives, like praising an actor for his good looks rather than his performance. We must class him among great French prose writers against his objections. At the close of the Memoirs he apologizes for being a sloppy stylist and explains that his only motive was to set down the chronicle of his time as swiftly as the thoughts came, and that he never bothered with matters of "composition." Moveover, he disdained the writer's rewards. He could not be sure he would ever have readers, for he insisted that his Memoirs be published long after his death. It never occurred to him that he was a man of letters, a vocation he considered inconsequential and frivolous.*

Saint-Simon was an artist in spite of himself, without conscious literary style, attention to language, or selection. He piles up detail indiscriminately, for he is not trying to write a literary description, but a complete description. Whatever his sins, they are not sins of omission. He is like those primitive painters who must paint every leaf on a tree, every quill on a porcupine, and the effect is strangely similar—sometimes awkward, sometimes overburdened, but artlessly inventive and crowded with life.

Thus, we admire Saint-Simon for reasons quite different from those for which he wanted to be admired. He was especially proud, for instance, of the several hundred pages he devoted to the various grades of Spanish grandees. But it is almost impossible for the modern reader to follow this fastidious nomenclature, better suited to gather dust on the back shelves of historical libraries.

We admire instead, his ability to renew and revivify the language, coin expressions, make an individual spring to life in one sentence, describe the "mechanics" that animate people and events. We are less interested in what he considered the essential part of his chronicle—the descriptions of battles and treaties, the origins of titles, the depredations on ducal privilege—and we sift through the riverbed of his recorded memories for the nuggets of gold he scarcely knew were there.

And yet, whether he knew it or not, Saint-Simon did have a literary technique, a kind of reportorial genius. His sources went from the highest to the lowest, from the King to downstairs maids. He was as honorable in his private life and affairs as he was unscrupulous when in search of information. Eavesdropping, snooping, and reading other people's mail were to him simply research techniques. Through his friendship with Torcy, the post office superintendent, he had access to secret government dispatches upon which he relied for his chapters on French foreign policy. He knew all the principals at court, and won the confidence of ministers like Pontchartrain and Chamillart, who gave him full accounts of cabinet meetings. He exploited the natural bent of women for gossip, and often spent his afternoons closeted with one or several ladies eager for such a good listener. He once spent eight consecutive hours with the well-informed princesse des Ursins, and wrote in his Memoirs that "the eight hours seemed like eight moments." He would ask ten persons the same question to get a fact straight, would hover near a conversational group in the Hall of Mirrors trying to pick up snatches of talk, would write hundreds of letters to run down minor details. And finally, he had the unofficial court register of the marquis de Dangeau, a dry but complete list of court events that Saint-Simon used as a skeleton for his memoirs. He stored up this exhaustive documentation in his library, to which he retired in 1739 for his prodigious writing task. In this laboratory of words, surrounded by notes, registers, official papers, genealogical histories, and more than six thousand books, he spent ten years creating the Memoirs.

The Memoirs have endured, not because of Saint-Simon's political theories or his futile court pursuits, but because of the power of his writing. Three of the four greatest French novelists of the last century and a half gratefully admitted their debt to the Memoirs: Stendhal, Balzac, and Proust. Saint-Simon has been *compared to Proust because both writers dealt with hermetic segments of a decaying society. But Saint-Simon was from the first an "insider," which Proust was not. This made the* Memoirs *possible and at the same time set their limitations. Proust chose as his subject the crumbling structure of French nobility at the end of the nineteenth century, as a painter chooses a landscape. But Proust was an outsider. He was invited to the right parties and knew the right people, but he was always tolerated as "le petit Marcel" and would have been the first to admit that he was a spectator, not a participant. Where Saint-Simon strove for inventory-like accuracy to describe a society of which he was a member, Proust took the elements he needed from a society of which he was a guest to create his own alternate structures. Proust, the conscious artist, controlled his material and gave it form. Saint-Simon, the unconscious artist, was controlled by the events he described, which dictated their form.*

Saint-Simon and Proust have been called the two worst snobs in French literature. But their treatment of snobbery is an illustration of their opposite methods. To Saint-Simon, snobbery was necessary for survival. In a court where everything was based on minute distinctions of rank, attentiveness to those distinctions was simply a matter of self-preservation. For Proust, snobbery is a literary device, the parable of a declining age when the distinctions were still upheld although they had become meaningless. Proust loves the great names of France for the musty odor they exhale and because they are a link with the past he was striving to recapture. Saint-Simon's whole effort is a legacy for the future—he wanted no more than to light the way for historians looking back down the dim corridors of seventeenth-century court life.

Saint-Simon's Rival (1720)

Philippe de Courcillon, marquis de Dangeau, kept a detailed diary of court life and the King's activity, which was a precious help to Saint-Simon. Dangeau made himself popular with the King

*through his love of gambling and determined adulation. There
is not a word of criticism either of the court or of the King in
his diary, which Saint-Simon scorned even though he made good
use of it. Dangeau died in 1720, a colonel in the infantry, a
provincial governor, and a member of the Académie Française.
But he had not obtained the peerage so fervently sought in fifty
years of sycophancy.*

As soon as he started coming to court, around the time the
Queen Mother died, he began to set down the events of the day
every evening, and he was faithful to his task up to the day he
died. He followed the style of a gazette, without any interpreta-
tion, and only noted the events themselves and their exact date,
without a word about their cause or about court intrigues and
behind-the-scenes activity. What leaps from the pages of his revolting diary (where the day's events seldom fill more than a
single page) are the baseness of a humble courtier, worship of
the master and everyone in or close to favor, insipid prodigality
and abject praise, relentless and suffocating clouds of incense for
the King's most trivial acts, supreme dullness from fear of offend-
ing, and a determination to excuse everything, particularly concerning the generals and others in the King's good graces, such
as Mme. de Maintenon and the ministers. . . .

It is hard to understand how a man could have the patience
and perseverence to work every day for more than fifty years
at something so diluted, dry, constrained, cautious, and literal
that it only scratches the surface and repels by its aridity. But
it must also be said that it would have been difficult for Dangeau
to have written real memoirs, which demand that the author be
a part of the court's interior mechanism. Although he almost
never left court, and only for brief moments, although he was a
member of distinguished circles and although he was liked and
even esteemed for his sense of honor and discretion, it is nonetheless true that he was never a part of anything, or initiated into
anything. His memoirs were like his shallow and frivolous life:
He only knew what everyone could see and was content to
attend feasts and festivities, of which his vanity makes much in
his memoirs; and yet he was never anything in particular. It
did happen that his friends, some of whom were persons of im-

portance, gave him information about their own affairs, but those instances were few and far between.

His few important friends knew too well the frivolous stuff he was made of to waste their time on him. Dangeau's intelligence was less than mediocre; he was futile, incompetent in everything, and content to take shadow for substance and feed on the wind. All his energies were devoted to propriety, inoffensiveness, fishing for compliments, and the acquisition, preservation, and enjoyment of a kind of consideration. He never realized that his vanity and self-conceit amused everyone including the King, or that practical jokes were made at his expense.

With all this, the memoirs are filled with a thousand facts suppressed in gazettes. They will greatly improve with age, and whoever wishes to write something solid about the period will find them very helpful to avoid confusion, because of their accurate chronology. Finally, they represent a precise portrait of the court's surface, its days, members, occupations, amusements, and the daily routine of the King and the rest of court. Nothing would be more valuable for history than to have similar memoirs for every reign since Charles V, which would throw a marvelous light on the futility of everything written about the periods.

Two final words about this singular author. He did not hide the fact that he was keeping a diary, for he had nothing to fear from its contents; but he never showed it, and it has only been seen since his death. It was published recently, after coming into the possession of his grandson the duc de Luynes, who had a few copies printed. Dangeau, who was incapable of scorn and wanted to be a member of everything, had early solicited and obtained a seat in the Académie Française (at his death, he was dean of the Académie), and another in the Académie des Sciences, although his knowledge of science was nil. He prided himself on being a member of these academies and hobnobbing with the illustrious, although the memoirs are filled with astonishing examples of crass ignorance concerning duchies and the dignities conferred by the Spanish court.

A FUNERAL SERVICE FOR THE DAUPHINE (1690)

When he was fifteen, Saint-Simon was allowed to accompany his father to a funeral mass at the Abbey of Saint-Denis near Paris. The mass was for Marie-Anne-Christine of Bavaria, wife of Monseigneur, grandson of Louis XIV and Dauphin. His report to his mother on the ceremony, which was attended by all the principal persons of the court, is his first known writing.

When everything was ready, ordered, and in place, we waited half a quarter hour, and then the double doors at the end of the choir opened to the sound of hand bells rung by twenty-four criers. Through the doors came acolytes bearing censers and taper stands, deacons and assistant deacons, cantors, and monks in their copes, and finally five prelates, that is to say: Three in mourning copes, followed by the deacon (with his assistant) also in mourning cope, and the celebrant, wearing vestments and a black chasuble. The bishops had their crosiers and white miters, and each was followed by two or three almoners in surplices. Preceded by vergers, the procession went toward the altar, which is on the right, between the platform on which the body of the dead princess was resting, and the monks' seats, which had been turned over to the princesses, Parlement, the High Council, the Board of Excise, and the town notables. The celebrants bowed before the altar, the nonofficiating clergy, the representation of the late King Louis the Just's body, whose memory is held in reverence,[1] the body of Mme. la Dauphine, and the princes and princesses. Then the music began to play, and the celebrants said mass.

Everyone knows how a pontifical requiem high mass is celebrated, so that I will limit myself to descriptions of the reverences during offertory and the other special parts of this funeral service. When the offertory came, an armchair was placed on the two steps crossing the choir, and folding chairs for the other

[1] Louis XIII, responsible for making the Saint-Simons a ducal family.

bishops, who were all wearing their miters, while behind them stood the officiating monks, the almoners, and the other servants. Seeing the prelates in place, the chief herald went up to them and executed a ceremonial reverence. For a ceremonial reverence, one must cross both feet and both legs and bend the knees without bending the body or head, as women customarily do; but women draw back or bend their bodies a little, which should not be done in a ceremonial reverence, since the knees should bend deeply without any movement of the body, which is proportionately lowered while remaining straight.

Monseigneur the duc de Bourgogne, accompanied only by his governor, went up to Madame[2] and paid her a special reverence. Madame received from one of her almoners a white wax candle, lit and studded with gold half-louis, and led by the duc de Bourgogne and his governor, she went up to the bishop of Meaux [Bossuet], who was celebrating the mass. After having paid her reverence with Monsieur le duc de Bourgogne, they knelt at the feet of the celebrating bishop on a square of black velvet. Having kissed his episcopal ring, the princess presented her candle, which the bishop handed to one of his almoners. There arose a dispute between the almoners and the monks over the money attached to the candle, which became so violent they almost came to blows. They broke the candle in two or three places to get the money, and jostled the bishop of Glandesves so that his miter would have fallen off if he had not held it with his hands. However, the argument was settled, with the almoners receiving all the offerings and then handing them over to the monks, whose community would profit from the proceeds.

How Saint-Simon Became Interested in Ducal Dignities (1711)

Ever since I can remember, I had collected examples of the loss of our dignity, and the occasions which had caused them. I had

[2] Madame, the second wife of Philippe d'Orléans (Monsieur, the brother of Louis XIV), was a princess (of Bavaria) like the dead Dauphine.

been interested in these matters since my earliest childhood and had studied them ever since. I had persistently applied myself to learn from the old ducs and duchesses who had been best-informed on the court of their time. I checked their information with other persons who had been at court, and checked it again with untitled persons, scholars and learned men well versed in the customs of the court and society from firsthand knowledge, and former valets. I would lead them to the subject during a conversation, and gradually make them tell what I wanted to get out of them. I took notes on the information I obtained. Thus I had all my material at hand, and I added the examples I had seen in my time at court. Without these advantages, I could not have compiled the information; the time required would have been prohibitive.

A Definition of History (1723)

This passage from the Foreword of the Memoirs *shows Saint-Simon driven by defeat at court into pessimism and resignation. The complete involvement in his own time, the obsessional attachment to rank, had soured to somber detachment. The same man who was able to convey a sense of epic magnitude to court minutiae could also write one of the most eloquent statements on the futility of life since Ecclesiastes.*

To write the history of one's country and one's time demands the thoughtful recollection of everything original and unimpeachable that one saw, knew, and was privy to on the world's stage, including the various mechanisms, often outwardly trivial, that controlled vital and far-reaching events. It is to explore step by step the nothingness of this world, of its fears, desires, hopes, disgraces, fortunes, and of its works; it is to convince oneself that all is nothing, because of the short and swift duration of all things and of the lives of men; it is the sharp recollection that happiness in this life is an illusion, and that peace and bliss are not to be found on earth; it is to show that if it were possible for the multitude mentioned here to anticipate the results of their efforts, their sweat, their cares, and their intrigues, all but a dozen at the most would have stopped at the start of their lives and abandoned all their ambitions and their most cherished designs; even the dozen know that the happiness they sought must end with death; the knowledge increases their regrets by intensifying their attachments, and cancels everything they had attained. . . .

History's advantage . . . is that it attacks and exposes only those who have been dead long enough so that no one is left to take their part. Thus, the reputation, destiny, and interests of the living are not affected and there can be no objections to seeing truth in all its purity. The reason is clear: He who writes the history of his time and attaches himself only to the truth without sparing anyone must be careful not to disclose his aim. He would have too much to fear from powerful persons directly or indirectly offended by the most cruel and palpable truths! He would be insane to expose himself to the faintest suspicion that he is the author. His work must ripen under lock and key and be passed on to his heirs, who would do well to leave it alone a generation or two and let it appear only when time has made it safe from resentment.

CONCLUSION OF THE MEMOIRS (1723)

Now I have finally reached the end I proposed to myself in these memoirs. The only good memoirs are those that are completely true, and the only true memoirs are written by those who have seen and taken part in the matters they are recounting, or who have been told about them by trustworthy eyewitnesses. Moreover, the author must love truth to the point of sacrificing everything else. I dare say that I embodied this last point, and am convinced that no one who knew me would disagree. It is even this love for truth that did the most harm to my personal fortunes. I felt this often, but preferred truth above all, and could never stoop to any disguise. Again, I loved truth even more than myself. . . .

There remains objectivity, an essential point, considered most difficult (or perhaps, I don't shrink from saying, impossible) for those who have seen and taken part in what they are writing. One is charmed by honest and sincere persons, irritated by the scoundrels who proliferate at court, and infuriated by those who have done one personal harm. Stoicism is a fine and noble chimera. If I claimed objectivity, it would be in vain. For it will be found in these memoirs that praise and blame flow naturally toward those who have affected me, and that I am cooler toward those who leave me indifferent. However, I always attack dishonesty and defend virtue, depending on the degree of virtue or vice. In spite of all this, I will pay myself the compliment (which I hope is borne out by the text of these memoirs) that I was forever on guard against my affections and aversions, and particularly the latter. I only wrote about this one or that one with the scales of justice in the other hand, mistrusting myself as I would an enemy, so that I would neither invent, exaggerate, nor omit, but do justice to everyone, and let truth in its purest form come to the surface. In this sense, I believe I have been completely objective, and I do not think there is any other course.

As for precision and truth, it can be seen from the memoirs themselves that almost everything comes from personal experience, or from those who took part in the events recounted. Their names are given, and they are above suspicion, as is my close relationship with them. I have indicated what I feel to be less certain, and I was not ashamed to admit what I did not know.

In this manner, the sources of the memoirs are firsthand. Their truth and authenticity cannot be doubted. And I believe I can say that until now no other memoirs have dealt with so many different matters in such depth and detail, or have provided such an informative and interesting whole.

Since I will never see them published, I can speak about them frankly. But if these memoirs ever see the light of day, I do not doubt they will excite a prodigious revolt. Everyone is attached to his family, his interests, his pretensions, and his illusions, none of which can suffer the least contradiction. If one is favored by truth, truth is a friend, but it does not necessarily favor one's interests. Those of whom one speaks well are not grateful: It was no more than the truth. The far greater number who are ill-treated are all the more furious because everything stated is borne out by the facts. . . .

I have one observation to make about some of my conversations, particularly those with Msgr. le duc de Bourgogne, M. le duc d'Orléans, M. de Beauvillier, the ministers, one with the duc du Maine, three or four with the late King, and more recently with Monsieur le Duc and many important people, in which I gave, received or disputed, opinions and advice. There are so many of them that I can understand how a reader who does not know me might believe they are the kind of invented speeches historians put in the mouth of generals, ambassadors, senators or conspirators to improve their books. But I protest, with the same truth that has guided my pen until now, that all these conversations are real and have been reported in the memoirs with complete scrupulousness. If there is one thing I can reproach myself for, it is weakening my part of the conversations in the report, for in the animation of the moment, one speaks with more strength and freedom than can be set down.

One flaw that has always bothered me in memoirs is that once the reader has put them down, he wonders what happened to the principal characters discussed. He would like to know immediately what became of them, without taking the trouble to pursue his research elsewhere. This is what I would like to remedy, if God gives me time. I will not be as precise as when I was a part of everything. Although Cardinal Fleury[1] never withheld anything I wanted to know about foreign or court affairs (often he mentioned them before I asked him), I listened indifferently, and when I was talking with ministers and other learned men I was even more apathetic. So that I fear any supplement or sequel to these memoirs will be filled with great blanks, obscure, very listless, and very different from what I have written so far. But at least the reader will be able to learn what happened to the characters who appeared in the memoirs until the death of Cardinal Fleury, which is all that I propose.

Shall I say a final word about the negligence of the style, the same words repeated too often, the overabundant synonyms, and particularly the obscurity that often comes from the length of

[1] André-Hercule, cardinal de Fleury (1653-1743), had been tutor of Louis XV and became misister of state in 1726.

the sentences and perhaps from repetition? I realize these defects but have been unable to avoid them. I was carried away by my subject matter, and was careless in setting it down, except to explain it well. I was never a scholar, and I could not help writing quickly. To correct my style and make it easier to read would mean recasting the whole work, and this task exceeds my strength and will. To correct what one has written, one must be able to write well, a claim I do not make, as can easily be seen here. I have cared only for accuracy and truth. I dare say that they are both to be found in my memoirs, that they are its law and its soul, and that the style deserves a measure of benign indulgence in their favor. It needs it so badly that I cannot promise improvement in this respect in the sequel I propose.

WHY SAINT-SIMON WROTE

This brief text is part of a preamble to Saint-Simon's notes on the peerages and duchies of his time. It serves as a rationale and introduction to all his work.

A sick person rejects many dishes without tasting them, and barely touches others before rejecting them.

In the same way, a mind languishing in a void considers many possibilities before attempting to fasten its weariness on any single one. Finally, reason prevails by providing inconsequential matters to reaccustom the mind by degrees; and since futility has never been to its taste, it does not long continue its browsing without exploring more thoroughly. Such was the origin and continuation of what can only be called a work of writing, to which one gives no more than the credit it deserves: That it was useful to amuse during the time of its composition, excellent after that to light the fire with, and perhaps also to show someone of limited instruction and indolent disposition, in an easy over-all glance, what he ignores and would do better not to ignore; a sort of composition where dates and certain genealogical and sometimes even historical facts were transcribed, and where one moved easily with the current of narration and reasoning, carried along by the subject matter because it was not worth the effort to hold back and only had merit for oneself and the amusement that could be derived from it. Self-enlightenment and personal satisfaction have been sought, along with memory's relief; and all this together has extended what was meant to be very brief.

Saint-Simon and His Contemporaries

If proof is needed that Saint-Simon never considered himself a writer, it can be found in his attitude toward the other literary figures of his time. Instead of judgments and comparisons, we find apathy and a measure of scorn for a profession he obviously considered as lacking in distinction. He devotes less space to the death of Mme. de Sevigné than to a faux pas by one of the King's valets, and even then, manages to leave the letters on which her reputation was based unmentioned. He is less interested in Racine's plays than in his social blunder in front of the King. His half-dozen lines on Voltaire have become famous, but for the wrong reasons.

1696—Mme. de Sevigné, a pleasant woman and an excellent companion, died at Grignan at her daughter's, who was her idol and did not deserve to be. I was a good friend of the young marquis de Grignan, her grandson. She had poise, natural graciousness, and an amiable wit, and in her conversation she could impart these qualities to those who lacked them. She was an excellent conversationalist, and knew all kinds of things while pretending to know nothing . . .

1696—The public lost a man celebrated for his wit, style, and knowledge of mankind: I mean La Bruyère, who died at Versailles of apoplexy. He imitated and surpassed Theophrastus with inimitable portraits of the men and women of our time in his new "Characters" . . .

1699—We lost the celebrated Racine, whose beautiful plays had made him famous. No one had a more agreeable or a greater store of wit. There was nothing of the poet in his manner, and everything of the honest and modest man, and toward the end, of the man of means. His friends were among the most illustrious at court and among men of letters. I leave it to the latter to describe him more eloquently than I could. To amuse the King and Mme. de Maintenon, and to occupy the young ladies of Saint-Cyr, he wrote two dramatic masterpieces, *Esther* and *Athalie*. They were all the more difficult to write because they are religious tragedies, devoid of romance, and historical truth had to be preserved out of respect for the holy scriptures. The comtesse d'Ayen and Mme. de Caylus excelled when the plays were shown before the King and a chosen few, in Mme. de Maintenon's apartment.

At Saint-Cyr, a very select company was admitted to see several performances. Racine and his friend Despréaux [Boileau] were commissioned to write a biography of the King. Thanks to this task, his plays, and his friends, he acquired certain privileges. Sometimes he was even received by Mme. de Maintenon, on days when the King had no ministers to see, such as Friday. In winter when bad weather made the day seem long, Racine would be summoned to amuse them. Unfortunately for him, he was very absent-minded.

One evening when he was with the King and Mme. de Maintenon, the conversation touched on the theatres of Paris. After exhausting the subject of the Opéra, they began to discuss the Comédie. The King inquired about plays and actors, and asked Racine why, as he had heard, the Comédie was in decline. Racine gave several reasons and then said the main reason was that because there were no young authors or new plays, the actors fell back on old plays, and among others the worthless and offensive plays of Scarron.[1] At this the poor widow blushed, not because the cripple's reputation had been attacked, but because his name had been mentioned in front of his successor. The King was embarrassed, and the sudden silence brought the unfortunate Racine to his senses. He realized into what pit his fatal absent-mindedness had made him fall. Of the three he was

[1] Scarron, it will be remembered, was Mme. de Maintenon's first husband.

the most upset, and did not dare raise his eyes or open his mouth. The surprise was so complete and unpleasant that it lasted more than several moments. Finally, the King sent Racine away, saying he had work to do. Completely bewildered, he found his way to his friend Cavoye's room and recounted his blunder. It was so momentous there was no patching it up. From that time, the King and Mme. de Maintenon never spoke to Racine again, or even looked at him. He was so deeply saddened that he languished, and died two years later.[2]

1711—Boileau Despréaux died. He was well known for his wit, his works, and particularly his satires. It was in this last manner that he excelled, although he was the best-natured fellow in the world. He had been commissioned to write the King's biography, but did almost no work on it.

1716—Arouet, the son of a notaire who served my father and myself until his death, was exiled and sent to Tulle for having written satiric and imprudent verse.[3] I would not even pause to set down this trifle had not this same Arouet become a famous poet and member of the Academy under the name of Voltaire. He had many tragic adventures and became a sort of celebrity in the republic of letters, and even attained a kind of importance in certain social circles.

[2] This account of Racine wasting away because of the King's disapproval is pure fantasy, and would have been more conceivable of Saint-Simon himself.

[3] The verse hinted at incest between the duc d'Orléans and his daughter, the duchesse de Berry.

SAINT-SIMON AND
THE "REPUBLIC OF LETTERS"

When Saint-Simon died in 1755, he was secure in the knowledge that the secret of his *Memoirs* had been kept. The government, however, had vague suspicions that the papers found in his possession concerned public affairs, and prudently impounded them. Five large wooden cases containing the *Memoirs* and other writings and documents remained in the trust of a notaire until 1760, when they were appropriated by the Foreign Affairs Ministry (much of the material is in the ministry's archives to this day). Word got out about the "sensational" nature of the *Memoirs,* and pirate editions began appearing in 1781, at first signed "Duc XXX," and eventually attributing the work to Saint-Simon.

In 1820, a marquis de Saint-Simon, distant cousin of the memoirist, was granted the rights to the papers by King Louis XVIII. It took him eight years to wrench the *Memoirs* from a ministry reluctant to give up its treasure, and he was never able to take possession of the other papers. He supervised the first complete edition of the *Memoirs,* which appeared in 1829. The manuscript consisted of 173 large in-folio copybooks, covered with a minute but regular handwriting, and numbered from pages 1 to 2,854. The copybooks had been carefully tied in small bundles with green string and placed in eleven calfskin portfolios stamped with Saint-Simon's coat of arms (on a field sable an argent cross bearing five shells gules) and a monogram. In a twelfth portfolio there was a table of contents.

The literary merit of the memoirs was not recognized for a long time. Shortsighted critics derided the negligence of Saint-Simon's style, his barbarous grammar, neologisms, repetitions, elliptical phrases, pleonasms, erratic punctuation, and impropriety. Saint-Simon's rehabilitation in the "republic of letters," from an "abominable" writer to "one of the three or four most gifted writers" in the French language is summed up in the following verdicts by a jury of his peers. Saint-Simon, for whom writing was a necessary evil and writers a motley lot, might have appreciated the irony.

MADAME DU DEFFAND, at whose salon many famous men of letters of the eighteenth century gathered, wrote to Horace Walpole in 1770:

"We are reading the memoirs of Saint-Simon out loud in the afternoons, and it is impossible for me not to regret your absence, for your delight would be inexpressible . . . the memoirs continue to amuse me, and as I enjoy reading in company, this will go on a long time; they would amuse you too, although the style is abominable and the portraits are badly drawn; the author was not a man of wit, but since he was in touch with everything, he has some curious and interesting things to tell . . ."

STENDHAL left a heavily annotated edition of the Memoirs. Among his marginalia:

"My only pleasures were Shakespeare and the memoirs of Saint-Simon . . . , a passion which I kept as long as my taste for spinach . . ."

"Saint-Simon's character: Nothing original or direct except on the subject of religion. All his other pleasures depended on others. He wanted consideration, and his weapon was a duchy. He would have made a very comical King. . . . Saint-Simon did not have much depth, but his style had depth and he expressed with depth certain ideas which were not too complicated for the reader. Saint-Simon was bilious and a Jansenist, but not profound."

"The language is degenerating and losing its character because vanity and conformity (which have already killed gaiety) forbid the use of words [such as Saint-Simon used]. Saint-Simon was a great writer, but a poor politician. Rereading the memoirs is like listening to good music a second time. At the third reading these notes will please me. They will be necessary to my state of mind. I write these notes at the third reading to guide me at the fourth . . ."

SAINTE-BEUVE wrote:

"The human spirit does not abound in masterpieces; do you realize that the scene in the apartments of Versailles after Monseigneur's death is a unique and incomparable work, that there is nothing like it in all of literature, and that there are no portraits to match it in all of history's museums? . . .

"You say the man had a narrow range, that he only saw detail? Good heavens! And what detail! Name us some immense and grandiose frescoes in painting, if this is not one. You mention Tacitus, whose work was admirably condensed, fashioned, shaped, polished and repolished, whose warm and bitter portraits had a somber golden hue: Do not repent, Frenchmen, for having had at the court of Versailles, at the heart of the human scramble, the little duke with the piercing eye, cruel, insatiable, always running and prying, ubiquitous, looting and ravaging everywhere, an irrepressible and reckless Tacitus. . . . And what is more, thanks to a comic vein intrepidly added, Saint-Simon is a Tacitus in the manner of Shakespeare . . ."

MARCEL PROUST, in *Pastiches et Mélanges,* used a true story about a man named Lemoine who claimed he could manufacture diamonds and was able to extort large sums of money from the De Beers people as the theme for parodies of nine writers, telling the same story in each of their styles. Among the writers were Balzac, Flaubert, Sainte-Beuve . . . and Saint-Simon. Aside from this indirect homage, several passages in *à la Recherche du Temps Perdu* show Proust's indebtedness to the style and subject matter of the Memoirs: The duc de Guèrmantes is described in counterpoint to Saint-Simon's portrait of Louis XIV; Aunt Léonie has the same tyrannical authority over Françoise, the maid, that the King had over his courtiers at Versailles. The following is a passage from Proust's pastiche of Saint-Simon:

"I found the Regent alone, without any of his surgeons or other servants, and saluted him with a brief and shallow bow, which he returned. 'Well, what is it now?' he asked in a kindly but annoyed tone. 'Since you order me to speak, Sire,' I replied, staring at him with fire so that he could not sustain my gaze, 'it is that you are about to lose the little respect and consideration (those were my terms) which the public still has for you . . .'

"And I described in terrible detail how abandoned he was at court, and what progress this neglect, and to use the real word, this contempt had made in the last few years. I reminded him—and sometimes when I wake up in the middle of the night and recall the boldness of my words, I still tremble—that several times he had been accused of poisoning the princes who barred his way to the throne; that no one doubted the great pile of diamonds he was about to accept as real would be used to attain the Spanish throne with the help of the court of Vienna, the Emperor, and Rome; that the detestable authority of the latter would lead him to repudiate Mme. d'Orléans, and that it was fortunate her last pregnancy had been fruitful, for otherwise the infamous rumors of poisoning would have started up again; that even though he wished the death of his wife, he could not be accused like his father of the Italian vice (again, these were my words), but that this was the only vice of which he could be absolved, for his affection for Mme. la duchesse de Berry seemed to many to be more than that of a father; and that although he had not inherited Monsieur's abominable tendencies, he was still his father's son in his love of perfume, which had led to his loss of favor with the King, who could not suffer scents . . . ; that there was still time to maintain his lofty position, but only one way, to have Lemoine arrested and banished, and never again let him enter France.

"M. le duc d'Orléans, who had cried out once or twice at the beginning of my discourse, afterward maintained the silence of a man who has been crushed by a great blow; but my final words prompted him to open his mouth. He was not an evil man, but decisions were not his strong point. 'What!' he said. 'Arrest him? And what if his invention is real?' "

HENRI DE MONTHERLANT, whose passion for Saint-Simon began at an early age, wrote the following in his *Textes sous l'Occupation: 1940–1944:*

"Three thousand large pages of compact manuscript, and not a single thought! Did he ever think during his entire life? One cannot tell by reading only the memoirs. He had political opinions, but everyone in France has political opinions, and they have nothing to do with intelligence. . . .

"Neither his soul nor his intelligence measured up to his extraordinary natural gifts. I painfully resolve to accept that a man who is among the three or four most gifted writers of our national literature does not have a trace of greatness in his character. Where the devil can greatness be found in Saint-Simon? He approached everything he saw, touched, accomplished, or projected, from its petty side. He was duke of hairsplitters. . . . Well, I am wrong, for one of his acts does not lack greatness. It is the act of writing these three thousand pages during thirty years, three thousand pages which he wrote to be read, fully conscious of their rare merit, three thousand pages that are his only work, his only claim to fame, and which he wrote after deciding that not one would appear during his lifetime. This passion for posthumous glory . . . does not go without a certain magnanimity.

"This marvelous farrago is the language of one of the two most dazzling artists in French literature (the other is Chateaubriand). Almost every style, next to his, seems thin and pedantic. . . . Saint-Simon invented the natural style, I mean the spoken language reviewed and corrected by literature. He takes the style he hears around him at court, a style that retains the sap and boldness of the court, and a certain coarseness that was and is the nobility's privilege (he tells the charming story about the little cat that came into the council chamber, which everyone wanted to chase, and which he wanted to keep. That is his style: He always keeps the little cat). . . .

"There is also something about him which democracies have in horror. Ours only tolerates Saint-Simon because it learned from him that Louis XIV never washed. And I believe the Americans do not even know he exists, or else confuse him with the socializing economist (it is well known that the greater a writer is in his own language, the less he is appreciated abroad)."

JEAN COCTEAU wrote in a 1953 letter to François-Régis Bastide, author of a penetrating study on Saint-Simon:
"Saint-Simon must be lived. . . . If Versailles becomes an illustrious ruin, it will be vital to keep the duke as the living soul of this empty shell. No one except Montaigne dipped such a pointed pen in such black ink. The pen of our duke made holes in the paper. His glances 'darted' (to use his own words)."

CLAUDE ROY, a contemporary novelist and essayist, devoted a passage to Saint-Simon in a book of criticism, *Le Commerce des Classiques*:
"Saint-Simon's example demonstrates this: Realism is not attained through objectivity, and only passion is realistic. The detached and indifferent eye sees nothing and fixes itself on nothing. There must be some live passion to give vision all its sharpness. You can only see clearly what strongly interests you; Saint-Simon's limits are in the quality of his passion. It is neither lofty nor noble. He has no great or profound aims, no really pure ambitions of the soul. He draws his vigor from the hatred, peevishness and fury of not having his proper rank. But even as it is, with all its pettiness and obsessiveness, Saint-Simon's passion is a marvelous fixing bath. Photographs that have been dipped in the acid bath of his resentment never fade. The gossip he dwells on, the passages he broods over, the portraits he ruminates about, become History. The great noble who was always wrong is finally, by force of vitriol, eternally right in the memory of men."

JEAN DE LA VARENDE, a writer of historical romances whose serious side was the study of Saint-Simon, wrote, in *Saint-Simon et sa Comédie Humaine*:
"In Saint-Simon's style there appears a sort of unvanquished gaiety, a juvenile quality that persists and keeps him under pressure. Curiosity is such a strong ferment with those lucky enough to possess it that it determines an expectation of the hour and the event, a brightening of the personality, a quick and lively appetite. The curious are always

alert, resourceful, and interested. Far from deliberately refusing melancholy, they ignore it. They may be sad, but they are never morose. . . . Besides, gaiety at court, at least on the surface, was mandatory. Moroseness was tantamount to exclusion from society. . . . And in his style, in his grammatical independence and unconcern for rules and syntax, he proves his frivolity and gaiety as a writer . . . his use of colloquialism denotes a basic good humor."

LYTTON STRACHEY wrote, in *Landmarks in French Literature*:
"Saint-Simon was a man of small intellect, with medieval ideas as to the structure of society, with an absurd belief in the fundamental importance of the minutest class distinctions, and with an obsession for dukedoms almost amounting to mania; but he had in addition an incredibly passionate temperament combined with an unparalleled power of observation; and these two qualities have made his book immortal. . . . His innumerable portraits are unsurpassed in literature. They spring into his pages bursting with life—individual, convincing, complete, and as various as humanity itself."

LOUIS AUCHINCLOSS, who seems to be the only American writer to have expressed himself on Saint-Simon, devoted a chapter to the Memoirs in *Reflections of a Jacobite* in which he said:
"Because he foresaw the pernicious effects of a bureaucratic government centered about an absolute monarch, Saint-Simon is often given more credit for political vaticination than he strictly deserves. We should remember that his own political solution was simply to restore the power of the nobles. It was the purest feudalism, and almost nobody but Saint-Simon, including his fellow peers, really wanted it. He was like a shrill Wall Street Republican in the days of the New Deal, predicting with some accuracy the evil consequences of red tape and high taxes, but recommending in their stead a return to the old, discredited system of laisser faire. The government of Louis XIV was at least an effort to cope with contemporary problems, while Saint-Simon, for all his perspicacity, had his eyes fixed on the past. One wonders if his project of restoring the feudal hierarchy would not have summoned a Robespierre from the masses a century before his time."

NANCY MITFORD, in an introduction to an English selection from the Memoirs entitled *Saint-Simon at Versailles*, wrote:
"As a writer his success was paramount. He was lucky to have such interesting people to write about. There has seldom been a dull Bourbon. Licentious or bigoted, noble or ignoble, they were nearly

all odd, original men with strong passions, unaccountable in their behavior. Louis XIV casts a dazzling glare on the pages of all the writers of his day; he was the most extraordinary member of this extraordinary family. Saint-Simon was able to observe him like a specimen under a microscope, and made the most of his opportunity. He hated the King, but he was not unfair to him. Indeed, his prejudices were usually justified."

HAROLD NICOLSON wrote about Saint-Simon in his study of the eighteenth century, *The Age of Reason*:

"Louis de Rouvroy, second duc de Saint-Simon, whose genius for observation and analysis renders him second only to Boswell as a diarist, remains a perplexing figure. There are moments when his lack of any sense of proportion, when his preoccupation with wholly unimportant things, persuade us that he was a stupid little man. At other moments, his gift of description, his astonishing insight into human character, fill us with admiration. There are passages even in his diary when he seems aware of the shallowness and falsity of the age that he painted with such brilliance, and when we detect a note of irony, almost a note of hatred and contempt, twanging like a brass wire through the minuets of his court gossip. . . . What is so disconcerting about Saint-Simon is that the clarity of his portrayal will suddenly become distorted by his obsessions and that we find ourselves pondering whether this intelligent annalist could discriminate between the significant and the trivial, between what was serious and what was not. Although he describes the genesis and the development of world-shattering events, although he provides us with vivid portraits of the figures of his time, we still ask ourselves, when we have finished the fascinating volumes of his memoirs, whether the man was a genius or a fool."

Finally, G. P. GOOCH, the prominent modern British historian, has said of him, in his *Courts and Cabinets*:

"In the ranks of the recorders Saint-Simon occupies a place apart. Like Pepys among the diarists, it is not a case of *primus inter pares* but of unchallengeable superiority. His *Memoirs* are unique in their vast bulk, their Venetian coloring, their Tacitean pungency, their power to bring a dead world to life. . . . His forecast [that publication of the *Memoirs* would produce a "prodigious revolt"] was correct, for skirmishes still continue on various sectors of his vast battlefield, and the work forms the most significant contribution to the history of France ever made by a single individual."

BIBLIOGRAPHY

Saint-Simon, Mémoires: Texte établi et annoté par Gonzague Truc. Bibliothèque de la Pléiade (Gallimard). 1961.

Duc de Sainte-Simon: Papiers en marge des mémoires, édition préfacée et annotée par François-Régis Bastide. Club Francais du Livre, 1954.

Saint-Simon par lui-meme: Images et textes présentés par François-Régis Bastide. Editions du Seuil, 1953.

M. le duc de Saint-Simon et sa Comédie Humaine. Jean de la Varende, Hachette, 1955.

Sur Saint-Simon. Emmanuel d'Astier, Gallimard, 1962.

Le Coeur Secret de Saint-Simon: Duc de Levis-Mirepoix, Edition de France, 1935.

INDEX

For ready reference, the reader is referred to the detailed Table of Contents at the beginning of the book, which, because of the arrangement of the material, will serve to locate many of the personages, events and anecdotes treated in the Memoirs. The persons, places and proper names listed here are those figuring in the actual scenes or anecdotes as related by Saint-Simon, rather than passing references; the King, for example, is mentioned continuously throughout the work, and his presence pervades it. By the same token, Saint-Simon himself is not listed in this index, though his presence is manifest on every page.